D0592500

Cooking
with Love

FLORENCE KERR HIRSCHFELD

Cooking
with Love

with decorations
by Grace Tulpa Chase

HOUGHTON MIFFLIN COMPANY BOSTON
THE RIVERSIDE PRESS CAMBRIDGE
1965

Copyright © 1965 by
FLORENCE KERR HIRSCHFELD
*All rights reserved including the right to
reproduce this book or parts thereof in any form
Library of Congress Catalog Card Number: 65-19314
Printed in the United States of America*

*To Leo
with Love*

Acknowledgments

• ♡ • ♡ • ♡ • ♡ • ♡ •

Man may well be an "island unto himself," his thoughts and spirit his alone, but no one is completely independent. This is especially true of "cookbooking." As in other art forms, hostesses are the recipients of timeless experimentation and legatees of the masters whose precepts we follow.

There is a constant interchange, the gifts of so many interested cooks, the generous expressions of innumerable friends and the irreplaceable effort of those with whom we are most closely affiliated. I thank them all for rallying, for the zest they add to my own. Without the glow of their warmth, the luster surrounding my efforts would be considerably dimmed.

In this devoted coterie of staunch supporters talented Naomi Zemans commands an irrefutable apex. Her understanding advice and counsel are constant encouragement; her confidence and superb editing are irreplaceable "manna from heaven." To her my gratitude and sincere appreciation. Delightful Eileen Gardner commuted to my workshop brimful of suggestions and ideas. Her presence contributed greatly to the excitement we enjoyed. The witty jibes of my patient, tasting, amused and interested husband heightened the challenge.

I repeat my thanks to all.

Florence Kurr Hirschfield

Preface

❤ ❤ ❤ ❤ ❤

I HAVE HAD a wonderful time accumulating these recipes and feel singularly qualified to chat about cooking activities because as mother, grandmother, clubwoman, busybody and Jack-of-all trades I represent that tremendous, powerful and active group known as HOUSEWIVES.

When I learned to cook, my second-best love affair began — second only to that with my loving and long-suffering spouse. Tolerating the testing, trying and devising, he has survived gastronomically and spiritually, stouthearted and sturdy as the structures he designs. Cooking involves every facet of culture and history, the development of our six senses, plus the seventh of fine discernment.

Like cup and saucer, foods mate with encounter, be it tête-à-tête or gala spectacular. With cooking as an interest, the pot of gold at rainbow's end fills with all the satisfying ingredients of accomplishment. It has brought me study, travel, history, companionship, therapy and pure enjoyment. It has equaled the unknown quantity I sought. Turn about is fair play, so this anthology is my return, the life and cooking pleasures of a contemporary hostess. In gratitude, I offer a toast

To COOKING — WITH LOVE

Contents

•♡•♡•♡•♡•♡•

Guideposts Along the Recipe Circuit

THE aim in this book has been toward flavorful preparation with clear directives.

Read the recipe carefully before proceeding. Check and assemble all ingredients, observing the possibility of advance preparation of any part or of the whole recipe.

Rather than a separate and lengthy list of short cuts, detours and directions, many helpful suggestions are distributed throughout this book where they can be best employed.

Ingredients, such as sauces and marinades, when capitalized are indexed. They appear in their proper categories or following a specific recipe.

The number of people served is included at the end of each recipe.

For accuracy, can sizes have been omitted; because of trends, can sizes are constantly changing. Therefore we indicate amounts by weight or measurement.

Unless otherwise stated sour cream is dairy sour cream; oven temperatures are all preheated; flour is all-purpose; butter is listed in cup measure (for more detail, read Reviewing Stand).

Flavor is the essence of cooking; I urge you to experiment with seasonings and adjust perfectly to your own taste.

The suggested courses following entrées, when italicized, are indexed and in their proper categories. Note that suggestions of these complements are not intended as full menus; rather as a springboard for your imagination. Other indexed recipes are those which are capitalized.

I stress naturalness and informality as the bulwark of conviviality. Combine entrée and pasta on one platter, and if possible, add a border of vegetable, thus simplifying your service and at the same time enlarging the possibilities for attractive arrangements.

All these recipes have been tested in my small functional kitchen, and I offer them without a qualm to my cooking contemporaries.

For more detailed suggestions browse through the final pages which embody many practical and decorative ideas.

Cooking
with Love

What About Hors d'Oeuvres?

• ♡ • ♡ • ♡ • ♡ • ♡ •

THE ROLE of hostess gives every woman the opportunity to star in her own right. No applause compares to the plaudits of happy guests. Their praise is well earned, for the least obvious arrangement represents careful thought, planning and effort.

Several keys open the door of hospitality: warm welcome, pleasant comfort, attention and interest in your guests, and the all-important dining. A cordial greeting sets the mood. Free circulation and movement are as important to guests' comfort as excellent service. If you have a bar, set it opposite the entrance, but as far away as possible. Ashtrays and cigarettes should be plentiful and well distributed, also something to nibble with drinks. Place hors d'oeuvres at another advantageous point. The informality of the host who acts as dispenser of beverages is conducive to conviviality.

Champagne is a refreshing change from whiskey or gin, enhanced by a plump strawberry in the bottom of the glass, adding color and flavor. There are other aperitif wines: the velvety red Dubonnet, Port, Byhrr, Vermouth, and Pernod. (The last three are best combined with other ingredients.) Try Dubonnet on the rocks with a twist of lemon, and for sheer simplicity, there is Port and the always reliable Sherry.

The length of the cocktail hour is flexible. If guests become restless, then the kitchen needs acceleration. Ofttimes the group becomes so engrossed that dinner may be pushed back to avoid breaking the spell. This accommodation is part of the hostess's responsibility, and with experience she meets challenging situations by an unobtrusive change. With good kitchen organization, the proper selection of dishes and service, the hostess-cook should thoroughly enjoy her own entertaining. It is this quality in a hostess which is transmitted to appreciative guests, and her cordial "Do come again" will not soon be forgotten.

Controversy

For years my optimistic and loving spouse has waged a one-man campaign against the too-prolific appetizers — out of respect for a thoughtful and carefully prepared dinner to follow. Living with a logical architecturally trained mind which recognizes that the shortest distance between two points is a straight line, I must pull my tangent ideas together, serve fewer and fewer choice morsels before the course dinner, but let my imagination run full *rein* for cocktail parties.

One Sunday night, two couples stopped in for cocktails. We had Miniature Pizzas (which I had made with one-half the recipe) plus

Stuffed Mushrooms   Chicken Chutney Salad
Wine Cheddar Cheese
Toasted Buttered Cocktail Rye   Sesame Crackers

The usual protest of "too much; how can we eat dinner?" ensued. I met it with a jaded eye, but secret delight. Very well, I thought, tonight I accept the challenge of the hors d'oeuvre battle, and you shall not eat a full dinner. After another cocktail, I raided the larder, and reentered with shining platters, girded for conquest. The emergency shelf and freezer had disclosed this bounty:

Cold Pickled Tongue   Hot Rye Bread*
Assorted Cheeses
Herkimer   Cheddar   Muenster
Strawberries with Hulls
(on a green plate)
Mustard-Gherkins   Sweet Pickles   Preserved Kumquats
Fruit Topped Cookies
Coffee   Sanka

From the freezer came

Rye Bread   Strawberries   Cookies

From the refrigerator

Tongue and Cheeses

The emergency cupboard offered

Mustard Gherkins   Sweet Pickles   Preserved Kumquats

At the Jockey Club in Madrid, the distinctive Blinis, unlike those served anywhere else I had ordered them, were a large puffy kind, lavishly spread with black caviar. This is how I translated their measurements.

PUFFY BLINIS WITH CAVIAR

3 eggs, separated	¼ cup milk
¼ cup flour	shortening for greasing skillet
½ teaspoon salt	4 ounces black caviar
1 teaspoon grated prepared or	1 cup sour cream
fresh orange peel	8 lemon wedges
⅛ teaspoon white pepper	¼ cup chopped onion

Beat egg yolks until thick and lemon colored. Add flour and salt; blend well, then beat in orange peel, pepper and milk. Beat egg whites until very stiff; fold into yolk mixture. Grease

* Pièce de résistance: place foil-wrapped frozen sliced rye bread in 450° oven for 15 minutes or until thoroughly heated.

a 6-inch skillet lightly; pour in 4 scant tablespoons batter, or use a scant ¼ cup measure as a ladle. Brown evenly on one side; turn and brown reverse side. Remove and spread each with ½ tablespoon caviar; roll; place seam side down and top with sour cream. Serve with lemon wedges and chopped onion. Makes 8 cakes.

For these, individual service is the most attractive.

Try this delicious substitute. Combine ¼ pound coarsely diced Nova Scotia salmon with 1 cup sour cream and fill the pancakes; roll and serve. They need no topping.

BLUE CHEESE PIE

1 tablespoon unflavored gelatine	⅛ teaspoon garlic powder
¼ cup cold water	(optional)
¼ cup half and half cream	½ cup sour cream
2 ounces (¼ cup) blue cheese	2 teaspoons Worcestershire
1 8-ounce package cream cheese, softened	1 8-inch baked pie shell

Garnish: sliced pimiento olives

Soak gelatine in water; add to cream in saucepan and stir over medium heat until gelatine is dissolved. Combine blue cheese, cream cheese, garlic powder, sour cream and Worcestershire; blend very thoroughly and stir into gelatine mixture. Pour into prepared pie crust; garnish with sliced pimiento olives. Place in refrigerator and chill until set.

A good dessert cheese to serve with fruit, or an interesting appetizer with relishes. It may be poured into a 2-cup mold instead of the pie shell. Turn out on a small platter and serve with crackers or melba rounds.

This freezes very well.

BUBBLING MUSHROOMS

16 large mushrooms
dash salt
dash savory
1 3-ounce package cream cheese

1 tablespoon sour cream
2 tablespoons minced chives,
    dried or fresh
butter for baking pan

Rinse mushrooms and remove stems; drain on paper toweling, then dust with salt and savory. Combine cream cheese, sour cream, and chives; blend well until creamy and smooth. Fill caps liberally with cheese mixture in smooth high mounds. Place on well-buttered baking pan and broil 7 to 8 minutes, 6 inches from heat. They will be browned and bubbling. Serves 4 to 5.

You may use one 3-ounce package prepared cream cheese with chives, blended with 1 tablespoon sweet or sour cream, or substitute minced green onion, fresh or dried, for the chives.

Re the mushroom stems, do not dispose of them as they are delicious sliced in sauces; or minced, a fine addition to stuffing for pancakes, poultry or sandwich spreads.

If you wish, steam the mushroom caps first (see Index).

CHEESE CHUTNEY PUFFS

½ pound Herkimer cheese, grated
½ teaspoon baking powder
¼ teaspoon curry powder
    (optional)
2 egg yolks

2 egg whites, beaten stiff
4 strips bacon, cooked crisp
    and crumbled
⅓ cup finely chopped chutney
24 1½-inch Toast Rounds

2 tablespoons softened butter

Combine cheese, baking powder, curry and yolks; fold in beaten whites. Mix bacon and chutney together carefully; spread Toast Rounds with butter and heap with bacon mixture. Cover with cheese mixture, carefully sealing the edges. Place on cooky sheet, and broil 6 inches from heat until lightly browned and puffed. Serve at once, or prepare an hour in advance and heat just before serving. Makes 24.

TOAST ROUNDS FOR CANAPÉS

Cut thinly sliced white bread into 2½-inch rounds, using cooky
cutter or rim of a glass. Toast under broiler on one side only;
spread untoasted side with softened butter and selected topping.

CHINA TOWN SHRIMP

½ pound shrimp, fresh or frozen   2 tablespoons fennel seeds
  3 slices bacon   (optional)
China Town Sauce
    Garnish: 1 cup crisp shredded lettuce, in ¼ inch strips

If you use fresh shrimp, peel them but do not remove the tails;
they add attractiveness. Clean and devein shrimp; make
"butterflies" by slitting along vein line but not through shrimp.
Steam 5 minutes if you have a steamer, or cook in salted water
3 minutes, until quite pink. Sauté bacon partially, one minute
on each side, in an oven-proof skillet. Remove bacon and drain
off fat, then cut each slice in thirds; place shrimp in one layer in
skillet and pour China Town Sauce evenly over all. Sprinkle
with fennel. Top with bacon pieces; place under broiler 6 inches
from heat and broil about 5 minutes until well heated. Spread
crisp shredded lettuce on platter and pour hot shrimps and sauce
over. The combination of hot shrimps and the cold lettuce is an
epicurean experience. Serves 4 as appetizer.

China Town Sauce

    3 tablespoons ketchup   1 tablespoon brown sugar
    1 tablespoon soy sauce   ¼ teaspoon powdered ginger
    1 tablespoon oil   ¼ teaspoon powdered garlic
    1 tablespoon honey   6 scallions, finely sliced
    2 tablespoons white vinegar   2 tablespoons apricot preserves

Combine all ingredients and blend well.

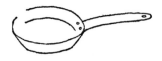

CLAM PUFFS

3 ounces cream cheese, softened	½ teaspoon Worcestershire
2 tablespoons sour cream or heavy cream	¼ teaspoon salt
	½ teaspoon grated onion
1 7-ounce can minced clams, drained	30 1½-inch toasted bread rounds
	paprika for dusting top

Blend cheese with cream; mix with clams, Worcestershire, salt and onion. Spread on toast rounds and place under broiler about 5 minutes, or until puffed and browned. Dust tops with paprika. Mixture may be made two days in advance and spread an hour in advance of serving. Broil as needed. Makes about 30 puffs.

The unusual ingredients of the Russian "Coulibiac" read like an ode to an epicure. The traditional recipe calls for a brioche crust, filled and rolled like a jelly roll, or filled and folded with a top and bottom layer of crust. My own version brings repeated requests for the recipe, which I have possessively retained until now. My schedule did not permit the time for raised dough, so I used Cream Cheese Pastry. For yeast dough, use recipe in Raised Fruit Cookies.

COULIBIAC TART

1 recipe Cream Cheese Pastry	¼ pound Nova Scotia or
2 hard-cooked eggs, coarsely chopped	¼ pound smoked salmon
	1 pound cooked shrimp, thinly sliced
1 cup sour cream	

Topping: dill weed, paprika

Remove half of dough from refrigerator; roll between 2 sheets of lightly floured wax paper. Pull paper away frequently as dough is rolled to prevent sticking and to allow the dough to spread. Roll it large enough to cover a 10-inch ovenware pie plate or low casserole and fit it into the pan. Spread the hard-cooked eggs over the dough, dotting with half the sour cream; layer first the salmon, then the shrimp. Dust with dill weed and dot with remaining sour cream. Roll out second half of dough and cover layered ingredients, sealing the edges firmly and tucking them inside the pan rim. Dust top of dough lightly with dill weed and paprika. Refrigerate until needed, and bake in 375° oven 45 minutes or until lightly browned. Delicious for luncheon with a green salad and a colorful fruit dessert. Serve with Dill Cream Sauce, if desired. Serves 6 as an entrée; 10 for an appetizer.

DILL CREAM SAUCE

1 cup sour cream	¼ teaspoon paprika
1 tablespoon lemon juice	¼ teaspoon oregano
¼ teaspoon salt	¼ teaspoon dill weed
dash cayenne	2 egg yolks, beaten

Combine all ingredients except egg yolks in top of double boiler; heat but do not permit them to come to a boil. Add ¼ cup of the heated liquid to the egg yolks very gradually, then pour egg mixture into the rest of the sauce, stirring to blend well. Serve warm but not boiling hot. Makes approximately 1 cup.

COQUILLE ST. JACQUES

1½ pounds scallops, coarsely chopped	3 tablespoons butter
½ cup dry white wine	3 tablespoons flour
½ teaspoon salt	1 cup scallop stock
dash cayenne	½ cup heavy cream
2 tablespoons finely chopped shallots or green onions	1 cup grated sharp cheese
	½ cup buttered, soft bread crumbs

Place scallops in saucepan with wine, salt, cayenne, and shallots. Bring to boil; cover and simmer 10 minutes; drain, reserving 1 cup stock. Melt butter and blend in flour; add stock and cream. Cook, stirring, until thickened; stir in cheese and scallops. Spoon into 6 large shells or individual baking dishes. Top with crumbs and bake in 400° oven 10 minutes or until browned. Serves 6.

It was in New Orleans, and we were dining in an ante bellum home, now a distinctive restaurant. Greeted by a dignified butler serving wine in the sitting room, we were ushered into the beautifully appointed dining room. A quiet charm and elegance wafted us into another era from which we were awakened by the service of piping hot Crab Lorenzo.

CRAB LORENZO

12 thin slices white bread
softened butter
½ pound crabmeat, fresh, frozen (defrosted) or canned
2 egg yolks, well beaten
½ cup melted butter
¼ cup lemon juice
¼ teaspoon salt
⅛ teaspoon paprika

¼ cup coarsely chopped mushrooms, fresh, freeze-dry or canned
1 tablespoon chopped green onions
2 tablespoons sherry
2 tablespoons grated Parmesan cheese

Cut two 2-inch rounds from each slice of bread; place on a cooky sheet and toast on both sides until lightly browned. Spread with softened butter and set aside. Pick over crabmeat to remove cartilage. Pour yolks into top of double boiler, over hot water. Do not let water touch bottom of pan; add butter gradually, stirring constantly with wire whisk or wooden spoon, then add lemon juice slowly, continuing to stir. Add salt and paprika, stir until thickened; remove from heat. Fold in mushrooms, onions, wine and crabmeat and mix gently. Place a teaspoonful on each toast round; sprinkle with Parmesan cheese and an added dash of paprika. Bake in 450° oven about 15 minutes until lightly browned or place under broiler about 5 minutes. Makes 2 dozen.

To use as an entrée, trim crusts from bread and cut into triangles before using. Proceed as above; garnish with anchovy strips if you desire, and serve 2 for each portion. Serves 6.

For either the canapés or the entrée, the recipe may be prepared well in advance; heat to serve.

With it I like to serve

Jellied Beet Consommé
Princess Salad and Chiffonade Dressing
Lemon Cheese Pie

DANISH TART

The province of Lorraine claims the original Quiche of France and in all likelihood this similar Tart was brought to Denmark with other historical French importations. My imagination places it in the Napoleonic era when the Count and Countess Bernadotte left France for Denmark, there to become the reigning King and Queen.

Flaky Pastry for 1 8-inch tart

1 cup flour	6 tablespoons solidly cold margarine or butter
¼ teaspoon salt	2 tablespoons cold water

Mix flour and salt; cut in 2 tablespoons butter with knife or pastry blender until consistency of cornmeal, then add second 2 tablespoons butter and cut until size of peas. Add just enough cold water to hold dough together. Shape into ball; wrap in wax paper and chill in refrigerator or freezer about 30 minutes. Remove and roll between 2 sheets of wax paper 10″ to 12″ rectangle; cover with shavings of butter from remaining 2 tablespoons. Fold dough over butter into thirds; roll out again; fold in thirds and chill thoroughly. Remove and roll ¼ inch thick into 11-inch circle. Remove top layer of wax paper; turn over onto 8-inch plate with paper on top and then peel it off. Fit dough loosely into pan; turn edges under at rim and press with tines of fork to make ridges. Chill ½ hour before baking. Prick slightly and place in 375° oven for 10 minutes until partially baked. Add Base Filling; cover with custard, return to 375° oven and bake 20 minutes or until custard is set. Serves 6.

This is a wonderful crust for other pies or tarts. Double the quantity to make 18 4-inch tarts or a double crust.

Base Filling Selections

Any two of the following may be spread over tart crust and covered with Custard Filling.

4 thin clices Canadian bacon, sautéed and cubed
6 slices bacon, fried crisp and crumbled
1 medium onion, thinly sliced
1 medium onion, finely chopped
½ cup sliced green onions
½ cup Danish blue cheese
½ cup chopped ham

The onion of either sort may be combined with ham or bacon.

Custard Filling

4 eggs, lightly beaten	½ teaspoon salt
2 cups half and half cream	¼ teaspoon white pepper
¼ teaspoon grated or ground nutmeg	1 tablespoon butter

Combine ingredients except butter; pour over Base Filling in tart shell; dot with butter and bake as directed.

If you do not have small tart shells, here is a very convenient way to "do it yourself." For the final rolling, place dough on a sheet of heavy duty aluminum foil and roll to ⅛ inch thickness. Cut foil and pastry into 3-inch circles, turn up sides of dough and foil to make tart shells. Proceed as for large tart.

QUICHE LORRAINE

For traditional Quiche Lorraine, use the recipe for Danish Tart with suggested crumbled bacon and custard as the filling.

SWISS CHEESE QUICHE

Omit the bacon from the traditional Quiche Lorraine and add ½ cup grated Swiss cheese to the custard filling. These may be used as individual tarts. For added flavor, blend in a tablespoon of grated onion.

EGG ROLLS

Skins

¾ cup sifted flour	pinch of sugar
1 tablespoon cornstarch	1½ cups water
1 teaspoon salt	sufficient salad or peanut oil
2 eggs, beaten	for sautéeing and deep frying

Sift flour, cornstarch and salt into bowl; beat in eggs and sugar. Add water slowly, beating constantly until batter is smooth. To make each egg roll skin, lightly grease a hot 6-inch skillet. Pour 3 tablespoons batter into skillet, tilting pan quickly to cover bottom. Bake until set; turn once and bake reverse side. Stack as finished while preparing balance. Place 2 tablespoons of filling on each pancake; fold opposite sides over filling and roll up from one open side to close roll. Pour oil into deep saucepan to a depth of 2 inches; heat to 375° or until a cube of bread toasts in 40 seconds. Place 3 or 4 Egg Rolls at a time in heated oil and fry until golden. Drain on paper towel and remove to baking sheet; place in 250° oven to keep warm. Slice each in thirds and serve with Mustard Sauce and Plum Sauce. Makes 18.

Filling

½ cup finely chopped celery	½ cup finely diced
¾ cup shredded cabbage	cooked beef
½ cup water	4 scallions, finely chopped
3 tablespoons salad oil	½ cup water chestnuts,
½ cup finely diced cooked	drained and finely chopped
shrimp	1 garlic clove, minced
¼ cup soy sauce	

Place celery, cabbage, and water in saucepan; bring to a boil and drain. Heat oil in skillet; add shrimp and beef; sauté 3 minutes, stirring constantly. Combine all ingredients and sauté 5 minutes, stirring well.

Rags to Riches

Strolling near the American Embassy in Rome, we chanced upon an obscure and faceless entranceway from which the most delicious odors emanated. Down three steps, a sharp turn, and we encountered a friendly, gay and completely sophisticated group of diners. My limited knowledge of Italian gave me the impression that these were professional people, of the art and gourmet level.

I developed a subtle swinging motion of the head during dinner in a decorous effort to see all. A striking black and white appetizer course was served and attacked with great gusto. The charming maître d'hôtel exclaimed, "Oh, madam, you must have it." "It" was a study in texture contrast, as well as color: Fagioli con Caviale; crisply cooked white navy beans, mixed with olive oil and lemon juice, topped with black caviar, and served in individual salad bowls.

FAGIOLI CON CAVIALE AL ROMANO
(White Beans with Caviar)

2 cups dried white pea beans (quick cooking or regular)	¼ teaspoon coarsely ground pepper
¼ cup olive oil	¼ cup caviar (domestic or imported)
2 tablespoons lemon juice	

Garnish: lemon wedges

Cook beans according to package directions; drain well and cool. Toss with oil, lemon juice, pepper, and turn into serving bowl. Spread caviar lightly over beans and toss before serving. Garnish with lemon wedges. For more formal service, use individual salad bowls. For a living room appetizer, have your guests serve themselves; pepper mill and Melba Toast at hand. Serves 6 to 8.

The Roman chef tosses the warm beans with ¼ cup Chianti.

GREEN ONION PIE

Milk Pastry

1 cup sifted flour   ½ teaspoon sugar
½ teaspoon salt   ½ cup butter or margarine
2 tablespoons milk

Sift flour with salt and sugar. Cut in butter as for pastry. Add milk and toss gently and quickly. Roll dough to fit a 9-inch pie plate. Flute edges.

Green Onion Filling

3 cups thinly sliced green   dash cayenne pepper
  onions and tops   ½ teaspoon caraway seeds
¼ cup butter or margarine   1 cup milk
1 teaspoon salt   1 cup sour cream
⅛ teaspoon pepper   2 eggs, slightly beaten

Cook onions in butter 5 minutes. Season with salt, pepper, cayenne and caraway seeds. Blend in milk, sour cream, and eggs. Turn into prepared pastry shell. Bake at 400° 15 minutes; reduce heat to 350° and bake 30 to 40 minutes longer, or until custard is set.

Serve hot as an appetizer or as a hot vegetable dish. Light cream may be used instead of milk.

GUACAMOLE

2 medium-sized ripe avocados   1 onion, grated
3 hard-cooked eggs, finely   1 teaspoon salt
  chopped   1 teaspoon lemon juice

Mash avocados; add finely chopped eggs, grated onion, salt and lemon juice. Blend well and serve with crackers, Melba Toast, or corn chips. Do not prepare too far in advance, as mixture tends to darken. However, should there be leftovers, they may be brightened with a drop or two of green coloring. The flavor lasts! Makes about 1½ cups.

JAPANESE CRAB BALLS

1 tablespoon butter	½ teaspoon salt
1 tablespoon flour	1 teaspoon lemon juice
½ cup milk, scalded	½ cup cornstarch
1 10-ounce package crabmeat or	vegetable oil
1 6½-ounce can crabmeat	

Heat butter in skillet; add flour and stir until mixture is thick and smooth. Add milk slowly, stirring until smooth and thickened; cook until it reaches the boiling point. Blend in crabmeat, salt, lemon juice, and chill. Shape into walnut-sized balls and roll each in cornstarch. Heat sufficient oil to cover, and deep-fry a few at a time in heated oil. Serve hot, with Plum Sauce and Mustard Sauce.

KARIC CRABMEAT CHOUX

3 6-ounce cans crabmeat	½ teaspoon curry
½ cup mayonnaise	8 drops tabasco
½ cup sour cream	juice of 1 lemon
¼ cup pickle relish	10 drops yellow coloring
6 stalks celery, finely chopped	(approximately)
2 teaspoons Worcestershire	1 recipe Tiny Cream Puffs

Devein crabmeat, and flake; combine all ingredients and blend well. Cut top from small choux (cream puffs) about ¼ of the way down; fill with a heaping teaspoon of crabmeat mixture and replace "hat." Fills about 4 dozen.

Though I had never encountered a recipe for Duck Pâté, there seemed no reason to ignore a plump morsel of liver, and this delicious, creamy spread results.

LIVER PÂTÉ CANARD

3 tablespoons butter or margarine	¼ teaspoon salt
1 duck liver or 3 chicken livers	2 hard-cooked eggs
1 small onion (approximately	½ teaspoon lemon juice
⅓ cup), coarsely chopped	1 teaspoon cognac

Heat the butter in a skillet; add liver and onions; sauté over medium heat until lightly browned, about 10 minutes; add salt. Combine liver and onions with eggs in a food mill or sieve and press through to a fine paste. Add lemon juice; blend; then mix in cognac. Place in a small mold or crock, about 4-ounce size, and chill. Spread on Melba Toast rounds or cocktail rye. Garnish with a sprig of watercress and a dusting of paprika. Makes about 1 dozen.

This recipe can be doubled or tripled with no problem.

MINIATURE PIZZAS

1 recipe dough for Raised Fruit Cookies
1 6-ounce can tomato paste
¼ cup grated Parmesan cheese
oregano
3 garlic-flavored frankfurters, cut in ¼-inch slices

Prepare the cooky dough; roll to ⅛-inch thickness, then cut into 2-inch rounds. Make a depression in each cooky and fill with ½ teaspoon tomato paste; sprinkle with oregano. Cover with a slice of frankfurter and top with ¼ teaspoon cheese. Bake in 450° oven until browned, about 10 minutes. Makes about 4 dozen.

This recipe may be made in advance and refrigerated until serving time, or may be baked and frozen, then reheated. If dough is a larger amount than needed, use excess for cookies to serve with coffee.

You may use prepared refrigerator biscuits instead of cooky dough; cut each in half and proceed as above.

For variety, substitute a rolled anchovy, a button mushroom or ½ pimiento olive for the frankfurter slice.

This is the lip-smackingest, messiest finger food in the category. The formal, hot, scented towels of Chinese dining would be a boon. Instead, have a goodly supply of paper napkins available.

ORANGE WINGS

10 chicken wings	1 teaspoon seasoned salt
2 tablespoons butter	½ cup orange marmalade

Rinse wings and dry on paper toweling, tucking the tip under the larger joint to form a triangle. Heat butter in skillet; sprinkle wings with seasoned salt and place in heated butter. Sauté over moderate heat until evenly browned on both sides, about 20 minutes. Spread with orange marmalade, continuing to sauté while basting frequently with pan drippings for another 20 minutes. Remove from skillet; drain on paper toweling and serve hot. They will be glazed and "sticky" good. Serves 4 to 5.

The wings may be cut in half and the tips discarded. This way they are a bit more manageable, but definitely on the dainty side.

Use the leg pieces, if you prefer, and prepare a larger quantity to use as an entrée.

This dish may be made in advance and reheated in a 325° oven. Do not drain when done; instead, set aside and baste when reheating. If made only a short time in advance, they may be drained and kept hot in the oven at 300° until served.

OYSTERS ROCKEFELLER

24 medium-sized oysters	½ clove garlic, minced
4 tablespoons melted butter	¼ teaspoon salt
1 tablespoon finely chopped	⅛ teaspoon paprika
onion or 1 tablespoon finely	1 cup cooked chopped spinach
chopped shallot	⅓ cup bread crumbs
2 tablespoons snipped parsley	2 tablespoons anisette (optional)

Remove oysters from shells; wash shells and replace oysters; or, place oysters in greased ovenware serving platter without shells. Heat 2 tablespoons of the butter; add onion, parsley and garlic; sauté lightly. Spread over oysters and dust with salt and paprika. Combine spinach, crumbs, anisette, and remaining 2 tablespoons butter. Spread over oysters. Bake in 400° oven 12 to 15 minutes, until lightly browned.

It is difficult to say how many people 24 oysters will serve, as it depends on the menu. As a first course, 6 are customary; with other hors d'oeuvres 3 should be ample. Of course, the question of appetites is always vague, and a definite hostess problem. We are not alone on that score.

Yucatan with its abundance of papaya combines it colorfully with prosciutto.

PROSCIUTTO PAPAYA

1 large papaya or	¼ pound prosciutto
1 small honeydew melon	(about 12 thin slices)
freshly ground pepper	

Garnish: 4 lime wedges, watercress

Cut melon in half, then in quarters; remove seeds and peel. Cut each quarter into 3 slices and drape a slice of prosciutto over each slice. Garnish with lime wedge and a sprig of watercress. Have a pepper mill at hand. Serves 4.

Necessity being the mother of invention, I have substituted thin slices of chipped beef for prosciutto.

PUMPERNICKEL CHEESE PIE

6 to 8 very thin slices pumper-	¼ cup melted butter
nickel bread	1 recipe Roquefort Wheel
Garnish	
20 large grapes, halved and	small bunches grapes
seeded	sliced apples

Use an 11-ounce package of sliced pumpernickel squares, or an unsliced pumpernickel loaf, and slice ¼-inch thick; remove crusts. Dip both sides in melted butter and place in 9-inch pie pan in single layer to line pan evenly. Trim around the edges and use leftover pieces to fill in the connecting openings. Prepare ingredients for Roquefort Wheel and pour into prepared pumpernickel pie crust, spreading evenly. Garnish with grape halves by placing them cut side down, close together around edge of pie; chill. Serve in wedges or from pan bordered with bunches of grapes and apple slices. Serves 10 as appetizer.

For an alternate garnish, trim with sliced pimiento olives.

For an alternate filling with a milder cheese flavor, prepare Blue Cheese Pie Filling.

ROQUEFORT WHEEL

1 tablespoon unflavored gelatine	½ pound Roquefort cheese
2 tablespoons water	1 teaspoon caraway seeds
2 tablespoons milk	½ teaspoon paprika
1 3-ounce package cream cheese	2 teaspoons Worcestershire
½ cup heavy cream, whipped	

Garnish: parsley, rose radishes

Soak gelatine in water 5 minutes; add milk then dissolve over heat while stirring. Beat cream cheese and Roquefort until fluffy; combine with caraway seeds, paprika and Worcestershire; mix until well blended. Add gelatine; mix and place in refrigerator until it starts to thicken. Fold in whipped cream and pour into a 9-inch well-greased pie pan; refrigerate again until set. Turn out on platter; arrange assorted crackers around the wheel of cheese. Garnish with parsley and rose radishes.

Use for filling Pumpernickel Cheese Pie or pour into baked pie crust and serve as Roquefort pie. Serves 12 for appetizer.

RAMAKI

1 8-ounce can water chestnuts, drained and halved	12 slices bacon, cut in thirds
1 cup wine vinegar (approximately)	6 tablespoons brown sugar

Marinate water chestnuts in vinegar to cover for a minimum of 1 hour; drain. Spread each ⅓ bacon slice with brown sugar, about ½ teaspoon or more. Place a half water chestnut on sugar-spread bacon; roll it in the strip and fasten with toothpick. Bake in 350° oven for 20 minutes; drain off accumulated grease and return to oven for about 10 minutes or until crisp and brown. Makes about 36 pieces.

To prepare in advance, remove from oven when grease is drained, set aside and reheat in 350° oven for 10 minutes when needed.

To freeze, remove after draining; cool and wrap for freezing. To serve, remove from freezer and heat in 375° oven 20 minutes.

RED CAVIAR POLKA DOTS

1 8-ounce package cream cheese	¼ teaspoon dill weed
2 tablespoons mayonnaise	¼ teaspoon salt
2 tablespoons sour cream	1½ teaspoons unflavored gelatine
½ teaspoon lemon juice	½ cup milk
¼ teaspoon onion powder or	¼ teaspoon Maggi or
¼ teaspoon onion juice	¼ teaspoon Worcestershire

1 4-ounce jar red caviar

Let cream cheese stand at room temperature until softened. Blend in mayonnaise, sour cream, lemon juice, onion powder, dill weed and salt; mix until very smooth. Combine gelatine with milk in a small saucepan, and let stand 5 minutes. Place over low heat and stir until dissolved; blend in Maggi and cheese mixtures. Fold in caviar gently, to avoid breaking delicate globules. Pour into greased 2-cup mold; place in refrigerator until set. Turn out on small platter; garnish with lemon wedges and border with caraway rye bread and/or crackers. Makes 2 cups. Serves 6 to 8.

I like the freshness of a pretty doily. Cut a piece of wax paper an inch larger in diameter than your mold and place it on the doily. Turn the mold out on the wax paper, place crackers around it and brighten the base with crisp watercress.

I serve shrimps with the mold if more appetizer is needed. Then I use a larger plate, rim the mold with the shrimps (use about 1 pound) and add a bowl of cocktail sauce nearby. The colors are worthy of note: pink, red, and green.

To unmold, dip the mold in and out of hot water very quickly; run a knife around edge of gelatine mixture and cover with a plate. Hold it firmly, turning the mold over in proper position; smack it smartly and raise it carefully and gently.

SHRIMP NORICE

2 pounds cooked shrimp, cleaned and deveined
Dressing Norice

Add shrimps to Dressing Norice and toss gently. Pour into serving bowl and refrigerate 15 to 20 minutes. Place bowl on platter and border with assorted crackers. Serves 6 to 8.

Dressing Norice

1 cup heavy cream, whipped	1 teaspoon chopped onion
1 cup mayonnaise	(optional)
1 teaspoon lemon juice	2 teaspoons curry

Prepare two days in advance of serving to blend flavors. Fold cream and mayonnaise together; blend in lemon juice, onion and curry. Cover and place in refrigerator.

SHRIMP VERMOUTH

2 tablespoons olive oil	⅛ teaspoon pepper, freshly
1 pound shrimp, cleaned	ground
and deveined	½ cup dry Vermouth
½ teaspoon salt	juice of 1 lemon (3 tablespoons)
1 tablespoon butter or margarine	

Heat oil in skillet; add shrimp and cook about 7 minutes, until golden brown, turning constantly. Sprinkle with salt and pepper; lower heat and add Vermouth, lemon juice and then butter. Allow to simmer 5 minutes. Spear with cocktail picks and serve immediately. Serves 4.

This is a last-minute gourmet "quickie."

SWEET AND SOUR MEAT BALLS

3 slices bread, crusts removed	½ cup ice water
2 pounds ground beef chuck	1 1-pound can tomatoes
1 small onion, grated	4 gingersnaps, crumbled
1 teaspoon salt	½ cup brown sugar
⅛ teaspoon pepper	½ cup white sugar
¼ teaspoon paprika	juice of 1½ lemons (4½ table-
1 egg	spoons)
	½ teaspoon salt

Soak bread in a cup of cold water; squeeze dry. Mix beef, onion, salt, pepper, paprika, egg, bread and ice water; form into small balls the size of walnuts. Sieve tomatoes directly into saucepan; add gingersnaps, sugars, then lemon juice and salt. Cook slowly, covered, until dissolved, then add meat balls and simmer 2 hours. Meat balls will be glazed, the sauce thickened. Serves 8 for appetizer.

TENDERLOIN SQUARES HAWAIIAN

1 pound beef tenderloin (cut in 1-inch cubes)
Hawaiian Marinade

Place beef in shallow pan in a single layer, and pour Hawaiian Marinade over cubes. Refrigerate 30 minutes; drain off the marinade and reserve for basting. Place under broiler 3 inches from heat and broil quickly, about 1 minute on each side or to your desired doneness. For delicious, "fun" eating have your guests prepare them over a living room hibachi. Serves 4 to 6 as an appetizer.

Hawaiian Marinade

2 tablespoons sake or sherry	1 teaspoon monosodium glutamate
⅛ teaspoon powdered ginger	⅛ teaspoon garlic salt
¼ cup brown sugar	2 tablespoons salad oil
½ cup soy sauce	⅛ teaspoon freshly ground pepper

Combine all ingredients and blend well. Makes about 1 cup.

TERIYAKI CHICKEN NOGUCHI

2 3-pound chickens, quartered	2 teaspoons salt
2 teaspoons sugar	Teriyaki Marinade

Place chicken quarters in one layer in shallow pan and sprinkle with sugar and salt; refrigerate overnight. Four hours before serving, pour Teriyaki Marinade over chicken; return to refrigerator and let stand 2 hours. Turn frequently so chcken is evenly flavored; drain, reserving Marinade for basting. Place in 350° oven and baste at once. Bake 1½ hours, turning the chickens and basting thoroughly every 15 minutes. The chicken will be glazed and shiny brown. To serve, cut into bite-sized pieces — a cleaver is an efficient tool for this operation, if you own one. Makes about 36 pieces; serves 10 to 12.

Teriyaki Marinade

1 cup sugar	2 teaspoons fresh ginger, finely
1 cup soy sauce	grated, or 2 teaspoons
1 teaspoon monosodium glutamate	powdered ginger
½ cup dry white wine or sake	

Combine ingredients and blend thoroughly. Makes 2½ cups marinade.

May be used for fish; see Fresh Salmon Teriyaki.

TINY MUSHROOM TARTS

24 baked 1-inch Flaky Tart Shells	Mushroom Filling
2 tablespoons grated Parmesan cheese	

Mushroom Filling

2 tablespoons butter	⅓ cup half and half
¾ cup chopped fresh mushrooms	cream or milk
(about 20 medium sized)	½ teaspoon salt
1 green onion, thinly sliced	⅛ teaspoon garlic
1½ teaspoons instantized flour	powder

Heat butter in skillet; add chopped mushrooms and green onions; sauté 5 minutes. Sprinkle with flour; add cream and

simmer until blended, about 5 additional minutes. Stir in salt
and garlic powder. Flaky Tart Shells, partially baked for 6
minutes, will allow for additional browning when reheated
with filling. Heap each with a generous teaspoon of filling;
sprinkle with cheese. Place in a 350° oven for 15 minutes.
Serve piping hot. Makes 24 tarts.

Flaky Tart Shells

1 cup sifted flour	⅓ cup shortening
½ teaspoon salt	2 tablespoons water

Mix flour and salt; cut in shortening with pastry blender until
texture of cornmeal. Sprinkle with water, then mix with fork
until dough forms a ball; shape until smooth. Roll on sheet of
heavy duty aluminum foil to ⅛-inch thickness. Cut foil and
pastry into 3-inch circles. Turn up side of dough and foil to
make tart shells; prick bottom. Bake at 450° for 6 to 8 minutes
until slightly brown. Fill and bake an additional 10 minutes or
until heated and browned. Makes 12 to 15 tarts.

These shells baked for only 6 to 8 minutes allow for additional
baking with Mushroom or other heated filling. To complete
shells for cold filling, bake a total of 15 minutes, or until nicely
browned.

Cream Cheese Assortment

Cream cheese is the housewife's boon. It can be a many-flavored
thing.

Basic mixture

1 8-ounce package cream cheese
2 tablespoons sour or sweet cream

Soften the cream cheese and blend thoroughly with cream.

For appetizers

Make marble-sized balls; roll in chopped nuts or chives; spear
on toothpicks.

Stuff prunes, apricots, figs, cherries or olives.

Make a sandwich of 2 thin slices of apple or pear; or with pecan or walnut halves. This variety may be used in salads as well.

Stuff celery, either small branches or large ones, cut in 1½-inch lengths. Stuff stalks of French endive, finocchio, or caps of fresh mushrooms. Stuff celery cabbage, replace stalks and tie to original shape, chill and cut crosswise in ¾-inch slices.

Neufchatel, which has ⅓ less calorie content, may be invariably substituted for cream cheese.

Combine basic mixture with one of the following

For canapés

1 teaspoon fresh dill or	⅓ cup chopped green onion
1 teaspoon dill weed	⅓ cup snipped parsley
4 slices crumbled bacon	1 tablespoon chutney

Spread on toast rounds or crackers, and top with one of the following:

anchovy fillets	3 or 4 capers
1 small smoked oyster	⅓ cup snipped parsley
1 tiny Danish shrimp	1 tablespoon chutney
½ teaspoon mashed sardines	cube of Nova Scotia salmon

If desired, they may be broiled until puffed and brown.

For dips

Blend with one of the following

1¾-ounce can anchovy fillets	½ cup pickle relish and
1 can sardines, mashed	2 tablespoons chopped pimiento
1 6-ounce can minced clams, drained	½ cup Blue cheese and
	1 tablespoon Worcestershire

Use cream cheese as a binder for chopped seafood or meat. Add horseradish, steak sauce, tabasco or other seasonings and herbs.

CAVIAR-FROSTED CREAM CHEESE

1 8-ounce package cream cheese
1 1¾-ounce jar caviar

Place cream cheese in center of 10-inch serving plate. Spread caviar over top and let stand at room temperature 7 or 8 hours; the cheese will absorb flavor. Border platter with toast rounds, crackers, olives, and rose radishes. This delicious appetizer serves 6.

Not quite as festive but similar and very good: cover the cheese with a coating of meat stock paste, or 1 tablespoon Worcestershire. Make several dents with a knife in surface of cheese to retain coating.

CREAM CHEESE AND BOLOGNA

Spread bologna with cheese and make cornucopias, or stack 5 slices cheese-spread bologna. Chill and cut in wedges; spear with toothpicks.

TOMATO TIDBITS

In our abundant land we accept tomatoes, this beautiful fruit, with complacency. In England, where they are plentiful only in season, they are found at the florists, each one carefully clothed in tissue. Their versatility is endless. Cherry or plum tomatoes, when in season, are delightful and colorful assets used as appetizers, garnishes or in salads.

For appetizers or salads, slit cherry or plum tomatoes ¾ through and stuff them with:

softened cream cheese   1 tiny Danish shrimp
1 small smoked oyster   1 teaspoon mashed sardines
1 teaspoon crab salad

For tasty variety add 4 slices crumbled bacon or try adding to an 8-ounce package of softened cream cheese one of the following, and blend well:

1 teaspoon fresh dill   1 teaspoon snipped parsley
1 teaspoon chopped green onion

For garnish

Make marble-sized balls, place in hollow side of peach, apricot, avocado or pear halves, fresh or canned.

For desserts

Arrange a plate of figlets, dried or fresh figs, dates, and tender prunes around an 8-ounce block of cream or Neufchatel cheese. Serve with crackers.

The fruits may be stuffed with cheese, also.

To plump the dried fruits, cover with boiling water and allow to stand 15 minutes. Drain well.

Accept the challenge and try your own ideas; they can be endless.

Soupçon of Soups

FROM the recording of a recipe for Avgholemono by Apicius in A.D. 200, to the great variety of today, soup has always been a singular favorite.

Monks of the feudal thirteenth century made soups an artistry. The eighteenth century produced bouillon as a base for innumerable sauced gourmet dishes, and these sauces were the dunkers' joy. When bouillon was cleared and strained into consommé another achievement was hailed — the consummate soup.

The American Revolution produced "pepper pot," and other thick soups arrived here from France via Canada. Distortion of the French "la chaudière" (the kettle) in which bouillabaisse is conceived, gave us our name for the popular chowders.

In any language, from every land, emerges a favorite soup, thick or thin, hot or cold, vegetable, fish or fowl, acclaimed and enjoyed throughout the world.

ANDALUSIAN GAZPACHO

1 medium onion, sliced	¼ cup fine dry bread crumbs
1 clove garlic, minced	½ teaspoon salt
1 cucumber, peeled and seeded	2 tablespoons vinegar
3 tomatoes, peeled and sliced	2 tablespoons olive oil
1 green pepper, seeded and sliced	1 cup tomato juice

dash cayenne

Garnish

| 1 cup soft bread cubes | 1 cucumber, diced |
| 1 onion, coarsely chopped | |

Combine onion, garlic, cucumber, tomatoes and green pepper in blender and give it a whirl, or purée through a food mill. Add bread crumbs and chill ½ hour in refrigerator. Blend in salt, vinegar, oil, tomato juice and cayenne; chill until serving time. Pour into cold bowls; add 1 ice cube for each. Pass a selection of garnishes in individual dishes. Serves 8.

Here is my favorite Gazpacho. After preparing it, the descriptive phrase "soup-salad" came to mind.

GAZPACHO MÍO

1 cup peeled tomato, cut in chunks (about 2 medium)	1 small clove garlic, minced
1 cup diced green pepper	¼ cup wine vinegar
1 cup diced celery	¼ cup salad or olive oil
1 cup diced cucumber	1 teaspoon salt
¼ cup sliced green onion	⅛ teaspoon freshly ground pepper
1 tablespoon snipped parsley	1 teaspoon Worcestershire
1 teaspoon snipped chives, fresh or frozen	2 cups tomato juice
	croutons

Combine tomato, green pepper, celery, cucumber, onion, parsley, chives and garlic in a wooden bowl and chop very fine. Blend with remaining ingredients, except croutons, in a refrigerator container and chill thoroughly for several hours or overnight. Serve in mugs or bowls. Pass croutons separately for topping. Serves 8.

Using leftovers I took 2 cups of this recipe and evolved "Frozen Gazpacho," a delicious mold, served as a soup or a salad. Supplement the amount, if necessary, with additional tomato juice.

GAZPACHO FRÍO

¼ cup (scant) cold water   1 tablespoon unflavored gelatine
1¾ cups Gazpacho Mío

Garnish
    ½ head iceberg   1 cucumber, unpeeled,
       lettuce, shredded   sliced

Sprinkle gelatine over cold water and let stand 5 minutes. Strain 1 cup of Gazpacho Mío into a saucepan and bring just to boiling; add moistened gelatine and stir until dissolved. Combine with remaining Gazpacho; blend well. Let stand in refrigerator until of jelly-like consistency. Pour into 4-ounce greased molds and refrigerate a minimum of 4 hours or until set. Turn out on bed of shredded lettuce and garnish with cucumber slices. (Run the tines of a fork down sides of cucumber before slicing.) Serves 4 to 5.

Smaller molds will serve more, of course.

Pour into cups or mugs to serve as a first course.

BOUILLON ROUGE

1 cup prepared beef borscht   1 tablespoon strained lemon juice
4 cups beef consommé   1 ounce black caviar (domestic
1½ tablespoons unflavored   or imported)
   gelatine   ½ cup sour cream
⅛ cup sherry   cinnamon or nutmeg

Combine borscht and consommé; bring to boiling point. Add gelatine to sherry and lemon juice; let stand 5 minutes, then add to consommé mixture and dissolve. Adjust seasoning. Add more lemon if desired, and a little sugar if needed. Cool thoroughly. Drop 1 teaspoon caviar in bottom of each bowl or cup. Pour in cold bouillon very carefully. Refrigerate until firm. Serve with a dollop of sour cream on each and a dusting of cinnamon or nutmeg. Serves 6.

Beet borscht is available in most markets.

A magazine contest gave impetus to this original recipe, using as many prepared food products as possible.

BROWN ONION SOUP

3 tablespoons butter
½ cup chopped onions, fresh or frozen
1 tablespoon flour
4 cups water
3 teaspoons instant beef bouillon or 3 beef bouillon cubes
1 16-gram package onion dip mix (approximately 1 tablespoon)
¼ teaspoon marjoram
4 slices bread, toasted
4 tablespoons grated Parmesan cheese

Heat butter in saucepan, add onions, sauté until lightly browned. Add flour, stir until lightly browned, then pour in water, bouillon, onion dip and marjoram. Bring to boil, reduce heat, cover and simmer 30 minutes. To serve, pour into 4 ovenware bowls or a 6-cup casserole. Place toast (either triangle half slices or rounds) on soup, sprinkle with cheese and place under broiler until melted and bubbly. Serve piping hot. Serves 4.

The slices from a round loaf of bread fit beautifully.

This substantial course preceded cold Roast Chicken — an extra bird from the freezer prepared for just such a need. With it

*Velvet Noodles   Peach Chutney
Walnut Fluff Cake*

CLARET CHERRY PUNCH OR SOUP

1 quart sweet cherries (1 pound)
1 quart water
¼ cup sugar
1 3-inch stick cinnamon
½ teaspoon salt
1 cup claret
¼ cup water
2 tablespoons minute tapioca
½ lemon, thinly sliced
2 egg yolks, well beaten

Topping: 1 cup sour cream, nutmeg, sprig of mint

Wash cherries; remove stems and pits, then combine in a large kettle with water, sugar, cinnamon, salt and claret. Bring to a boil; reduce heat and simmer, covered, for 10 minutes. Mix water and tapioca; let stand 5 minutes, add to cherry liquid; add lemon slices. Bring to a boil again, then pour gradually over well-beaten egg yolks. Cool; refrigerate to chill thoroughly. Serve with a dollop of sour cream and a dusting of nutmeg. A sprig of mint is the essential to make this a julep. Serves 8 to 10.

Serve this in the living room in 6-ounce tall stemmed glasses. Sesame crackers are a good accompaniment. Try substituting other fruits or berries, either fresh or dried. The dried fruits in combinations are delicious. As part of the infinite variety, use sherry or white wine instead of claret.

I like to take advantage of the distinctive flavor of cherry pits. Tie them in a piece of linen or cheesecloth and cook with the cherries. Remove before adding cherry stock to the egg yolks.

CONSOMMÉ BELLEVUE

3 cups bouillon	½ cup whipped cream
3 cups clam juice	2 tablespoons minced parsley

Combine bouillon and clam juice; heat thoroughly. Serve in bouillon cups topped with a dollop of whipped cream and a sprinkling of parsley. Serves 6.

CURRY CUCUMBER BISQUE

2 cucumbers	1 teaspoon salt
2 scallions, minced or green, onions (white only) minced	⅛ teaspoon white pepper
	1 teaspoon curry
2 tablespoons butter or margarine	½ teaspoon oregano
6 cups chicken broth or consommé	⅛ teaspoon rosemary, crushed

Peel cucumbers, quarter lengthwise, remove seeds and chop coarsely. Place in pan with scallions and butter; simmer 10 minutes. Add broth, and remaining ingredients. Check seasoning as you add salt and pepper, as your broth may have a sufficient amount. Simmer 15 to 20 minutes. Serve with sesame seed crackers. Serves 6.

For convenience use canned consommé or bouillon cubes and water, as directed.

FRESH TOMATO BOUILLON

2 tablespoons butter
4 scallions, thinly sliced, or ½ medium onion, coarsely chopped
1 garlic clove, minced (optional)
6 medium tomatoes, cut in chunks (approximately 4 cups)
⅛ teaspoon freshly ground pepper

4 teaspoons sugar
1 stalk celery, thinly sliced
1 cup water
3 beef bouillon cubes
1 teaspoon salt
½ teaspoon celery salt
½ teaspoon oregano
½ teaspoon fennel (optional)

Garnish: avocado cubes or crumbled bacon

Heat butter in saucepan; add scallions and garlic; sauté until browned. Add tomatoes; simmer 5 minutes, then add remaining ingredients; simmer covered 20 minutes. Press through food mill or coarse sieve; top with avocado cubes or sprinkle with bacon. Makes 1 quart. Serves 6.

Serve this soup hot or cold, and if hot, serve with cooked rice.

For a thick tomato soup, peel the tomatoes before cooking, and do not strain.

When tomatoes are out of season substitute 1 quart tomato juice, or 1 1-pound 14-ounce can peeled tomatoes.

Fennel has a distinctive licorice-like taste and is an interesting seasoning; it is an optional ingredient, as the recipe is delicious without it.

JELLIED BEET CONSOMMÉ

1 1-pound 13-ounce can beets
1 cup beet liquid from can (plus sufficient water if needed)
3 10-ounce cans beef consommé
¼ teaspoon dill weed (optional)

2 tablespoons unflavored gelatine
¼ cup sherry
1 tablespoon lemon juice

Garnish: ½ cup sour cream, 1¾-ounce can caviar (domestic)

Drain liquid from beets and add water to make 1 cup. Reserve beets for another day. Add gelatine to ¼ cup beet liquid; soak for 5 minutes. Heat consommé; add gelatine mixture, stir until dissolved, then add remaining beet liquid, sherry, lemon juice and dill weed. Taste for needed salt. Pour into bouillon cups; place in refrigerator to congeal. To serve, scoop a teaspoon jellied soup from center and replace with a tablespoon of sour cream; top with caviar. Serves 6 to 8.

For another "look"

1. Chop canned beets fine; sprinkle over jellied soup and garnish with a sprig of watercress. Serve sour cream separately.
2. Place a teaspoon of caviar in bottom of each bouillon cup and fill with gelatine mixture. Chill bouillon in refrigerator until of jelly-like consistency. Top with a spoonful of sour cream.

MISTRESS FLOOD'S CLAM CHOWDER

2 7-ounce cans minced clams	1 10-ounce can tomato sauce
3 10-ounce cans clam juice	1 1-pound can stewed tomatoes
1 teaspoon salt	1 clove garlic, minced
¼ teaspoon thyme	1 stalk celery, finely diced
1 stalk celery with leaves	1 large leek, diced, or
1 whole onion	½ onion, chopped
4 tablespoons chicken fat	¼ pound haddock, diced
¼ cup flour	2 potatoes, diced
½ tablespoon curry powder	2 large green peppers, diced
1 teaspoon chopped parsley	

Drain juice of clams into large saucepan; set clams aside. Add clam juice, salt, thyme, celery stalk, whole onion; cover and simmer ½ hour. Remove vegetables and discard them. In another saucepan melt chicken fat; add flour and curry powder; cook this roux over low heat until smooth, bubbly and lightly browned. Stir a small amount of hot clam broth into roux until blended; return to clam broth, then add tomato sauce and canned tomatoes. Heat and add garlic, celery, leek, haddock and potatoes; cook 15 minutes and add green peppers, then cook an additional 10 minutes. Adjust seasonings to taste; add reserved drained clams; heat and serve at once, sprinkled with parsley. Makes about 3 quarts.

OYSTER CHOWDER

1 cup finely diced potatoes	4 tablespoons butter
½ cup finely diced carrots	1 cup fresh mushrooms, sliced
½ cup finely diced celery	1 tablespoon flour
1 whole small onion	1 cup half and half cream
½ cup finely diced green pepper	½ teaspoon seasoned salt
2 cups water	½ teaspoon seafood seasoning
½ teaspoon salt	pinch of thyme
1 bay leaf	1 teaspoon Worcestershire
⅛ teaspoon garlic powder	¼ cup dry white wine
1½ cups oysters	2 tablespoons snipped parsley

Combine potatoes, carrots, celery, onion, green pepper, water, salt, bay leaf, and garlic powder in saucepan. Bring to boiling; reduce heat and simmer 15 minutes. Drain oysters, adding liquid to vegetables; reserve oysters. Heat 2 tablespoons butter in skillet; add mushrooms, sauté 2 minutes, then add mushrooms to vegetables. Add remaining 2 tablespoons butter to skillet; stir in flour and heat until bubbly and smooth. Pour in cream gradually, stirring until smooth and blended. Add to vegetables and blend in seasoned salt, seafood seasoning, thyme, Worcestershire and wine. Adjust seasoning; bring to boil and simmer 5 minutes; add oysters, simmer additional 5 minutes or until edges of oysters curl. Pour into bowls; sprinkle with parsley and serve at once with salted crackers. Makes 7 cups.

The chowder may be made in advance except for the last-minute addition of the oysters.

SOPA DE LIMA

4 cups chicken bouillon	6 thin slices fresh lime
2 tablespoons lime juice or	fish-shaped crackers or
lemon juice	fritos

Heat bouillon to boiling; remove from heat; add lime juice. Pour into bouillon cups, garnish with lime slices and serve with the little fish-shaped crackers or fritos. Serves 6.

This is another version of the historic avgholemono soup which dates from A.D. 200. In Yucatan the lime replaces the lemon, and this soup is served with tortillas. For convenience I have added the fritos and little fish crackers.

Turkey Routine

To store leftover turkey is a cumbersome bore. I employ a method of procedure which disposes of the problem and the bird. It evolved from the preparation of our favorite Turkey Soup which must be cooked as soon as possible.

First remove the dark meat from legs and thighs in large pieces; wrap and freeze or store for immediate use. Delicious reheated with a basting of barbecue sauce.

Slice the breast, wrapping convenient portions in separate packages. Good to have on hand for Club Sandwiches or other combinations, for a cold platter or layered hot, as for a sauced Florentine or Divan casserole (with broccoli or spinach).

The larger chunky pieces of dark and light meat are fine with a White Sauce, served on toast or rice. Freeze the pieces in foil or plastic wrap; defrost before adding to sauce.

The small bits are far from useless; freeze them in 1-cup quantities and defrost when needed. Chop for sandwich fillings; grind for mousses, hot or cold, or mold a pâté.

Now for the soup.

TURKEY SOUP

Do not delay in preparing this soup of turkey bones. The flavor is far better and the dressing which adheres to the bones is used at once, as it should be.

turkey bones and leftover skin	dash powdered ginger
10 cups cold water	⅛ teaspoon white pepper
1 onion	1 tablespoon salt
3 large carrots	1 teaspoon poultry seasoning
5 stalks celery and leaves	3 onion bouillon cubes
1 teaspoon sugar	leftover gravy, if any

Crush the carcass if very large and place it in large kettle with the remaining bones and skin. Cover with cold water; add the onion (without removing outer dark leaves as they add color to the soup); add carrots, celery, sugar, ginger, pepper, salt and poultry seasoning. Bring to a boil, reduce heat; cover and simmer 2 hours. Add bouillon cubes and any leftover gravy. Adjust seasonings, adding salt if necessary. Simmer an additional 30 minutes. Strain through a sieve and serve with rice or noodles. Makes about 2½ quarts.

For a thicker soup, strain through a colander. Remove the bits of meat from the bones and add them. Stir in ⅓ cup slivered almonds for added texture and taste.

VICHYSSOISE

4 tablespoons butter	5 potatoes, peeled and
6 onions, sliced	quartered
4 leeks (no green), sliced	1 quart milk
6 cups chicken broth	1 pint half and half cream
1 pint heavy cream	

The quality of this recipe depends, in part, on the unblemished whiteness. Heat butter in large saucepan; add onions and leeks, cover and simmer until soft. Do not brown. Pour in chicken broth and add potatoes; cover and simmer 45 minutes. Sieve through food mill or strainer. Return to saucepan, add milk, and half and half cream; bring to a boil. Strain again; cool and add heavy cream. Refrigerate overnight. Makes 4 quarts.

You may use canned chicken broth, or 8 bouillon cubes dissolved in 6 cups of boiling water.

ZUCCHINI BISQUE

1 pound zucchini	½ cup chopped green onions
2 cups rich chicken broth or	½ cup Chablis or other white
1 10-ounce can chicken	wine
consommé, undiluted	2 tablespoons butter (optional)
½ teaspoon salt	

Wash zucchini; cut off ends but do not pare; slice or dice. There will be about 4 cups of the vegetable; combine in a saucepan with the broth and onion; cook 8 to 10 minutes or until zucchini is tender. Mash vegetables or give them a whirl in the blender. Combine with wine, butter, and salt. Heat. Serve with Italian breadsticks. Makes about 1 quart.

This recipe emphasizes the use of a good wine. The optional use of the butter is worth observing too. Though butter does add flavor, this creamy bisque is delicious without it, and the elimination of butter puts the recipe in the low calorie category.

There is a temptation to use long-neglected or inferior wines for cooking purposes. It is a mistake, as good wines make for exquisite preparations and no attempt should be made to disguise them in otherwise fine recipes.

This recipe is an import from Santa Margharita on the Italian Riviera. We had followed an epicure's suggestion to a nondescript little restaurant where the food belied the modesty. The Zuppa di Pesce was served from a cart; the fish transferred to individual bowls from a tremendous platter, then covered with the broth from a steaming tureen, the bread passed separately, and a slice dropped atop each bowl.

ZUPPA DI PESCE

3 pounds assorted sliced fish (trout, cod, salmon, haddock)	½ cup dry white wine
	1 quart water
1½ teaspoons salt	1 onion, sliced
¼ teaspoon coarsely ground pepper	1 stalk celery, with leaves
	2 tablespoons lemon juice or vinegar
1 cup salad or olive oil	
1 clove garlic, minced	2 teaspoons salt
2 tablespoons snipped parsley	1 bay leaf
½ teaspoon thyme	1 pound lobster or lobster tails, raw, cleaned
2 tablespoons tomato paste or catsup	½ pound shrimp, raw, cleaned

Cut fish into squares of approximately 3 inches; wash, dry and rub with salt and pepper. Heat oil in large saucepan; add fish and brown lightly on both sides. Add garlic, parsley, thyme, tomato paste and wine. Mix gently so that fish does not break; set aside. Pour water into saucepan; add onion, celery, lemon juice, salt, bay leaf and bring to a boil. Add lobster and shrimp and cook at moderate heat 5 minutes. Remove lobster and shrimp from liquid; peel both and return shells to liquid in pan. Simmer 20 minutes; strain over sautéed fish. Add lobster and shrimp; adjust seasoning, adding salt and pepper if needed. Bring to boiling; reduce heat and simmer very slowly 10 minutes. Stir gently to prevent sticking. Serve with crusty Fried Bread. Serves 6 to 8.

FRIED BREAD

Sauté ½-inch slices of Italian or French bread in olive or salad oil until lightly browned on both sides.

Fathoms of Fish

Fish as a food is as old as civilization, a true social climber since the Roman era when it was the food of the poor man. As a fish epicure, Aristotle gave it status, and today its popularity grows. One of our large fisheries distributes 276 fish items, and restaurants devoted to the delicacies of sea, lake and stream multiply daily, vying in a multiplicity of recipes.

When you buy fresh fish, make these few observations: Look the fish in the eye and be certain he responds with a bright stare.

His flesh should be firm and elastic to the touch.

The gills must be bright and pink, and the smell appealingly fresh.

Treat fish with consideration, as it is delicate and not a good "keeper."

Refrigerate it quickly.

Quick-frozen fish is fresh-catch.

One-third pound solid edible fish will serve one person.

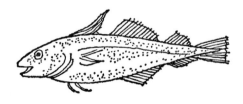

BOILED SHRIMP WITH HERBS

This is a flavorful seasoning, good when complementing a bland recipe.

1 pound raw shrimp	1 tablespoon caraway seeds
2 teaspoons salt	¼ teaspoon fennel seed
1 teaspoon lemon juice	⅛ teaspoon crushed red peppers
1 quart boiling water	

Wash shrimp. Place salt, lemon juice, caraway seeds, fennel and red pepper in boiling water; add shrimp and cook 5 minutes. Allow shrimp to cool in the stock, then remove and rinse. Peel shrimp; remove tails if used for a salad or creamed dish; allow tails to remain for dipping, barbecuing, or as "finger" food.

Shrimp de Jonghe is a famous Chicago origination. Here we vary it with crabmeat.

CRABMEAT DE JONGHE

1 6-ounce package frozen defrosted or ½ pound fresh crabmeat	⅓ cup dry bread crumbs
1 clove garlic, minced	¼ teaspoon seafood seasoning
1 tablespoon chopped parsley	4 tablespoons butter, at room temperature
1 green onion, minced	
½ teaspoon salt	¼ cup half and half cream
⅛ teaspoon freshly ground pepper	Polonaise Butter

Remove cartilage and bony pieces from crabmeat. Combine garlic, parsley, onion, salt, pepper, bread crumbs and seafood seasoning with butter and blend to a paste. Mix with cream, then add crabmeat in chunks. Turn into 4 buttered ramekins or shells; spread tops with Polonaise Butter. Bake at 400° for 15 minutes or until thoroughly heated and bubbly. Serves 4 as an appetizer. For an entrée, double the recipe.

Polonaise Butter

2 tablespoons butter	¼ cup bread crumbs

Melt butter in saucepan; add bread crumbs; mix and sauté until browned.

For Shrimp de Jonghe, use 1 pound cooked fresh shrimp, shelled and deveined; if they are large, split in two lengthwise. In some localities broken shrimp are available and serve equally well.

CRAB LOUIS

2 cups crabmeat, fresh, frozen or canned	3 hard-cooked eggs, quartered
	2 large tomatoes, cut in sixths
1 head iceberg lettuce, shredded	Louis Dressing

Remove cartilage from crabmeat and separate coarsely. Arrange a bed of lettuce on salad plates and heap crabmeat in center; pattern eggs and tomatoes around. Pour Louis Dressing generously over all. Serves 4 to 6.

Louis Dressing

1 cup mayonnaise	¼ cup chili sauce
⅓ cup sour cream	1 teaspoon grated onion
2 tablespoons snipped parsley	2 tablespoons French Dressing

Combine all ingredients and blend well.

FILLED FISH BERCY

2 slices white bread	1½ teaspoons salt
water to cover	¼ teaspoon pepper
1 pound filleted and boned carp, flounder or haddock	2 eggs, beaten
	3 tablespoons salad oil
1 pound filleted and boned trout	3 tablespoons butter
2 onions, peeled	2 onions, finely sliced
1 celery root, pared and sliced	2 cups cooked spaghetti
1 teaspoon sugar	Sauce Bercy
⅛ teaspoon marjoram	parsley

Soak white bread in water; drain and squeeze dry. Put carp, trout, onions, celery root, and drained bread through fine blade of food grinder. Place in bowl; add sugar, marjoram, salt, pepper, and eggs. Mix and blend well; it may be beaten in electric mixer to assure smoothness. Use a ⅓-cup measure to form uniform patties, then slip a knife around edge and unmold onto 9″ x 13″ shallow greased baking pan. Pour in oil and dot each patty with butter. Add sliced onions and bake in 400° oven 25 minutes. Baste often with pan drippings; reduce heat to 325° and bake an additional 20 to 25 minutes or until set and very lightly browned. Place each patty in buttered individual ovenware dishes and heat spaghetti with Sauce Bercy; around each patty, circle approximately ¼ cup spaghetti. Sprinkle with parsley; serve piping hot. Makes 12 patties; serves 6 as entrée and 12 as appetizer.

This may be arranged in dishes in advance and reheated in 375° oven for 15 minutes.

The patties freeze well.

Saucy Bercy

3 tablespoons butter	1 teaspoon seafood or poultry
3 tablespoons flour	seasoning
4 tablespoons chopped shallots	½ teaspoon salt
or green onions	⅛ teaspoon paprika
1 cup half and half cream	½ cup dry white wine
1 tablespoon snipped parsley	

Heat butter in skillet; add flour and then shallots; blend until heated and bubbly. After removing fish from pan, add cream to drippings, scraping well. Add to butter mixture, cooking until smooth; blend in seafood seasoning, salt and paprika; add wine and parsley. Heat, but do not boil. Makes 1½ cups.

Filled Fish Bercy is delicious hot or cold, and may be simply served with prepared horseradish as an accompaniment, either as appetizer or main course.

It freezes very well. Thaw first and reheat with the sauce.

FILLET OF SOLE DE NARANJA

The glowing copper utensils in Spain serve the dual purpose of cooking and presentation. This Fillet of Sole de Naranja was served in a large shallow double-handled pan reflecting the color of the orange wedges.

2 pounds fillet of sole, turbot,
   or other firm fish
1 tablespoon soy sauce
4 tablespoons olive oil
6 small shallots, minced with
   green tops or 3 green onions
½ pound sliced mushrooms
Garnish
   orange wedges
   paprika

½ cup white wine
¼ cup orange juice
2 tablespoons orange
   Cointreau or brandy
½ teaspoon salt
⅛ teaspoon coarsely
   ground pepper

2 tablespoons minced
   parsley

Dry fish with paper toweling and sprinkle with soy sauce. Pour 2 tablespoons olive oil in ovenware serving casserole; add half each of shallots and mushrooms; then place fish over. Cover with remaining olive oil, shallots and mushrooms. Add wine, orange juice and cointreau; sprinkle with salt and pepper. Bake in 350° oven about 40 minutes or until fish flakes easily with a fork and is lightly browned. Garnish with orange wedges, bright green parsley and paprika. Serve sizzling from the baking dish. Serves 6.

FRESH SALMON TERIYAKI

4 fresh salmon steaks
2 teaspoons salt
Garnish
   1 bunch watercress

2 teaspoons sugar
1 recipe Teriyaki Marinade

½ cup freshly grated horseradish

Sprinkle salmon with salt and sugar; place in single layer in shallow pan and refrigerate overnight. Remove 2½ hours before serving; pour Teriyaki Marinade over fish and refrigerate again for 2 hours, turning occasionally. Drain, reserving marinade and place under preheated broiler, 6 inches from heat. Broil 10 minutes on each side, turning only once; baste while broiling. Serve at once. Garnish with watercress and strands of freshly grated horseradish. Serves 4.

Though a delicious entrée worthy often of a start from scratch, this recipe lends itself with equal distinction to the problematical use of fish leftovers.

FISH MOUSSAKA

2 cups cooked rice (⅔ cup raw)	1 green pepper, coarsely
1 medium, sliced Sautéed Eggplant	chopped
4 Sautéed Fish Fillets, fresh or frozen	½ teaspoon ground cumin
(about 1½ to 2 pounds) sole	(optional)
or perch	¼ teaspoon garlic powder
1 15-ounce can tomato sauce	½ teaspoon salt
2 tablespoons chopped parsley	¼ teaspoon pepper
1 egg, beaten	

Butter a 2-quart casserole and spread a layer of half the rice; make a layer of eggplant, then a layer of fish and cover with the remaining rice. Combine tomato sauce, parsley, green pepper, cumin, garlic powder, salt and pepper, and pour over casserole contents. Pour beaten egg over all and bake in 350° oven 20 to 30 minutes, or until well heated. Serves 4 to 6.

Here we like the refreshing flavor of a seasoned salad such as Wax Bean Relish; add the Date and Nut Torte for a compatible Middle Eastern finale.

Sautéed Fish Fillets

1½ pounds fish fillets	2 tablespoons water or
vegetable shortening sufficient	2 tablespoons white wine
to cover skillet 1 inch deep	1 teaspoon salt
1 egg, beaten	dash cayenne

If fillets are frozen, defrost according to package directions. Rinse, dry with paper towels. Heat shortening in skillet to 370°; at this temperature a cube of bread dropped in fat will brown in one minute. Combine beaten egg and water or wine, salt and cayenne; dip fish in mixture. Place fish in heated shortening; brown about 2 or 3 minutes on each side; do not permit it to get dry, just golden. Drain on paper towels and use as directed.

The sautéed fish may be served with a Tartar Sauce or with Buttered Almonds, or with a Grape Sauce.

Sautéed Eggplant

¼ cup salad oil or shortening	½ teaspoon salt
1 eggplant, cut in ¼ inch slices, pared	¼ teaspoon pepper

Heat oil; sprinkle eggplant slices with salt and pepper; sauté on both sides until golden, 6 to 8 minutes.

An invitation from Richard Himmel, noted interior designer, and his diminutive wife, Ellie, is prophetic of an adventuresome event. The interesting decor of his home extends to imaginative serving pieces, such as the fish platter, circa 1830, on which this recipe was served.

GLAZED COLD TROUT

4 12-ounce trout, fresh or frozen, defrosted
2 teaspoons salt   Wine Court Bouillon

Salt the fish and let stand for half an hour on wax paper. Add to Wine Court Bouillon. There should be enough liquid to cover trout in one layer. Cover, bring to boil; reduce heat and simmer 3 minutes, then turn them over. The fish should flake easily; test with a fork from inside. Remove to platter; peel off top skin, cool, drain and refrigerate.

Wine Court Bouillon

2 cups water or fish stock	1 bay leaf
2 cups dry white wine	4 tablespoons tarragon vinegar
1 onion stuck with 6 cloves	1½ tablespoons sugar
2 large carrots cut in 2-inch lengths	½ teaspoon thyme (optional)
	1 teaspoon salt

Combine all ingredients in a saucepan, bring to a boil, then simmer 5 minutes.

For glaze	*Decorations*
2 cups clarified bouillon	cooked carrots from bouillon
1 egg white and shell	12 3-inch strips green onion
1 tablespoon unflavored	12 capers
gelatine	1 bunch watercress
⅓ cup water	diced aspic

To clarify bouillon, strain into a saucepan, reserving carrots; add slightly beaten egg white and shell. Bring to a boil and simmer 3 minutes. Soak gelatine in water and dissolve over low heat, stirring constantly. Strain bouillon through a piece of muslin into a bowl and add gelatine, stirring until dissolved. Refrigerate until of jelly-like consistency.

To decorate trout

Cut reserved cooked carrots into ¼-inch slices. With a flower or truffle cutter stamp out several "daisies." Arrange 3 toward head of trout, using strips of green onion for stem. Place a caper in the center of each carrot "flower." Pour slightly thickened gelatine over fish. Press lightly on decorations to anchor them in place. Set in refrigerator to harden. If necessary, fish may be glazed a second time. If gelatine becomes too congealed, stir it over hot water for a minute before brushing over fish. Pour extra aspic (congealed gelatine) in a shallow pan. Let it set until firm and cut into small squares for a garnish around the fish. Add sprigs of bright green watercress and quartered tomatoes. Serves 4.

This may be served as an entrée or first course. The fish may be masked in jelly without decorations, but I enjoy making it beautiful. Truly, though it sounds like an involved procedure, it is only a bit time-consuming, not difficult. Best of all, it can be prepared a day in advance.

DILL SAUCE FOR GLAZED TROUT

½ cup mayonnaise	2 teaspoons dill weed
4 teaspoons prepared mustard	4 teaspoons prepared horseradish
	2 teaspoons sugar

Combine all ingredients and chill well. Makes ½ cup.

HONG KONG SHRIMP

1 pound raw shrimp, shelled and deveined	1 6-ounce can water chestnuts, drained and sliced
1 tablespoon sherry (optional)	1 teaspoon salt
3 tablespoons salad oil	1 cup chicken stock
1 cup celery	2 tablespoons cornstarch
1 cup cooked peas	1 tablespoon cold water
1 6-ounce can bamboo shoots, drained	Chinese noodles

Cut shrimp lengthwise; do not cut through but spread open to "butterfly." Sprinkle with sherry. Heat 2 tablespoons oil over high heat in skillet; add shrimp and sauté until they curl and turn creamy white in color. Do not overcook; remove shrimp and set aside. Add remaining tablespoon of oil to pan; sauté celery for 1 minute, then add peas, bamboo shoots, water chestnuts and salt. Pour in stock and bring to a boil. Mix cornstarch with cold water; add to the vegetables and cook until sauce thickens, about 5 minutes. Add shrimp and bring to a fast boil. Serve on a heated platter surrounded with Chinese noodles. Makes 3 to 4 servings.

Southern Hospitality

A New Orleans love story of the eighteenth century relates that a delayed husband was wont to bring home an Oyster Loaf as a peace offering. A pearl in the oyster, too?

LA MÉDIATRICE
(Peacemaker's Oyster Loaf)

1 15-inch loaf French bread	1 tablespoon snipped parsley
6 tablespoons butter	1 teaspoon salt
2 dozen oysters	3 drops Tabasco
½ cup half and half cream	¼ teaspoon garlic powder
2 tablespoons chopped celery	(optional)

Slice off top of loaf and set aside to use as cover. Remove soft bread, leaving a shell of crust. Melt 2 tablespoons butter in skillet, add soft bread and stir over heat until lightly browned. Remove from skillet and set aside. Drain oysters, reserving liquid for basting. Heat 2 more tablespoons butter in same skillet; add oysters and sauté lightly only until edges curl. Add cream, celery, parsley, salt, Tabasco, and the sautéed bread crumbs. Fill bread shell, cover with bread top and brush with remaining 2 tablespoons butter. Place in a greased shallow pan and bake in 375° oven 5 minutes, then baste with oyster liquid. Bake about 25 minutes in all, basting two more times. Slice 1 inch thick and serve piping hot. Serves 6.

With this I like

> *Asparagus Ring   Caprice Salad*
> *Jam Cake*

OL' SOUTH BAKED OYSTERS

2 quarts oysters, drained	1 tablespoon Worcestershire
½ cup finely chopped parsley	2 tablespoons lemon juice
½ cup finely chopped shallots or onions	½ cup melted butter or margarine
	2 cups fine cracker crumbs
1 teaspoon salt	½ teaspoon seasoned salt
⅛ teaspoon pepper	⅛ teaspoon freshly ground
4 drops Tabasco	pepper
¾ cup half and half cream	

Grease a shallow 2-quart baking dish and pour in half the oysters. Combine parsley, shallots, salt, pepper, Tabasco, Worcestershire, lemon juice, and butter. Sprinkle half of this mixture over oysters and then spread half the crumbs on this layer. Repeat the three layers: oysters, seasonings, and crumbs; dust with seasoned salt and pepper. With a small knife make about 10 evenly spaced ½-inch holes through the layers. Pour the cream into them, being careful not to moisten crumbs. Place in 375° oven and bake 30 minutes or until firm. Serves 12 to 15.

SALMON SOUFFLÉ

3 tablespoons butter
3 tablespoons flour
1 cup hot milk
5 egg yolks, slightly beaten
½ teaspoon salt
½ teaspoon seasoned salt
¼ teaspoon dry mustard
1 tablespoon Worcestershire

1 teaspoon grated onion
½ teaspoon seafood seasoning or
 ½ teaspoon tarragon
 (optional)
2 cups cooked salmon or 1
 1-pound can, drained
6 egg whites, beaten stiff
Hollandaise sauce

Melt butter in saucepan; add flour and stir until smooth; add milk, stir till thickened and smooth. Set aside to cool. Beat in egg yolks gradually, then add salt, seasoned salt, mustard, Worcestershire, onion and seafood seasoning. Flake salmon medium fine; carefully remove bones. Blend into the egg yolk mixture; fold in beaten whites gently with a rubber spatula or other flat utensil. Do not mix too thoroughly. Pour into greased 2-quart soufflé dish; cut a 3-inch strip of heavy duty foil and secure with tape around top of soufflé dish to protect soufflé as it rises. Place in 375° oven and bake 35 to 45 minutes until nicely browned. Serve with Hollandaise Sauce, using the extra egg yolk for the sauce. Serves 4 to 5.

I have served the Salmon Soufflé for luncheon or supper with

Cauliflower Salad   Monkey Bread
Blueberry Cheese Cake

SCALLOPS TAPAI

3 tablespoons butter
¼ teaspoon garlic powder
1 small onion, finely chopped
1 pound scallops, fresh or
 frozen
1 tablespoon flour

½ teaspoon salt
1 teaspoon curry powder
2 tablespoons gin or
 dry vermouth
½ cup half and half cream
 and milk

¼ pound Sautéed Mushrooms

Garnish
¼ cup finely chopped
 parsley

4 slices toast, halved and
 buttered

Heat butter in skillet; add garlic powder with onion and sauté about 3 minutes, until tender but not browned. Quarter large scallops or halve small ones and sprinkle with flour; add to onion mixture and brown quickly; toss to prevent sticking, and to blend evenly. Add salt, curry, gin, cream, and mushrooms; heat to blend well. Serve from skillet or ovenware serving dish; sprinkle with parsley; border with crisp toast points. Serves 6 for appetizer, 4 as entrée.

Sautéed Mushrooms

Slice mushrooms through stem and cap; add to 1 tablespoon melted butter in skillet. Sauté 3 minutes over moderate heat, stirring gently.

SHRIMP EPICURE

1 clove garlic, minced	2 tablespoons Worcestershire
¼ cup parsley, minced	½ cup butter
¼ cup chives or green onion tops	Wine Sauce
	¼ cup bread crumbs
2½ pounds shrimp, cooked and cleaned	2 tablespoons grated sharp cheese

Combine garlic, parsley and chives; chop finely or place in blender and give a quick whirl. Sauté shrimp in butter 5 minutes; add garlic mixture and Worcestershire sauce; toss lightly. Place in 1½ quart casserole and pour Wine Sauce over all. Sprinkle with crumbs and grated cheese; brown under broiler, about 5 minutes. Serves 6 to 8.

Wine Sauce

¼ cup butter	⅛ teaspoon freshly ground pepper
1½ teaspoons arrowroot	1 10-ounce can consommé
½ teaspoon salt	2 teaspoons lemon juice
2 tablespoons white wine	

Melt butter; add arrowroot, salt and pepper; stir until smooth. Add consommé, stirring constantly; cook 5 minutes. Add lemon juice and wine; heat quickly.

SHRIMP SALAD

1½ pounds fresh or frozen shrimp, cooked, shelled and deveined
lettuce   Marinade for Shrimp

Garnish: artichoke hearts, hard-cooked eggs, radish roses

Marinade for Shrimp

3 tablespoons oil	¼ teaspoon salt
3 tablespoons malt vinegar	¼ teaspoon curry, or
⅛ teaspoon freshly ground pepper	to taste (optional)

Combine all ingredients; blend well.

Marinate shrimp a minimum of 1 hour before serving. To serve, drain; place 5 or 6 shrimp per person on a bed of lettuce; garnish with artichoke hearts, sliced egg and radish roses. Serves 4.

An excellent first course. For luncheon, serve with Finger Sandwiches.

Serve Creamy Mayonnaise separately. For 1 pound of shrimp combine ½ cup mayonnaise with ½ cup sour cream.

SHRIMP RÉMOULADE

1 head iceberg lettuce, shredded	6 thick tomato slices
2 pounds fresh shrimp cooked and cleaned	1 tablespoon chopped parsley
	Rémoulade Sauce

Arrange shredded lettuce generously on salad plates; top with thick tomato slices and circle shrimp on tomato. Cover with Rémoulade Sauce and sprinkle with chopped parsley. Serves 6.

Rémoulade Sauce

1 cup mayonnaise	1 teaspoon dry mustard
½ clove garlic, minced	1 teaspoon anchovy paste
1 tablespoon chopped parsley	1 teaspoon chopped chives
1 tablespoon capers	1 teaspoon Worcestershire
juice of ½ lemon (1½ tablespoons)	1 teaspoon dry tarragon,
2 hard-cooked eggs, finely chopped	chopped

Combine all ingredients and beat with rotary beater or in blender.

SOLE IN EGG ROLL

16 small fillets of sole	½ teaspoon salt
1 cup Seasoned Flour	⅛ teaspoon paprika
½ cup shortening	4 egg whites, beaten stiff
4 egg yolks, beaten	½ teaspoon monosodium glutamate
4 tablespoons shortening	

Rinse fillets and dry on paper toweling. Dredge each piece with Seasoned Flour. Heat shortening, in two large skillets if necessary, so fish lies flat. Sauté 10 minutes on each side, over medium heat. Cool and refrigerate overnight. Combine yolks with salt and paprika; fold in beaten whites, as for omelet; add monosodium glutamate. Heat 4 tablespoons shortening in two skillets if necessary. Dip each piece of fish in the egg mixture until well covered with a thick froth. Place in pan of heated shortening and sauté slowly 10 minutes on each side. Have the pieces well separated in pan. Arrange fillets on platter like spokes of a wheel, intersperse with cucumber cups filled with tartar sauce. Add crisp watercress and tomatoes for color. Serves 8.

You may use 4-pound trout, filleted into serving pieces for this interesting recipe.

Seasoned Flour

1 cup flour	½ teaspoon pepper
1 tablespoon paprika	1 tablespoon salt

Mix ingredients together. This flour may be used for fish or chicken. Use ¼ the amount for each 2 pounds of fowl or 1 pound of fish.

Shimmering Smelts

Smelts are native New Englanders, but an emergency in 1906 transplanted them to Lake Michigan, when the landlocked salmon faced famine. Planted to give sustenance to larger fish, they survived to become "food, fit for the gods" and gourmets. These silvery beauties spawn in April, when the midwestern shorelines are bordered with the gleaming lights of night fishermen. Huge nets scoop up the shimmering catch by the hundreds. The meat is sweet, lean and delicate, with bones so feathery they may be eaten. Cook them with or without the heads, but do not spare the butter.

SMELTS AU GOURMET

1 pound smelts	1 teaspoon salt
1 cup cracker meal	¼ pound butter
¼ teaspoon freshly ground	¼ teaspoon garlic
pepper	salt (optional)

Wipe the smelts dry with paper toweling. Dredge in mixture of cracker meal, pepper, and salt. Heat butter in skillet; add smelts and fry 3 minutes on each side until evenly browned. Turn carefully only once as they are very delicate. Place in rows on platter, garnished with crisp parsley and lemon wedges. Serves 3.

SKILLET SMELTS
(or Baked)

1 pound smelts, fresh or	2 tablespoons butter
frozen, defrosted	½ cup white wine
1 teaspoon salt	2 tablespoons cracker crumbs
¼ teaspoon white pepper	3 tablespoons melted
½ teaspoon seafood salt or ½	butter
teaspoon seasoned salt	¼ teaspoon garlic salt
1 clove garlic, minced	(optional)

It is not necessary to remove the heads, and the edible feathery bones can also remain. Wipe smelts with damp paper toweling, and place in single layer in electric skillet or ovenware pan. Dust with salt, pepper, seasoned salt; spread with garlic and dot with butter. Pour wine around fish; cover and cook over high heat about 6 minutes when wine should be absorbed. Sprinkle with crumbs and pour melted butter over; place under broiler until browned and heated, about 5 minutes. Add 2 tablespoons grated cheese if desired. Serve at once with Tartar Sauce. Serves 3.

This recipe came from Starkville, Mississippi, with the notation that it can be served as a "light luncheon or supper entrée" or as an accompaniment to a meat entrée. It's a man's dish too.

SOUTHERN SQUASH AND SHRIMP CASSEROLE

2 pounds yellow summer squash
2 tablespoons butter
2 large onions, thinly sliced
2 eggs, well beaten
½ pound cooked shrimp,
    cleaned and deveined

¾ teaspoon salt
⅛ teaspoon coarsely ground
    pepper
¼ cup dried breadcrumbs
1 tablespoon butter

Scrub squash and cut off ends. Slice or cut into small cubes. Place in a saucepan and add water to the depth of 1 inch; cover and cook over moderate heat 15 to 20 minutes, or just until tender. Drain well and mash. Heat butter, add onions, sauté until soft and golden but not brown. Stir squash, onions, shrimp, salt, and pepper into beaten eggs. Blend thoroughly and turn into well-greased 1-quart casserole. Dust with bread crumbs; dot with 1 tablespoon butter and bake in a 350° oven 45 minutes or until puffed and nicely browned. Serves 6.

For a heartier dish, add another ½ pound shrimp, and fold in 1 3-ounce package cream cheese, cut in small pieces. Please try it both ways.

I like it especially with Baked Ham, hot or cold.

As an entrée it goes well with

Perfection Salad   *Cherry Muffins*
Rum Mocha Russe

TROUT DE JONGHE

4 trout, about ¾ pound each, fresh or frozen	4 slices lemon
	4 teaspoons butter
1 recipe Crabmeat de Jonghe	salt and pepper

Garnish: radish roses, parsley

If frozen, defrost trout; do not remove heads as fish will lose their form. Bone, if necessary, then wash and dry. Press ¼ cup Crabmeat (or Shrimp) de Jonghe into each cavity. Place each stuffed fish on a strip of heavy duty foil; top each with slices of lemon and dot with butter. Seal foil airtight, but leave room for steam to circulate within. Place on baking pan in 400° oven. Bake 15 minutes; then open foil and bake 10 minutes additional. Remove from foil onto platter and pour pan juices over fish. Sprinkle with salt and pepper. Garnish with radish roses, nested in crisp parsley. Serves 4.

With this I like

Danish Dill Potatoes   *Green Tomato Relish*
Chocolate Soufflé — Sauce Marsala

TROUT IN RAISIN SAUCE

5 pounds trout or pike in 1-inch slices	½ cup dark brown sugar
	½ teaspoon cinnamon
2 tablespoons salt	1 cup raisins
1 quart white vinegar	6 whole peppercorns
1 large onion, diced	6 bay leaves
3 tablespoons white sugar	8 gingersnaps, crumbled
2 quarts water	2 large lemons, sliced

Place fish in glass pan or bowl and salt each slice well. Marinate in vinegar; let stand overnight in refrigerator. Next day pour off vinegar and discard. Place onion and white sugar in skillet; heat slowly, stirring until sugar becomes syrupy and carmelizes; sugar and onion should be golden. Add 2 quarts water, brown sugar, cinnamon, raisins, peppercorns and bay leaves. Bring to a boil and adjust seasonings. Add fish and cook uncovered, slowly, 45 minutes. Add gingersnaps, sliced lemons, and simmer an additional 15 minutes. May be served hot or cold. Serves 10 to 12.

An excellent first course, in smaller portions, as well as an entrée. May be made in advance as it can be refrigerated for several days. The flavors "marry" well.

Though most recipes add lemon slices with the water, sugar, cinnamon, and other seasonings, I like to add them for the last 15 minutes only, to preserve form and color for more attractive appearance.

WHITEFISH PARMESAN

3 pounds whitefish	1 cup sour cream
½ teaspoon salt	1 10-ounce can tomato soup
½ cup grated Parmesan cheese	

Clean fish; do not remove backbone. Wipe with paper toweling and place in greased shallow pan; sprinkle lightly with salt. Combine sour cream and soup; spread evenly over fish and sprinkle with cheese. Place in 350° oven and bake 30 to 45 minutes or until fish flakes easily when tested with a fork. Garnish with watercress and lemon wedges. Serves 6.

Pike may be prepared this same way.

Poultry Perspective

CHICKEN is the generic term for barnyard fowl of unending variety and varied origins. The multiplicity of preparations is a cogent comparison, a wealth of imaginative combinations.

The birds are of many shapes, sizes and colors, conforming fashion-like to the dining mode of each era.

The ancient Persians held cooking contests featuring fowl; later the Greeks added a force-feeding program and glazed the fatted poultry to a cooked patina. Napoleon added Chicken Marengo in honor of a triumphal encounter.

Today, the array of poultry recipes is arresting, the developed inheritance from many lands and significant traditions.

One can only envision a housewife paraphrasing while thumbing through the recipes, "How do I make thee, let me count the ways," while her spouse laments the effort of decision but savors the result with masculine gusto.

Poultry

BREAST OF CHICKEN FLORENTINE

4 whole chicken breasts, boned
1 teaspoon salt

Filling

1 10-ounce package frozen spinach, defrosted and drained
½ cup seasoned bread crumbs
1 egg
¼ teaspoon seasoned salt

1 teaspoon seasoned salt
Seasoned Sherry
Mushroom Sauce

¼ cup butter or margarine
¼ teaspoon dehydrated minced onion
⅛ teaspoon garlic powder
¼ teaspoon salt

Garnish: Radish roses, parsley

Combine filling ingredients and blend well. Spread chicken breasts on flat surface, skin side down, and place 1 heaping tablespoon of filling on each. Turn in 2 opposite sides and roll from open end, sealing well. Fasten with toothpicks; sprinkle with salt and seasoned salt. Place in a shallow pan and bake in a 350° oven 35 to 45 minutes, basting with Seasoned Sherry. Remove chicken when fork-tender and lightly browned. To serve, place on heated platter and cover with Mushroom Sauce. Garnish with bouquet of radish roses on a bed of parsley. Serves 4.

Seasoned Sherry

1 teaspoon salt
½ teaspoon seasoned salt

¼ cup sherry
¼ cup butter, melted

Blend ingredients and use to baste chicken while baking.

Mushroom Sauce

½ pound fresh mushrooms, sliced
2 tablespoons butter or margarine

¼ cup water
1 teaspoon cornstarch

Place mushrooms in skillet with butter and water. Cover and

steam 5 minutes. Make a paste of cornstarch and water; return to pan; add pan drippings from chicken and simmer 10 minutes. Pour over chicken on platter.

For an enticing luncheon, serve these in addition

Bouillon Rouge

Orange Noodle Soufflé   *Flower Pots Glacés*

Coffee

BREASTS OF CHICKEN BRISTOL

6 whole chicken breasts, boned	1 cup diced celery
2 teaspoons salt	1 medium onion, finely diced
½ teaspoon pepper	½ pound fresh mushrooms, sliced
1 cup raw wild rice or raw	½ teaspoon salt
long grain rice	paprika
¾ cup butter or margarine	Sherry Fruit Sauce

Dry chicken breasts with paper toweling; dust with salt and pepper; set aside at room temperature. Cook the rice (see Index) and place in large bowl. Heat ¼ cup butter in skillet and add celery and onion, sautéing until lightly browned; add to rice. Heat second ¼ cup butter in same skillet; add mushrooms, salt, and sauté 5 minutes; add to rice. Be certain to include all pan drippings; add ¼ teaspoon salt and toss lightly, blending well. Place boned breasts on smooth surface, skin side down and opened, then flatten firmly with hands. Spoon a sufficient amount of rice mixture on each for filling, then enclose it by bringing sides of breasts together as for a package. Fasten securely with toothpicks, shaping to look like squab chickens; place in shallow baking pan, seam side down. Brush with remaining ¼ cup softened butter and dust liberally with paprika. Bake in 375° oven 1 hour and 15 minutes, basting frequently. Pour 1 cup Sherry Fruit Sauce over breasts to form a glaze; reduce heat to 250° and bake 10 minutes; baste again with more sauce and bake an additional 10 minutes. Remove breasts to warm platter. Add remaining sauce to pan drippings and heat thoroughly. Pour a small quantity over breasts and serve remainder separately. Serves 6.

Sherry Fruit Sauce

½ 6-ounce can frozen orange juice
defrosted
1 cup pineapple juice

½ cup brown sugar
3 teaspoons cornstarch
2 tablespoons cold water

¾ cup cooking sherry

Combine orange juice, pineapple juice and brown sugar in saucepan; bring to a simmer. Make a paste of cornstarch and water; add to fruit juice mixture. Simmer about 5 minutes, until clear, then blend in sherry. Makes about 2 cups.

CHICKEN BREAST PARMIGIANA

3 whole chicken breasts
2 teaspoons salt
¼ teaspoon freshly
ground pepper
1 egg, beaten
¾ cup seasoned prepared
bread crumbs
¼ cup butter or margarine

¼ cup salad oil
2 teaspoons oregano
1 teaspoon sweet basil
6 slices Mozzarella cheese
6 tablespoons tomato sauce
¼ cup grated Parmesan cheese
1 cup water
2 tablespoons chopped parsley

Divide each chicken breast in half and season with 1 teaspoon salt and pepper. Dip each half in egg, then coat evenly in crumbs and place in refrigerator for 15 minutes or longer. Heat butter and salad oil together in large skillet; add coated chicken and sauté over moderate heat until golden brown. Remove breasts to a casserole; arrange in a single layer and sprinkle with the second teaspoon salt, oregano, and basil. Cover each piece with a slice of Mozzarella cheese; top cheese with 1 tablespoon tomato sauce and sprinkle ¼ cup Parmesan cheese over all. Pour water on bottom of casserole, but not over chicken. Place in 350° oven and bake 45 minutes. To serve, sprinkle with chopped parsley. Serves 6.

The preparation which precedes baking may be done in the

morning or the previous day. Allow an extra 10 minutes to heat through when removed from the refrigerator. Serve with Green Buttered Noodles.

An excellent recipe for thin veal steaks.

CHEDDAR CHICKEN KIEV

6 whole chicken breasts, boned	2 eggs, slightly beaten
1½ teaspoons salt	¾ cup fine dry bread crumbs
½ cup flour (approximately)	shortening for frying

Cheddar Filling

2 tablespoons butter or margarine	½ cup half and half cream
½ cup fresh mushrooms, finely chopped	¼ teaspoon salt
2 tablespoons flour	pinch cayenne
	1¼ cups shredded sharp Cheddar cheese

Heat butter in medium saucepan; add mushrooms and sauté about 5 minutes; blend in flour until smooth, then stir in cream, salt and cayenne. Simmer until mixture becomes very thick. Stir in cheese and simmer slowly, stirring constantly until cheese is melted. Turn into 8-inch pie plate and chill until firm, approximately 1 hour.

While filling is chilling, remove skin from chicken breasts and place bone side up, between sheets of plastic wrap or wax paper. Pound with wooden mallet or edge of saucer, working out from center until breast fillets are about ¼-inch thick. Peel off wrap; overlap pieces where breast was split and pin together with toothpicks; sprinkle with salt. Remove cold firm Cheddar Filling from refrigerator and cut into 6 equal portions; shape into short cylinders, then place one on each chicken breast. Fold sides of chicken over ends of filling and roll tightly in opposite direction. Fasten with poultry pins or toothpicks. Dust rolls with flour; dip in beaten egg, then roll in bread crumbs. Place in shallow pan; cover with wax paper or plastic wrap and refrigerate a minimum of 2 hours. One hour before serving, melt shortening in saucepan to a depth of 3 inches and heat to 375°. (A cube of bread dropped into the fat will brown in 40 seconds at 375°.) Add cold chicken; fry 8 minutes or until lightly browned; remove and drain on paper towels. Place in shallow dish in one layer; bake in 325° oven 30 to 45 minutes or until tender. Serve on piping hot platter and border with Fruit Pyramids; alternate with sprigs of crisp parsley for contrast, a dash of paprika for cheer and flavor. Serves 6.

Substitute 1 cup of cold butter for Cheese Filling; form into 6 cylinders. (They may be sprinkled with ¼ cup chopped chives. *Voilà* — Chicken Kiev.)

For a good flavor combination, balance with these as part of your menu

Noodles in Pecan Crust

Fruit Pyramids   *Mousse au Chocolat*

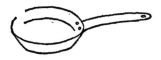

Curry powder is a blend of spices and herbs, mainly turmeric, cumin, and sage. Curry is not a spice, but a preparation. East Indian recipes are of great variety and their cooks urge your own combination of seasonings. We had chicken curry in Thailand, and when questioned the chef replied, "All cooking must be done with glee." So I used turmeric and cinnamon, and proceeded with abandon, coming up with this Chicken Curry Glee.

CHICKEN CURRY GLEE

1 2- to 3-pound fryer, disjointed	¼ teaspoon ginger
4 tablespoons butter	1 teaspoon pumpkin pie spice
1½ teaspoons seasoned salt	1 onion, chopped
¼ teaspoon turmeric	½ teaspoon cardamom powder
dash cayenne	½ teaspoon sesame seeds

Curry Accompaniments

Dry the chicken; heat 3 tablespoons butter in electric skillet, heavy Dutch oven or stove skillet. Add chicken, skin side down, and sprinkle with seasoned salt, turmeric, cayenne and ginger. Sauté until browned and turn over on other side; sprinkle with pumpkin pie spice, onion, cardamom powder and sesame seeds. Dot with remaining tablespoon of butter; cover and simmer about one hour or until done. Shake the pan or move pieces around to prevent them from sticking. The electric skillet should be at 300°; however, as heating varies, use your own judgment to keep it at a simmer. Serve in Raisin Rice Ring, with small bowls of Curry Accompaniments such as flaked coconut, chopped peanuts and chutney. The electric skillet offers the bonus of cooking and serving from the same dish.

CHICKEN JUPITER

6 chicken breasts, boned, or	2 eggs, slightly beaten
2 fryers, quartered	1½ cups finely crushed cornflake
1 teaspoon salt	crumbs
1 teaspoon seasoned salt	1 cup shortening, vegetable
½ teaspoon crushed thyme	or butter
½ teaspoon paprika	Jupiter Sauce

Clean chicken and dry with paper toweling. Combine salt, seasoned salt, thyme and paprika; dust evenly with the mixture. If using breasts, tuck in ends and shape to resemble individual caponettes; fasten with skewers (lacing pins). Dip each in egg to coat well, then in cornflake crumbs until completely covered. Allow to stand in refrigerator several hours or overnight. Heat shortening in skillet; it should be about 1 inch deep. Add prepared breasts and fry over medium heat until light brown on both sides, about 10 minutes. Remove and place on toweling or brown paper to drain excess fat. Arrange in shallow baking pan and spoon over half the recipe of Jupiter Sauce, reserving remainder to serve separately. Cover tightly with foil and bake in 350° oven ½ hour. Remove foil; baste, and bake uncovered an additional ½ hour or until fork-tender. To serve, place on hot platter; combine pan drippings with remaining Jupiter Sauce, artichokes and pineapple; heat and pour over chicken, arranging sauce ingredients attractively. Pass additional sauce separately. Serve piping hot. Serves 6.

Jupiter Sauce

1 13½ ounce can pineapple chunks, drained	2 tablespoons water
3 cups pineapple juice and water	½ teaspoon curry powder
	¼ teaspoon dry mustard
3 tablespoons lemon juice	½ teaspoon salt
1 tablespoon sugar	1 13-ounce can artichoke hearts, drained
2½ tablespoons cornstarch	½ pound mushrooms, sautéed

Set pineapple chunks aside. Add sufficient water to pineapple juice to make 3 cups; add lemon juice and sugar. Pour into saucepan, bring to a boil. Make a paste of cornstarch and water; add to juices and simmer, stirring until clear and slightly thickened. Blend in curry, mustard and salt.

To serve, add pineapple chunks, artichoke hearts, and mushrooms with liquid in which they were sautéed. Makes about 4 cups.

The sauce, with or without pineapple chunks and artichoke hearts, is delicious and may be used with plain baked chicken or other poultry.

To sauté mushrooms (a steamed variation)

½ pound mushrooms (cut stems even with caps)
2 tablespoons butter   2 tablespoons water

Heat butter in saucepan, add mushrooms, heat and add water. Cover tightly, steam about 5 minutes.

Although the chicken without pineapple chunks, artichoke hearts, or mushrooms is delicious and attractive, the addition, plus salad and dessert, makes a complete menu.

For dinner I serve it with a first course of

Green Onion Pie

the accompaniments of

Asparagus in Pepper Rings   Saffron Rice
Cornets Dolce

CHICKEN LOBSTER MARENGO

4 chicken breasts, halved
1 teaspoon salt
¼ teaspoon pepper
½ teaspoon seasoned salt
¼ cup butter or margarine
2 tablespoons sherry
2 tablespoons prepared seasoned
    chicken stock base or butter
½ pound mushrooms, sliced

2 tablespoons flour
1½ cups chicken broth
1 tablespoon tomato paste
1 bay leaf, crushed
2 tablespoons chopped chives
½ teaspoon salt
⅛ teaspoon pepper
2 10-ounce packages frozen
    lobster tails

3 fresh tomatoes, quartered

Sprinkle breasts with salt, pepper and seasoned salt. Heat butter in large skillet; add breasts and sauté until golden. Sprinkle with sherry. Remove to a shallow baking dish; add prepared chicken stock base; cover tightly with aluminum foil and bake in 300° oven 30 minutes or until tender. Add mushrooms to butter remaining in skillet and sauté 5 minutes. Blend in flour; add broth and simmer, stirring, until thickened. Add tomato paste, bay leaf, chives, salt and pepper; simmer an additional 15 minutes. In another saucepan, cook lobster tails according to package directions. Remove meat from shell, then cut into thin slices and add to sauce; add tomatoes and simmer about 5 minutes, just enough to heat tomatoes and lobster meat. Serve hot chicken breasts on large platter; top with sauce, arranging tomatoes and lobster as attractive garnish. Serve with rice or thin boiled spaghetti. Serves 6 to 8.

It was at the Petit Bedon in Paris, we were introduced to glamorous chicken en casserole. In translation, this is a reasonable facsimile.

CHICKEN PASTORALE

1 3-pound roaster or fryer
Mushroom Dressing Pastorale
½ teaspoon salt
¼ teaspoon seasoned salt
pinch paprika
¼ cup butter or margarine
2 tablespoons chopped parsley
2 shallots or green onions,
thinly sliced
1 10-ounce can chicken broth
3 carrots, quartered, cut in
3-inch lengths
1 teaspoon mushroom
powder
2 tablespoons dry white wine
(optional)
1 16-ounce jar small boiled
onions, drained

Wipe chicken with damp cloth; stuff lightly with Mushroom Dressing and fasten opening with lacing pins and string. Truss legs to tail; tuck wings under and tie together, but not across breast, then rub with salt, seasoned salt, and paprika. Heat butter in saucepan; add chicken and brown evenly on all sides. Add parsley and shallots; brown another 5 minutes. Pour in broth; add carrots; sprinkle chicken with mushroom powder and cover tightly. Reduce heat to a simmer; turn chicken frequently to cook evenly. Cook about one hour or until thigh is tender, moistening with white wine; add onions and reheat. If chicken is not sufficiently browned, pop it under the broiler for 5 minutes. Carve at table, serving each a portion of Mushroom Dressing, carrots, and onions. Serves 4.

Mushroom Dressing Pastorale

1 cup soft bread crumbs,
firmly packed
3 tablespoons melted butter
1 clove garlic, minced
1 egg, beaten
½ teaspoon crushed rosemary
2 tablespoons snipped parsley
½ teaspoon salt
1 2½ ounce jar mushroom stems
and pieces, drained

Toss all ingredients lightly, blending well. Sufficient for 1 3-pound fryer.

With this I serve

Salad Bella with Bouquet Dressing
Curried Tomatoes   *Wild Rice*
Glazed Crêpes

GALINHA (CHICKEN) BRAZILIAN STYLE

1 roasting chicken, 4 to 5   1 clove garlic, minced
pounds   2 teaspoons salt
½ cup wine vinegar   Stuffing Brasiliera
3 slices bacon

Wash chicken; drain and wipe dry with paper toweling. Combine vinegar, garlic and salt, rub into chicken and let stand ½ hour. Fill cavity with stuffing; close opening with lacing pins and string. Tie legs together, then tie to tail; fold wings under to form a base. Cover with bacon strips; place on heavy duty aluminum foil and seal well, allowing enough room for air space. Place in shallow pan and bake in 375° oven 2 hours. Open foil; remove bacon strips from top of chicken and bake until brown and tender. Serve with Carrot Farofa. Serves 4 to 6.

Stuffing Brasiliera

raw chicken giblets, chopped   1 teaspoon salt
1 tablespoon butter   ⅛ teaspoon pepper
1 tablespoon parsley   4 slices white bread
¼ cup chopped onion   ½ cup wine
1 cup purée of chestnuts

Add giblets to heated butter in saucepan and sauté 20 minutes. Add parsley, onion, salt and pepper, mix well. Combine bread, wine, and chestnuts; blend thoroughly and add to giblet mixture. Makes about 2 cups stuffing.

OLD-FASHIONED ROAST CHICKEN

1 3- to 4-pound roasting chicken or capon	½ teaspoon paprika
1 teaspoon salt	1 onion
½ teaspoon poultry seasoning	1 stalk celery with leaves
½ teaspoon seasoned salt	4 tablespoons butter, softened
	Wine Basting Sauce

Garnish: 1 1-pound jar spiced apples, parsley

Dry chicken with paper toweling and sprinkle with salt, poultry seasoning, seasoned salt and paprika. Place in shallow roaster; insert onion and celery into cavity; spread with butter. Roast in 325° oven 20 to 30 minutes per pound, or until tender. Baste frequently with Wine Basting Sauce. To serve, disjoint chicken, and arrange on platter with spiced apples, parsley and Broiled Potatoes. Serves 6.

Wine Basting Sauce

1 10-ounce can chicken broth	¼ teaspoon crushed rosemary
¼ cup white wine	1 teaspoon sugar
	½ teaspoon seasoned salt

Combine all ingredients in saucepan; heat to baste. Use for chicken or other roasts. Makes 1½ cups.

If a thicker sauce is desired, add 1 tablespoon instantized flour to each cup of pan drippings. Scrape the pan bottom very well.

SKILLET CHICKEN MANDARIN

8 chicken wings	2 cups orange juice, fresh or frozen
4 thighs and legs, disjointed	
4 tablespoons flour	2 tablespoons finely chopped candied ginger
½ teaspoon ground savory	
1½ teaspoons salt	½ teaspoon sugar
⅛ teaspoon ground pepper	½ pound fresh mushrooms, halved lengthwise
6 tablespoons vegetable shortening	
	½ teaspoon paprika

Garnish: 1 11-ounce can Mandarin oranges, parsley sprigs

Wash and dry chicken pieces. Combine flour, savory, salt and pepper in paper bag; add chicken pieces a few at a time, and coat thoroughly. Heat shortening in a Dutch oven or large skillet with cover; add coated chicken and sauté over moderate heat until light brown. Sauté one layer at a time, using two skillets if necessary. When brown place all in one skillet; add seasoned flour mixture if any remains and pour 1½ cups of the orange juice over the chicken; sprinkle with ginger. Cover and bring to a boil; reduce heat and simmer about 30 minutes or until tender. Add sugar to remaining half cup of orange juice and pour over chicken. Add mushrooms, pushing pieces of chicken aside so that mushrooms are immersed in sauce. Dust with paprika; cover and simmer slowly 10 minutes. Garnish with Mandarin oranges and sprigs of parsley. Serves 4 to 6.

With this I serve

Chinese Fluffy Rice   *Tomato Salad*
Chocolate Coconut Nests
Iced Tea   *Hot Coffee*

CHINESE SQUAB

6 squabs, quartered	2 cups fresh asparagus
⅔ cup salad oil	½-inch slices
2 cups sliced mushrooms	2 cups chicken bouillon
1 11-ounce can water chestnuts,	½ cup sherry or sake
drained and sliced	¼ cup soy sauce
¼ cup cornstarch	

Place squabs in large skillet in heated oil; cover and cook, turning frequently until tender. Add mushrooms, water chestnuts, asparagus, and chicken stock. Cover and cook 5 minutes; remove to hot serving dish. Prepare sauce by adding stock to pan juices, sufficient to make 3 cups; add sherry and soy sauce. Make a paste of ¼ cup pan juices and cornstarch and add to sauce. Bring to boil; reduce heat, simmer 5 minutes and pour over squab and vegetables. Border with Chutney Peaches. Serves 6.

With this I serve

Just Noodle Pudding   *Cream Puffs Jermyn Street*

CORNISH HENS NORMANDY

6 Cornish hens
2 teaspoons salt
¼ teaspoon white pepper
½ teaspoon nutmeg
2 tablespoons lemon juice
1 clove garlic, minced (optional)
½ cup butter or margarine, melted

1 cup orange juice or ½ cup
   orange juice and ½ cup
   white wine
2 cups Orange Sauce
   (approximate)

Garnish: Orange slices and parsley

Dry hens with paper toweling. Combine salt, pepper, nutmeg, lemon juice and garlic and rub well into skin of hens; place them in shallow baking pan with ends of legs tied together. Pour butter over hens and place in 350° oven to roast for 15 minutes. Pour orange juice (or combination orange juice and wine) over hens; roast 45 minutes additional, basting frequently with pan juices, until hens are tender. The leg meat will be soft and the hens golden brown. Remove from pan and keep warm on hot platter while preparing Orange Sauce; then pour half the sauce over hens and garnish with orange slices and parsley. Serve remaining sauce separately. Serves 6.

Orange Sauce

2 cups liquid (pan drippings plus
   sufficient orange juice)
2 tablespoons butter

2 tablespoons flour
2 tablespoons Cointreau or
   orange Curaçao

2 oranges cut into ½-inch slices (optional)

Pour pan drippings from roaster and add sufficient orange juice to make 2 cups liquid. Melt butter in saucepan; add flour and stir until smooth and bubbly. Add orange juice mixture slowly, stirring until heated and blended. Stir in Cointreau and orange slices; simmer 5 minutes. Adjust seasonings, adding salt if necessary and ⅛ teaspoon nutmeg, if desired.

For 6 guests, serve this with the Cornish Hens

Rice Mounds   *Tomatoes Polonaise*
Charlotte Russe

Adaptables

This recipe may be used for duckling. Roast a 5-pound fowl about 2½ to 3 hours, or until golden brown. Roast in 400° oven for first hour without basting. Drain off fat and then proceed as for Cornish hens, reducing heat to 350°. If, when tender, the pan drippings are too fat, skim until clear, then add orange juice and wine to make the two cups needed.

Eye appeal is always important and Cornish Hens can be adapted to interesting compositions. Place them on platter with "tails" pointing toward a center of mounded rice. Arrange baked Tomatoes Polonaise between hens, and tuck bunches of watercress, crisp and green on both sides of tomatoes. Sprinkle rice with snipped parsley or paprika.

TAM O'SHANTER HENS
(Baked)

3 Cornish hens or broilers	½ cup Scotch whisky or cognac
1 tablespoon lime juice	2 teaspoons meat stock paste
3 teaspoons salt	1 tablespoon Worcestershire
½ cup (¼ pound) butter, softened	1 tablespoon instantized flour
1 tablespoon dry mustard	1 cup half and half cream

Garnish: Pears and Spice

Dry hens with paper toweling and rub with lime juice and salt, both inside and out. Make a paste of butter and mustard and coat birds. Place in shallow roaster and bake in 350° oven; baste frequently with pan drippings until tender; about 1 hour and 15 minutes. Remove from oven; heat ¼ cup Scotch in ladle; pour over hens and flame. Split hens in halves and place on platter to keep warm. Add remaining ¼ cup Scotch to roaster; scrape bits from pan; add meat stock paste and Worcestershire.

Bring to boil, and if desired, strain into small saucepan. Add flour and heat, simmering for 5 minutes, then add cream and bring to boiling. Adjust seasonings; — pour piping hot over birds. Garnish with Pears and Spice. Serves 6.

TAM O'SHANTER HENS
(Steamed)

With this method, the hens become moist and juicy. Use ingredients for Baked Hens; dry them with paper toweling; rub with lime juice and salt, inside and out, as for baked hens. Place in steamer or on rack over water in saucepan; cover and steam 30 minutes. Cut in halves; rub with a paste of mustard and butter and place in shallow roaster. Place in 400° oven and bake 30 minutes, basting frequently with pan drippings. When tender, remove to hot platter and proceed as above for Scotch-flavored sauce. Serves 6.

In a charming cellar restaurant structured with rough-hewn beams, we were served from a kitchen of minute proportions by the hostess-proprietor. The dish equaled her pride in the recipe, which she generously gave me.

CANARD ST. GERMAINE

5- to 6-pound duck
2 teaspoons salt
½ teaspoon pepper
2 tablespoons olive or salad oil
1 cup red wine
2 tablespoons sugar
2 tablespoons vinegar
1 cup soup stock or 1 chicken bouillon cube in 1 cup boiling water
½ cup orange juice

3 tablespoons grated orange rind
2 tablespoons lemon juice
1 tablespoon grated lemon
1 1-pound can bing cherries, drained
juice from cherries
½ teaspoon rosemary
additional red wine for sauce
2 tablespoons brandy or wine

Clean duck carefully and cut into serving pieces. Combine salt and pepper; rub into duck. Heat oil in large skillet; add duck and brown evenly and well. Remove to covered casserole or Dutch oven and place in 475° oven; roast uncovered for 20 minutes; drain off fat. Reduce temperature to 350°; pour wine over duck then cover tightly and continue to roast for one hour. Drain drippings into skillet in which duck was browned; skim off excess fat. To skimmed drippings, add sugar, vinegar, soup stock, orange juice and rind; add lemon juice and rind, cherry juice and rosemary. Blend well and heat to boiling, scraping up brown bits from pan. Drain any fat from duck; cover with sauce, close roaster tightly and roast again, a total of 2 to 3 hours or until tender. Remove duck to heated platter. Strain and measure pan drippings; add salt and pepper if necessary and add sufficient wine to make 2 cups. Make a paste of flour and brandy; add to sauce and pour into saucepan. Cook, stirring constantly, until thickened. Add whole cherries; heat and pour a small amount over duck; pass remainder separately. Serves 4.

Here at home I serve it with simply cooked

Wild Rice
Curried Tomatoes   *Salad Bella*
Glazed Crêpes

DUCKLING MADEIRA

1 4- to 5-pound duckling	Apple Kraut Stuffing
1 tablespoon lemon juice	1 apple, cored and quartered
1 teaspoon salt	½ teaspoon marjoram
1 teaspoon seasoned salt	½ teaspoon tarragon
½ teaspoon garlic powder	1 tablespoon melted butter
1 cup Madeira or white wine	

Wash duck and pat dry with paper toweling. Rub inside and out with lemon juice then sprinkle evenly with salt, seasoned salt and garlic powder. Fill with Apple Kraut Stuffing; lace or sew opening of cavity and tuck wings under back of duck. Insert quartered apple in neck cavity and fasten skin with lacing pins or picks. Place in shallow roasting pan and sprinkle with marjoram and tarragon; brush with melted butter. Prick duck in all fat places with sharp fork to allow to drain. Place in 450° oven for 15 minutes then reduce heat to 350°. Drain off fat as it collects in pan. Roast one hour; drain off fat, then baste with ¼ cup wine and repeat basting three more times. Cook additional 1½ hours, about 30 minutes to the pound, or until tender. If not brown enough, raise heat to 450° for 15 more minutes. Remove duck from roaster and cut into serving pieces; arrange with Apple Kraut Stuffing on platter and keep warm while preparing Madeira Sauce. Serves 4 to 5.

Apple Kraut Stuffing

2 tablespoons butter or other shortening	2 apples, peeled, cored, and coarsely chopped
1 medium onion, coarsely chopped	2½ cups sauerkraut, drained
	4 cloves
	1½ teaspoons caraway seeds

Heat shortening in skillet; add onion and sauté until golden brown. Add apples; sauté for one minute then add kraut, cloves and caraway seeds. Mix well and heat thoroughly. Makes 3 cups of stuffing, sufficient for 1 duck or 1 goose.

Madeira Sauce

Skim fat from roaster and add 1½ cups stock made from giblets, blending with brown bits scraped from bottom. Pour through sieve into saucepan; add ¼ cup cream and adjust seasonings. Pour part over duck and serve remainder separately. Makes about 2 cups.

If you prefer stronger flavor add wine to taste. Heat thoroughly.

Roast Duck Bonus

Though seldom used, duck fat is an alternate shortening for salt pork or other rendered poultry fats. This recipe produced almost 2 cups of strained fat, enhanced by the wine aroma. Stored in small crocks, it will keep a long while under refrigeration.

WHOLE DUCKLING APRICOT

1 4-pound duckling	1 teaspoon meat stock paste
1 teaspoon salt	1 clove garlic, minced
1 teaspoon seasoned salt	(optional)
1 teaspoon poultry seasoning	¼ teaspoon marjoram
½ teaspoon paprika	1 teaspoon salt
2 tablespoons butter	½ thinly sliced lemon
1 cup canned apricot nectar	1 medium onion, sliced
¼ cup apricot liqueur or cognac	2 teaspoons arrowroot or 1
½ cup water	tablespoon cornstarch

Garnish: 1 1-pound can whole apricots, 1 9-ounce can sliced pineapple

Clean duck and rub inside and out with salt, seasoned salt, poultry seasoning and paprika. Prick tail end and other fatty parts with a fork to allow fat to drain quickly as it sautés. Heat butter in skillet; add duck and brown evenly about 20 minutes. Remove duck to roaster and cover. Place in 325° oven and bake 1 hour, then drain off fat thoroughly. Now drain fat from skillet in which duck was browned and into it pour apricot nectar, liqueur, water, meat stock paste, garlic, marjoram and salt. Heat and mix well, scraping bits from bottom of pan; pour over duck and add sliced lemon and onion. Roast uncovered for 45 minutes or until fork tender. If duck is not sufficiently browned, place under broiler, watching carefully. Remove to platter; drain off pan juices; remove fat if there is too much for your liking and mix ¼ cup pan juices with arrowroot to make a paste. Return to pan (there should be about 2 cups) and add more fruit juice if necessary. Simmer 5 minutes until clear and pour over duck. Garnish with whole apricots on pineapple slices. Serve with Chinese Fluffy Rice shaped in a ring and centered with tiny canned peas. Serves 4.

This recipe is equally good for goose or wild duck. Though it may sound "busy" it is a simple procedure.

On a Wednesday night we were four for dinner. Our menu was simple but the oversized turkey made an abundancy.

WEDNESDAY'S MENU

Tiny Mushroom Tarts   *Stuffed Endive*
Champagned Turkey
Fruited Noodle Pudding   *Roasted Onions*
Bibb Lettuce with Bean Sprouts
Orange Torte

CHAMPAGNED TURKEY

1 12-pound turkey, tied and trussed	1 teaspoon paprika
2 teaspoons freshly ground	2 tablespoons salt
pepper	¼ pound butter, melted

Wipe the bird with damp toweling, then dry. Press pepper firmly into skin; sprinkle with paprika and salt. Place on back in a shallow roaster and pour melted butter over all. Cover loosely with foil and place in 325° oven. Roast 1 hour; remove foil and continue to roast, basting frequently with pan drippings, approximately 3 more hours, or until tender. When done the thigh joint should move easily and the leg should be tender. Remove to a heated platter and allow to stand 15 minutes before carving. Garnish with parsley and a bouquet of grapefruit roses. Serve Champagned Sauce separately. Serves 10 to 12.

If a turkey without dressing is unfinished business for you, use one of your choice or consult the Index.

CHAMPAGNED SAUCE

1 cup pan drippings, skimmed	2 tablespoons cognac
1 cup domestic champagne	½ pound thinly sliced mushrooms
1 cup half and half cream	(optional)

Remove turkey to platter and skim off excess fat from pan drippings. Place roaster over heat; pour in champagne and blend well, scraping brown bits from bottom. Add mushrooms; bring to a boil and cook quickly for 5 minutes. Reduce heat; stir in cream and cognac. Serve separately, piping hot.

For a glaze

Baste with undiluted defrosted orange juice or ½ cup melted currant jelly. Omit champagne in the gravy.

Both suggestions for the champagne gravy and the glaze may be used for other poultry.

For leftover turkey, see recipe for Turkey Soup or Casserole Tomorrow.

One need not be a hunter to enjoy quail. Many markets, in most parts of the country, sell the domestic variety, dressed and ready for preparation.

QUAIL IN CRIBS

6 quail, dressed and halved	⅓ cup water
1½ teaspoons salt	6 hard rolls
freshly ground pepper	Brandy Pears
¾ cup butter	watercress

Dust quail with salt and pepper. Heat ½ cup butter in skillet; add quail and sauté until evenly browned. Add water; place in 325° oven; cover tightly and steam 20 to 30 minutes or until tender. While quail are steaming, prepare rolls by splitting in half and removing centers to form "cribs"; place in 325° oven until browned; brush with remaining ¼ cup butter. To serve place ½ quail on each half roll. Garnish with Brandy Pears and frame with watercress. Serves 6.

Though quail are rich, they do not make bountiful portions, so I serve substantial complements, such as

Noodle Spinach Ring — Mushroom Center
Icy Lime Pie

Stuffings

CORN PUDDING MICHIANA
(Vegetable or Stuffing)

2 eggs, slightly beaten
1 16-ounce can corn niblets
1 12-ounce can cream style corn
½ cup grated carrots
¼ cup finely diced green pepper

¾ cup soft bread crumbs (1½ to 2 slices in ¼-inch cubes)
¼ cup finely chopped onion, dry or frozen
1½ teaspoons salt

Topping
1 tablespoon dry bread crumbs

1 tablespoon butter

Combine all ingredients and mix well. Turn into a well-greased 1-quart baking dish; sprinkle with bread crumbs and dot with butter. Place in a 350° oven and bake 45 minutes to one hour until lightly browned. To serve, dust with paprika. Serves 6.

Use this pudding as stuffing for Crown Roast of Pork or Lamb. It is an excellent combination.

CORN BREAD DRESSING

turkey gizzard, heart and neck
1 onion
2 celery stalks
1 tablespoon chopped parsley
1 teaspoon salt
water to cover

8 cups crumbled corn bread
2 eggs
2 tablespoons rum
1 teaspoon poultry seasoning
salt to taste
¼ cup melted butter

Wash giblets and place in small saucepan with onion, celery stalks, parsley and 1 teaspoon salt. Cover with water and bring to a boil; reduce heat and simmer until tender. Remove meat from neck and grind with gizzard and heart. Combine with corn bread; add poultry seasoning and salt to taste. Mix well and toss with rum. Add giblet broth sufficient to moisten and ¼ cup melted butter, then blend evenly. Stuff cavity lightly as this dressing will swell while baking. Sufficient for a 15-pound bird.

6 cups dressing fills an 8-pound turkey.
10 cups fills a 14-pound turkey.
12 to 13 cups for an 18-pounder.

DRESSING MARGO
(Smoked Oyster Stuffing for Turkey)

1 7-ounce package seasoned
    prepared croutons
1 cup milk
1 cup coarsely chopped celery
1 medium-sized onion, finely
    chopped

½ cup raisins, preferably
    white
½ cup coarsely chopped walnuts
1 1-ounce can smoked oysters,
    chopped
½ cup butter or margarine

Place seasoned croutons in large bowl and add milk. Add remaining ingredients and toss lightly; adjust seasonings, adding salt if needed. Fill cavity loosely, as dressing swells in roasting. Sufficient for a 7- to 10-pound fowl; double the recipe for a 12 to 15 pound turkey.

WILD RICE DRESSING

1 cup wild rice, washed and
    drained
3 cups water
1½ teaspoons salt
¼ cup butter
1 medium onion, finely
    chopped

½ cup slivered almonds
½ pound fresh mushrooms,
    sliced
2 tablespoons minced parsley
¼ teaspoon ground cloves
    (optional)
1 teaspoon seasoned salt

Wash rice and soak overnight; drain well. Bring water to boil; add salt and rice; cover tightly and cook about 35 minutes until tender. Drain if necessary. Heat butter in skillet; add onion, almonds and mushrooms; sauté 3 minutes. Blend in parsley, cloves and seasoned salt; mix well. Makes approximately 4 cups.

Delicious with game or domestic fowl, or use as meat accompaniment.

The Good Egg

A Chinese custom heralds the arrival of a new baby with a gift basket of eggs to relatives and friends.

The Good Egg

A first on the pantry list, the egg is an ingredient and a garnish; and a succulent entry for breakfast, lunch or supper entrée.

As Mark Twain said, "Put all your eggs in the one basket, and—

WATCH THAT BASKET."

EDIBLE BASKETS

Croustades Petites

1. Cut 2-inch slices from a loaf of day-old unsliced bread. Remove bread from center of slice, leaving a shell ¼ inch thick; dip in melted butter and bake in 350° oven 10 minutes or until toasted a golden brown.
2. Use hard rolls instead of bread loaf; slice off tops evenly.
3. Cut hamburger buns in half; remove soft bread leaving shell and toast.
4. Remove crusts from thin slices of white bread; brush both sides with melted butter and press into 3-inch muffin tins to form cups; place in 350° oven and bake 10 minutes or until toasted.

5. Use a puff pastry, small cream puffs or baking powder biscuits.

Nests

1. Sautéed slices of thin bologna will curl to form cups.
2. Press duchess potatoes, (mashed) through a cooky press to form nests.
3. Mound stiffly beaten egg whites on a slice of toast and sprinkle with salt and pepper; make a depression and drop in yolk. Bake in 350° oven 10 minutes or until set.
4. Drop whole egg into a nest of creamed spinach and bake as above.
5. Buttered, toasted English Muffins are always a standby.
6. Cut a 2-inch hole in center of bread slice; sauté one side in butter, turn on reverse side and drop egg in center; salt, cover and steam slowly until set. A framed egg —
7. A cooked prepared artichoke makes a deep nest for a poached egg; serve with Hollandaise or other sauce.

Large Croustade

May be made of a whole loaf of round or oblong bread.
1. Remove soft crumbs and toast as for Petites Croustades. Retain top slice for cover.
2. Use Puff Pastry or make a shell of Choux Paste for a large Cream Puff container.

About Eggs

To break the shell, crack it gently but firmly on a flat surface.

As a safeguard against yolk breakage, and a check on freshness before cooking, open each egg separately into a sauce dish before sliding it into the heated butter or water for poaching.

To hard-cook eggs

Have eggs at room temperature; boil for 15 minutes in simmering water to cover. Move about several times while cooking to center the yolk. When done, plunge them immediately into cold water to prevent a green rim from forming around the yolk. DO NOT OVERCOOK.

To present them attractively

Halve or quarter with fluted cutter. To halve, cut egg with sharp knife; forming points in egg white; separate white carefully and remove yolk. Points will form a crown. Cut a sliver from bottom of each half to stand evenly. Refill with prepared yolks as for Deviled Eggs. Top with rolled anchovy, smoked oyster, red or black caviar, sprig of parsley, paprika, or a fillip of your own ingenuity.

Unbeaten egg whites may be frozen. Defrost and use as needed. They can be utilized for baking without concern. Mark number of egg whites on container before freezing.

Have egg whites at room temperature before beating. More volume results.

The French use a wash of whole eggs or yolks mixed with water, a Dorure, to "gild" pastry. We prosaically call it "brushing."

The egg is a staple of history over which poets have waxed lyrical and cooks have connived.

They are

Used as decoration, eaten hot or cold, soft or hard.

Used as a binder in baking, for sauces and for ground meats or fish.

Used to clarify soups and gelatines.

An emulsion in dressings.

Good to the last drop — add the shell to the contents of a pot of old fashioned coffee for a clear cup of the brew.

PARTY DEVILED EGGS

1 dozen hard-cooked eggs	2 teaspoons minced onion
⅓ cup mayonnaise	dash Tabasco
1 tablespoon prepared mustard	1 tablespoon sweet pickle relish

Peel eggs; cut in halves crosswise, using fluted vegetable cutter for a special party look, cut small slice from each end to form a base. Remove yolks carefully so as not to damage whites, then mash or press through a strainer. Mix with mayonnaise, mustard and other seasonings. To refill whites, spiral yolk mixture from fluted tip of pastry tube. Cover lightly and chill.

Vary the filling with poultry, salmon, sardines, seafoods.

Vary the yolk mixture with addition of anchovy paste, or a choice of herbs and spices.

In his *Dictionary of Cuisine*, Alexandre Dumas records a recipe for an Arabian Omelet given him by the chief cook of the Bey's royal household. The main ingredient is an ostrich egg, each "good for 10 hen's eggs." Here is my interpretation of this exotic dish.

ARABIAN OMELET

1 clove garlic	¼ teaspoon pepper
10 eggs	4 tablespoons butter
½ teaspoon salt	Arabian Sauce

Rub bottom of bowl with cut clove of garlic; add eggs, salt, and pepper; beat well. Heat butter in large skillet; pour in eggs; cook over medium heat, drawing from edge of pan to center to allow eggs to run underneath. When set, pour Arabian Sauce over omelet and fold in half. Slide onto a heated platter. Serves 6.

Arabian Sauce

4 tablespoons butter or olive oil
1 onion, coarsely chopped
1 green pepper, coarsely
    chopped

2 large tomatoes, peeled, seeded,
    and chopped
½ teaspoon salt
dash cayenne
8 anchovy filets, drained and halved

Heat butter in skillet; add onion and green pepper and sauté lightly until soft, but not brown. Add tomatoes, salt and cayenne; simmer until tomato juice is reduced and sauce is thickened; add anchovy filets.

The sauce may be prepared in advance; add anchovies when reheating to pour over omelet.

BRUNCH EGGS IN CROUSTADE SHELLS

6 eggs
¼ cup half and half cream
2 tablespoons butter
⅔ teaspoon salt
⅛ teaspoon freshly ground pepper

1 teaspoon minced onion
¼ pound sautéed sliced
    mushrooms
1 teaspoon Worcestershire
    (optional)

1 teaspoon minced parsley

Garnish

4 Croustades Petites
paprika

2 tablespoons snipped
    parsley

Beat eggs and cream together slightly. Heat butter in skillet; add eggs and cook over low heat. With a fork, draw eggs from edge of pan to center so uncooked egg runs underneath. When almost set, add remaining ingredients, mixing evenly. Fill prepared Croustades. Sprinkle with snipped parsley; dust with paprika, and tuck a sprig of parsley under Croustade for flourish. Serves 4.

Try adding a dash of sherry just before removing eggs from pan. Or, add 2 tablespoons grated Parmesan cheese at the last minute. Two tablespoons of cream cheese, crumbled, may be added with salt, pepper.

This is a good skillet dish for lunch, brunch or late supper. The ingredients can be assembled early; make the Croustades ahead of time.

CHEDDAR CURRY OMELET

A beautifully puffed, soufflé-like omelet.

3 tablespoons green onions, finely sliced or 1 tablespoon grated dry onion
6 tablespoons butter or 6 tablespoons margarine
6 tablespoons flour

1 teaspoon salt
¾ teaspoon curry powder
1½ cups milk
6 egg whites
6 egg yolks
½ cup grated Cheddar cheese

Sauté the onion lightly in butter or margarine; stir in flour, salt, curry powder; cook, stirring constantly, until just bubbly. Blend in milk; continue cooking and stirring until sauce is very thick; boil one minute. Cool. Beat egg whites until they form soft peaks; beat egg yolks until thick and lemon colored. Beat cooled sauce very slowly into egg yolks; fold in beaten whites. Pour into a well-buttered 10-inch electric skillet or ovenware pan. Cook in electric skillet at 300° (unless otherwise indicated), 50 minutes. For oven method, bake in ovenware skillet at 325° for 30 minutes. Sprinkle cheese over top of omelet and cook additional 5 minutes. Serve immediately. Serves 6.

We enjoyed this brunch combination

Cheddar Curry Omelet   *Pineapple Shells Manoa*
Fruit Dressing Manoa
Simple Simon Coffee Cake

CIRCLED EGGS

12 strips bacon
1½ teaspoons Worcestershire
6 eggs

dash salt
dash pepper
Tabasco

Optional

½ teaspoon chervil or ½ teaspoon snipped parsley
or ½ teaspoon catsup

Sauté bacon just until soft, about 2 minutes on each side. Butter muffin pan; circle each cup with two strips of partially cooked bacon. Drop ¼ teaspoon Worcestershire into each cup, then drop an egg into each one. Dust with salt and pepper and add a drop of Tabasco. Place in 350° oven and bake about 15 minutes or until set to your desire. Remove and serve on toast rounds or fried apple slices. Serves 6.

For a different flavor, sprinkle eggs with chervil or parsley, or drop ½ teaspoon of catsup in bottom of each cup before adding eggs. Or you may want to use Holland-Ease Sauce.

EGG FOO YONG

2 tablespoons shortening	¼ cup salad or peanut oil
½ pound fresh mushrooms, sliced or ½ cup canned, sliced mushrooms, drained	1 tablespoon soy sauce
	1 cup cooked veal, chicken, lamb or pork, cut in
½ cup coarsely chopped onion	¼″ x 2″ slices
1 cup bean sprouts	5 eggs, well beaten
¼ teaspoon salt	

Melt shortening, add mushrooms and onion; sauté for 3 minutes. Combine with remaining ingredients in large bowl; blend lightly. Heat oil in 10-inch skillet. Drop ½ cup of mixture for each pancake into heated oil, and brown lightly. Turn over and brown reverse side. Makes 6 pancakes. Serve with Foo Yong Sauce.

Foo Yong Sauce

2 tablespoons cornstarch	2 chicken bouillon cubes
1½ cups water	1 tablespoon soy sauce
2 teaspoons molasses or dark syrup	

Mix cornstarch with ¼ cup of the water to make a smooth paste. Combine with remaining ingredients. Simmer until smooth and clear and bouillon cubes are dissolved.

For Shrimp Foo Yong, substitute 1 cup coarsely diced shrimp for meat or chicken.

EGG ARTIFLORES

6 artichokes, cooked	Hollandaise Sauce
1 recipe Creamed Spinach	pinch of paprika
6 poached eggs	

Garnish: slices of olive or truffle

Cook artichokes (see Index); keep them warm. Prepare spinach while artichokes are cooking; keep hot over low heat; poach the eggs. Set each artichoke on a luncheon plate, fill cavities with spinach, place an egg in each artichoke on top of the spinach. Cover with Hollandaise, dust with paprika; a slice of olive or truffle on each makes this lovely dish complete. Serves 6.

Orange Tea Biscuits, a fruit compote and cake would complete this brunch.

Artichokes are versatile cups for many combinations of your choice. Vary both fillings and sauces.

The spinach may be omitted.

Crumbled bacon may be sprinkled on egg.

Serve with Curry Soy Sauce.

Chill and fill artichokes with

seafood
hard-cooked eggs and tomatoes
avocado and citrus fruits

EGGS BENEDICT REVISED

A simple twist to the traditional.

4 English muffins, toasted and buttered	8 poached eggs
	Holland-Ease Sauce
1 4½-ounce can deviled ham or ½ cup minced tongue	2 tablespoons snipped chives or parsley

Spread cut side of muffins with deviled ham; place a poached egg on each and pour Holland-Ease Sauce over. Sprinkle with chives, and serve hot as possible. Serves 4.

EGGS FONDUE

Swiss Cheese

6 eggs, lightly beaten
⅛ teaspoon white pepper or
    freshly ground black pepper

½ cup Swiss or Gruyère Swiss
    Cheese
½ teaspoon salt
1 tablespoon butter

Beat eggs, salt, and pepper together; cut cheese into small strips and add to eggs. Heat butter in skillet, pour in egg mixture, and draw the eggs to the center as they become firm at outside edge. Cook just until firm, but not hard. Or cook until of consistency preferred. Serves 4.

Serve with Wondrous Popovers, preserves and crisp bacon.

EGGS FONDUE

Cream Cheese

6 eggs
½ teaspoon salt
⅛ teaspoon pepper

1 3-ounce package cream cheese,
    cut in small pieces
1 tablespoon butter

Proceed as for Swiss Cheese.

FRUITED HAM AND SUNNY EGGS

2 ½-inch slices tenderized ham
4 slices fresh or canned
    pineapple
2 firm bananas, cut lengthwise
    watercress

¼ cup brown sugar
2 tablespoons butter or
    margarine
⅛ teaspoon salt

Cut gashes in fat around ham slice to prevent curling; place in skillet and sauté 5 minutes on each side. Cut each ham slice in half and place pineapple slice topped with ½ banana on each portion. Combine sugar, butter, and salt in saucepan and simmer until sugar is dissolved. Pour over ham and cook 10 minutes, basting frequently. Place slices on platter alternately with Sunny Eggs and watercress. Add slices of bacon for more substantial service. Serves 4.

SUNNY EGGS

2 tablespoons butter or margarine   4 eggs
salt and pepper to taste

Heat butter in covered skillet; butter is hot enough when a drop of water sizzles in it. Break eggs gently into heated butter; cover and cook 3 to 4 minutes or until of desired firmness. Season with salt and pepper.

Banana bread is good with this. You also might want to add crisp bacon slices for contrasting texture.

Originally a Basque recipe, this special omelet has been embraced by Paris and its environs. The journey has left its mark of changes, but the flavor of Southern France remains, though we first ate it in the shadow of Notre Dame.

PIPÉRADE

2 tablespoons butter or oil   1 clove garlic, minced
8 slices Canadian bacon or ham   ½ teaspoon salt
1 large onion, coarsely chopped   ⅛ teaspoon sugar
1 green pepper, thinly sliced   2 tablespoons butter
1 1-pound can tomatoes, drained   8 eggs, well beaten
2 tablespoons chopped parsley

Heat butter or oil in a saucepan; add Canadian bacon and sauté until lightly browned. (If ham is used, have the slices cut ¼-inch thick and then into eight 3-inch strips.) Set aside. For sauce, add onion and green pepper to the butter in the pan and sauté slowly until soft but not browned. Stir in tomatoes, garlic, salt, and sugar; simmer slowly about 10 minutes until liquid has been absorbed. Set aside and keep hot.

Heat 2 tablespoons butter in another skillet, add eggs, and as eggs cook bring them from the edge of the skillet to the center with a fork, until just set. Pour sauce over eggs, mixing sufficiently to blend slightly. Arrange on hot serving platter; top with bacon or ham strips, and sprinkle with parsley. Serves 6.

Instead of the Canadian bacon, substitute 6 slices bacon and cut them in ½-inch squares. Sauté until crisp; drain and keep warm. Use as topping.

For Sunday supper include

Spinach Salad or French Endive   Vinaigrette Dressing
Cinnamon Toast de Luxe
Apple Strips

SWISS CHEESE PUFF

(La Gougère)

1 cup water	1½ cups sifted flour
½ cup butter	4 large eggs
1 teaspoon salt	1¼ cups finely diced imported
⅛ teaspoon coarsely ground	Swiss or Gruyère cheese
pepper	yolk of egg, beaten (optional)

Pour water into saucepan; add butter, salt, and pepper. Bring to boiling and melt butter, then remove from heat. Pour in flour, all at once, stirring to blend. Return to heat and stir batter vigorously with a wooden spoon until it forms a ball and pulls away from sides of pan. Let cool 5 minutes, then add eggs, one at a time, beating well after each addition until blended. Beat in 1 cup of the diced cheese. Butter a 6-cup casserole thickly; drop rounded tablespoons of dough into casserole, one next to the other, forming a circle. Smooth top and inside of circle and sprinkle with remaining ¼ cup diced cheese. If a shiny crust is desired, brush with beaten egg. Place in 350° oven and bake 50 minutes to one hour until crust is firm and brown. Serves 6.

May be served hot as an hors d'oeuvre or luncheon entrée. It is a cross between a cream puff and a soufflé and is delicious. Serve with artichokes and bibb lettuce or similar type of salad.

Or serve individually in 6 soufflé dishes.

SPANISH OMELET

4 egg yolks	⅛ teaspoon white pepper
½ teaspoon salt	4 egg whites
¼ teaspoon cream of tartar	1 tablespoon salad oil

Beat yolks until thick and lemon colored. Add salt and cream of tartar to egg whites and beat until stiff, but not dry. Fold yolks and pepper into beaten egg whites. Heat oil in 10-inch skillet (when sufficiently heated, a drop of water will sputter when added). Push the batter into skillet. Reduce heat to very low and cook about 10 minutes, until omelet is lightly browned, then place in 350° oven for 10 to 15 minutes or until set. Remove to platter and cover with Spanish Sauce. Cut in wedges to serve. Serves 6.

May be baked in ovenware serving skillet; just cover with sauce without removing omelet.

Spanish Sauce

2 tablespoons butter or margarine	2 chopped fresh tomatoes
1 small green pepper, coarsely chopped	½ cup sliced fresh mushrooms or 1 4-ounce can stems and pieces drained
½ small onion, coarsely chopped	
¼ cup finely diced celery	½ teaspoon salt
8 stuffed pimiento olives, sliced	¼ teaspoon oregano

Heat butter in saucepan; add green pepper, onion and celery and sauté 5 minutes. Add tomatoes, mushrooms, salt, oregano and olives. Simmer 15 minutes or until reduced to thickness of heavy sauce. Serve very hot.

Hot off
the Griddle

$\bullet\,\heartsuit\,\bullet\,\heartsuit\,\bullet\,\heartsuit\,\bullet\,\heartsuit\,\bullet\,\heartsuit\,\bullet$

AMSTEL APPLE FLAPPEN

5 large tart apples	1 tablespoon brown sugar
¼ cup sugar	1 12-ounce can beer
1 teaspoon cinnamon	peanut or salad oil for deep
2 cups flour	frying
1 teaspoon salt	confectioners' sugar

Peel whole apples; core and slice in ½-inch rounds. Combine 2 tablespoons sugar and cinnamon and dredge slices evenly. Pour remaining 2 tablespoons sugar in a bowl and add flour, salt and brown sugar. Stir in ½ can of the beer very quickly, then add second half. Dip apple slices into batter, then place in heated oil, 370°, and fry until golden, about 3 to 5 minutes. Drain on paper toweling and dust with confectioners' sugar. Serve piping hot. Serves 5 to 6.

If you have no thermometer, test by dropping a cube of bread in the oil; at 370° it will brown in one minute.

If you like sauces with the fritters serve with frozen strawberries, raspberries or blueberries, defrosted.

APPLE PANCAKE BOWL

Pancake Shell (Bowl)	½ cup milk
3 eggs, beaten	1 tablespoon soft butter or
½ cup buttermilk pancake mix	margarine

Beat eggs until foamy. Add remaining ingredients and blend, then beat vigorously. Pour into greased 9-inch ovenproof baking pan or pieplate. Bake at 450° 15 minutes. Pour filling into shell, and serve warm or cold, as desired. Serves 2.

Filling

2 tablespoons sugar	dash salt
⅛ teaspoon cinnamon	¾ cup cold water
1 tablespoon cornstarch	1 teaspoon lemon juice
1 cup cooked apples, drained or canned sliced apples	

Mix sugar, cinnamon, cornstarch and salt. Slowly add water and stir until blended. Cook over medium heat about 12–15 minutes, till thickened. Sprinkle lemon juice over apples; add apples and cook 2 to 3 additional minutes.

BUTTERMILK GRIDDLE CAKES

1 cup sifted flour	1¼ cups buttermilk or
½ teaspoon soda	soured milk
½ teaspoon salt	1 tablespoon butter or
1 egg, beaten	margarine, melted

Resift flour with soda and salt. Combine beaten egg, buttermilk, and melted shortening; add to flour mixture gradually, beating only until smooth after each addition. Pour about 2 tablespoons of batter on hot, lightly greased griddle for each pancake. Brown on one side until light and bubbly; turn and brown other side. Makes about 12 griddle cakes. Serve with Hot Buttered Sugar.

HOT BUTTERED SUGAR

½ cup brown sugar, firmly packed   2 tablespoons water
2 tablespoons butter

Combine all ingredients in saucepan; heat until bubbly and serve in warmer.

CHEESE BLINTZES

2 eggs, well beaten   ½ teaspoon sugar
1 tablespoon sour cream   ⅛ teaspoon salt
1 cup milk   butter or margarine for browning
½ cup flour plus 1 tablespoon   Cheese Filling

Combine eggs, sour cream, milk, flour, sugar, and salt; beat well. Place in refrigerator and let stand 30 minutes. Grease an 8-inch skillet lightly. Pour in sufficient batter to cover bottom, about 2 tablespoons, and cook on one side; then spread on wax paper browned side up. Spread 2 tablespoons Cheese Filling on browned side of each pancake. Fold 2 opposite sides in, and roll up from open end. Heat 2 tablespoons butter in skillet; add rolled blintzes and brown quickly on both sides. Serve with sour cream or jelly. Makes about 14 blintzes.

Cheese Filling

½ pound small curd   sugar to taste
    cottage cheese   (about 1 tablespoon)
1 egg, beaten   salt to taste
¼ cup raisins (optional)   (about ¼ teaspoon)

Mix cheese, egg, sugar, salt, and raisins together. Blend evenly.

CHIFFON COTTAGE CHEESE PANCAKES

3 eggs   2 tablespoons flour
1 cup creamed cottage cheese   dash salt

Beat all ingredients together in electric mixer, beating well. Brush griddle with oil or butter and drop batter in dollar size cakes, using about 1 teaspoon for each. Brown lightly on each side and serve at once with maple syrup. Makes about 60 dollar-sized cakes. Serves 6.

Divide recipe by one-third, if desired. Though the quantity sounds exorbitant, each pancake is but a melting morsel.

SILVER DOLLAR PANCAKES

¾ cup flour	1 cup milk
1 teaspoon sugar	2 egg yolks
pinch of salt	1 teaspoon baking powder
1 cup sour cream	2 egg whites, stiffly beaten
butter for greasing pan	

Combine the flour, sugar, and salt; beat in sour cream, milk, egg yolks and finally the baking powder. Fold in the egg whites gently until mixed through. Grease a large skillet lightly over moderately high heat; pour in 1 tablespoon of batter for each pancake. Brown lightly and turn once to brown reverse side. Serve with confectioners' sugar. Makes 48 pancakes.

Use a child's toy pancake turner, the kind one buys in a variety store. Like the Three Bears: the regular pancake turner is too large, the spatula too small, and the doll pancake turner exactly right.

The Norwegian pancake griddle makes a perfect small circle.

SOUR CREAM WAFFLES

2 cups sour cream	⅛ teaspoon salt
1 cup plus 2 tablespoons flour	⅛ teaspoon sugar
3 eggs	1 teaspoon baking soda
1 tablespoon hot water	

Beat sour cream, flour, eggs, salt, and sugar until smooth. Mix soda with hot water, add to batter and blend well. Bake in preheated waffle iron. Waffle is done when batter stops steaming. Bake longer for a crisper crust. Makes 6 waffles.

SWEET CREAM WAFFLES

4 eggs, separated   2 cups flour
1 cup half and half cream   4 tablespoons butter or
½ teaspoon salt   margarine, melted
2 teaspoons baking powder

Combine egg yolks and cream and beat thoroughly. Sift dry ingredients together and add to yolks and cream; blend thoroughly. Add melted butter. Beat egg whites until stiff and fold into yolk mixture. Bake in preheated waffle iron. Makes 6 waffles.

The Flame

Through the ages, from cave to modern kitchen, woman has always been confronted with the questions "What shall I wear?" and "What shall we eat?" Just as her rawhide costume of the ages has developed into the luxuriously styled furs of today, so has the raw meat and flinted fire become the Steak Tartare and the Flame of this era.

The Flame may be the "cook-ins" of chafing dish and hibachi, the "cook-outs" of the barbecue pit, or the more or less concealed heat of the modern stove, on which so many delectables are prepared.

There is a sampling of varied entrées in the following section with complementary courses suggested for taste, texture and eye appeal. The embellishment of additional accompaniments has been left for your own selection, arrayed in the proper categories, and indexed informatively.

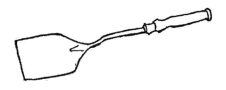

For your eating pleasure and to enhance the menu of each specific occasion, add your choice of hors d'oeuvre, soup, pasta or salad. Appreciative cheers will echo Brillat-Savarin's oft quoted comment, that "to know how to eat — is to know how to live."

Beef

ROAST BEEF U.S.A.
Standing Rib Roast

With this slow-cooking method there is little shrinkage, and meat roasts evenly. Set the temperature at 325°. Wipe the roast with paper toweling. You may or may not salt and pepper the meat. It does not penetrate and some think the salt prevents even browning. Place the meat, fat side up, in a shallow roaster; it will stand on rib ends and needs no rack.

For both experienced and inexperienced cooks, a meat thermometer is a must, eliminating all question of proper doneness. Be certain it does not touch any bone.

Do not sear the meat.

Do not add water.

Do not baste.

Do not cover the pan.

Time the roast so that it can stand 15 to 25 minutes before serving. It will slice more easily, and give you time to prepare the gravy.

The meat thermometer registers the degrees which correspond to the doneness: 140° for rare, 160° for medium, 170° for well done. A 3 to 4 rib roast will serve 3 persons per pound. If you have no thermometer, roast according to the following table for 325° oven. Beginning with meat at room temperature

Roast 20 to 22 minutes per pound for rare.
Roast 24 to 27 minutes per pound for medium.
Roast 30 to 33 minutes per pound for well done.

England and a joint of beef are as compatible as a cup and saucer, or gluttonous Henry VIII stripping a bone. His atrocious manners may have activated Erasmus' famous sixteenth century book on etiquette. English cooking has not enjoyed gourmet fame in the past, though today, swept up in the vogue of international experimentation with "soups to sauces," their cuisine is fast gaining deserved approval.

BEEF OF ENGLAND

3 ribs (about 9–10 pounds)	¼ cup Browned Flour
¼ cup butter or margarine	⅛ teaspoon pepper
1 tablespoon dry mustard	1 cup red wine
2 teaspoons salt	

Remove roast from refrigerator 2 hours before roasting. Rub well with softened butter. Combine dry mustard, Browned Flour, and pepper; coat roast evenly. Do not use salt. Let stand so flavors "marry." Place on a rack in 450° oven; roast for 20 minutes; reduce heat to 325°; baste intermittently with warmed wine.

Roast 15 minutes per pound for rare.
Roast 18 minutes per pound for medium.
Roast 20–25 minutes per pound for well done.

Time roast carefully and remove 15 minutes before serving time. (This causes flavors and meat to set, and it will carve more easily.) Salt just before serving.

Browned Flour

Place flour in a pan in 400° oven, and watch carefully as it browns quickly. Stir occasionally until golden.

Four Tips for Roasting Beef

1. Use prime beef for the best roasts.
2. Take beef from refrigerator at least 2 hours before roasting.
3. Do not salt beef until serving time as it forms a crust which prevents meat from browning evenly. A consensus.

4. Allow to stand on warm dish for 15 to 20 minutes at edge of open oven before carving.

BEEF FILLET FRESNO

16 large prunes
¾ cup strong tea or
   dry white wine
32 pecan halves
2 pounds beef tenderloin

4 tablespoons butter, melted
3 carrots, quartered
3 onions, cut in ½-inch slices
½ cup Madeira or dry white wine
parsley

Soak prunes in tea several hours or overnight. Drain and pit; fill each cavity with 2 pecan halves; set aside. Lard the beef by tying a large piece of suet on top, or skewer 2 pieces of bacon over meat. Either acts as a self-baster. Pour half the butter into shallow baking pan and place fillet in it; add carrots and onions, and bake 20 minutes in 450° oven. Remove suet and pour wine and remaining butter over fillet. Bake 30 minutes in all for rare; 45 minutes for medium rare. Baste with pan drippings. For last 5 minutes place prunes around beef and baste again with pan drippings. Place beef on platter; cut in ¾-inch slices and border with carrots, onion slices, and prunes; add a bouquet of parsley. Serves 5 to 6.

Prunes may be filled with Pâté de Foie Gras or Liver Paste.

This luscious entrée needs only simple embellishment to become a complete dinner. I served

Salad Siena   *Rum Torte*

BEEF FONDUE BOURGUIGNONNE

3 pounds lean fillet of beef,
   cut in ¾-inch cubes
    Assorted sauces

oil, or oil and butter
combined, heated

A dramatic conversation piece served as appetizer or main course. This cook-it-yourself recipe is assembled at the table, with the container for the cooking oil as centerpiece. The oil container must be quite deep. Use earthenware, a chafing or fondue dish, kept hot over a burner. Pour oil into the container to a depth of 3 inches. A slice of bread in the bottom will prevent splattering. Arrange the raw meat attractively on a platter, garnished with parsley, radishes, or carrot strips, and place bowls of sauce conveniently. Present each guest with a long-handled fork, on which to spear a cube of beef, and a second one or a dinner fork to which he can transfer it, as the fondue fork becomes very hot. The beef is dipped in the fat for about one minute, or to taste, then allowed to cool while switching forks and preparing the second cube. The cooked piece is then dipped in sauce, or a combination of sauces. Keep additional oil heating in the kitchen for ready replacement. Serves 6 as entrée.

With this fun do-it-together, I served several sauces

Mustard	Horseradish	Béarnaise
Tartar	Garlic Butter	Hollandaise

We found the cross between the Swiss Beef Bourguignon and Japanese Tempura in Piemonte, northern Italy. The cooking sauce had more flavor and was called

LA BAGNA CAUDA

½ cup butter
½ cup olive or salad oil
1 garlic clove, minced

1 2-ounce can anchovies, drained and chopped or 3 tablespoons anchovy paste

Combine ingredients in chafing dish or fondue pan and heat to boiling.

Use 3 pounds beef cubes and cook on fondue forks as for Beef Fondue Bourguignonne.

The following vegetables may be added with the beef cubes:

Fresh Green Pepper	Mushrooms	Celery
Cauliflowerets	Zucchini	Broccoli

Serve with chunks of Italian bread; 2 sets of forks; plenty of paper napkins.

BEEF IN BEEF BLANKETS

2 pounds thin beef round, cut
into 6 slices, 3" x 2"
½ pound round steak, ground
¼ cup finely chopped onions
½ teaspoon salt
¼ teaspoon freshly ground
pepper
½ teaspoon Bouquet Garni
(herb mixture)

¼ cup dry bread crumbs
1 teaspoon Worcestershire
2 teaspoons seasoned salt
1 tablespoon vegetable shortening or margarine
¼ cup tomato juice
¼ cup red wine
1 slice rye bread
1 tablespoon meat stock paste

Pound beef slices very thin with edge of saucer or kitchen cleaver. Combine ground round steak with onions, salt, pepper, bouquet garni, crumbs and Worcestershire sauce. Place 2 tablespoons of this mixture on each slice of pounded beef; roll up and tie with string. Dust with seasoned salt. Heat shortening in saucepan; add beef rolls and brown evenly over moderate heat; add tomato juice, wine, and rye bread (as a thickener); cover tightly. Place in 325° oven for 1½ hours; check occasionally and add more liquid if needed; adjust seasonings. Add meat stock paste; heat well. Serve with Gnocchi alla Romana, dusted with snipped parsley. Serves 6.

If preferred, ½ cup tomato juice may be used and wine omitted.

BEEF TONGUE MALAGA

1 3- 4-pound pickled tongue
1 teaspoon pickling spice

1 clove garlic (optional)
Raisin Sauce del Sol

Place tongue in saucepan; cover with cold water; bring to a boil. Add garlic and spice. Cover; simmer about 1 hour for each pound, or until very tender when tested with a fork. After cooking 1 hour, taste liquid and if it is very salty, drain off water and cover with fresh water. Continue cooking for proper amount of time. When tender, allow to cool in stock in which it was cooked; remove and peel off skin, then trim tongue by cutting off root with fat and bones. Starting with curve of heavy end, slice diagonally, making portions ½ inch thick. In this way, longer slices may be obtained from small end.

Place slices in saucepan and cover with Raisin Sauce del Sol; heat thoroughly and arrange on serving platter. Border platter with Cucumber Cups filled with Horseradish Cream. Serves 4 to 6.

Raisin Sauce Del Sol

1 cup tomato juice	⅓ cup raisins
½ cup brown sugar	1 teaspoon instantized flour or
½ teaspoon lemon juice	1 teaspoon flour mixed
¼ teaspoon salt	with water

Combine ingredients in saucepan; simmer about 10 minutes, until clear and slightly thickened. Pour over tongue; serve extra sauce separately. Very good with ham, too.

You may prefer fresh tongue. Simmer in salted water to cover, (about 1 tablespoon salt); add garlic clove, a teaspoon pickling spices and a medium onion. Adjust seasonings to taste as it cooks, proceeding as for pickled tongue. However, do not drain off any water. Cooking time is the same and the sauce a good complement.

Fresh tongue is gray in color, the pickled or smoked a more appetizing red.

Really good eating with

Italian Beans
Chocolate Whipped Cream Cake

BRAISED STEAK HUNGARIAN STYLE

2 pounds rump or round steak, 1 inch thick	1½ teaspoons seasoned salt
4 slices bacon, diced	¼ cup finely chopped sweet pickles
1 large onion, coarsely chopped	½ cup water
⅛ teaspoon freshly ground pepper	1 beef bouillon cube
1½ teaspoons paprika	½ cup sour cream

Cut the beef into 8 pieces of the same size. Fry bacon until crisp, then remove with a slotted spoon and set aside. Add onion to bacon fat in sauce pan and sauté until lightly browned, then add beef and sauté again until evenly seared and lightly browned. Add paprika, seasoned salt, pickles, diced cooked bacon, water and bouillon cube. Cover and simmer slowly until meat is tender, about 1½ hours. Check as it cooks, and add water if needed. Ten minutes before serving, add sour cream and heat thoroughly at very low heat. To serve, place meat on heated platter and pour gravy over. If there is too much, serve remainder in sauceboat. Serves 4.

Spaetzle are a good accompaniment, delicious with the gravy, or use Butter Dumplings.

Autocrat of the Kitchen

The appropriate menu is always a hostess' concern when planning for guests. There is a choice between the ultra-gourmet foods, or those of personal preference. The latter was the decision when a Pot Roast with Potato Pancakes was selected as the entrée. The cook was so informed and, as an afterthought, instructed: "Please Ora, use the finger bowls." "No ma'am," she responded promptly, "not with pot roast."

When the master of the house appeared for dinner, his lady said, "Ora and I don't agree on the subject of finger bowls, but she is so fond of you, I don't think she'll refuse." Good-humoredly he pushed open the kitchen door, but before he had his foot inside, a voice declared "No sir, they can think your wife is crazy, but they ain't gonna think I am."

However, it is not always what is served, but how it is presented, and we must disagree with Ora. So don't abandon your lovely appointments with the formal service of yesteryear. Rather enjoy them all in the lighthearted and informal manner of today.

BRAZILIAN POT ROAST

4 pounds lean beef, round
  or rump
1 teaspoon salt
2 tablespoons lemon juice
3 slices bacon
1 clove garlic, minced
⅔ cup chopped onion

¼ cup chopped parsley
4 whole cloves
½ teaspoon cinnamon
½ bay leaf
1 teaspoon sugar
1 cup canned tomatoes or 3 small
  fresh tomatoes, chopped

1 cup orange juice

Wipe meat with paper towels, season with salt and lemon juice. Sauté bacon until crisp in Dutch oven or saucepan (one with its own cover); remove bacon; add meat to remaining fat in pan and brown evenly. Combine garlic, onion, parsley, cloves, cinnamon, bay leaf, sugar and tomatoes; add to beef. Crumble sautéed bacon over meat. Bring to a boil; reduce heat; cover and simmer 10 minutes. Add orange juice and simmer, covered, about 3 hours or until fork-tender. As meat should cook "short," check that liquid does not dry out, and add small amount of water, if necessary. Serve sliced on heated platter; border with Glazed Oranges, interlaced with crisp parsley. Serves 6.

Though a pot roast may sound prosaic, these accompaniments make it party fare

Brussels Sprouts Bacchus   Buttered Broad Noodles
Strawberry Cloud Cake

Whenever we get a yen for Chinese food, which is quite often, we take ourselves to Ruth Moy's Restaurant. Mrs. Moy sent me this recipe with the postscript: "That's how I cook it at home."

CHINESE BEEF AND GREEN PEPPERS

1 pound fillet of beef, thinly sliced	½ medium Spanish onion, thinly sliced
2 tablespoons soy sauce	2 cups boiling water
1½ teaspoons cornstarch	¼ teaspoon salt
2 green peppers, sliced in ¼-inch strips	1 teaspoon fresh or dry ginger
	1 teaspoon cornstarch

4 tablespoons peanut oil for sautéing

Sauce Mixture for Beef

4 tablespoons sherry	½ teaspoon sugar
2 tablespoons soy sauce	1 teaspoon bead molasses
½ teaspoon salt	

Sprinkle fillet strips with soy sauce; dust with 1½ teaspoons cornstarch; toss well and set aside. Place peppers and onion in boiling water and blanch 2 minutes; drain. Combine salt, ginger and 1 teaspoon cornstarch; toss with peppers and onion. Combine sherry, soy sauce, salt and sugar; reserve. Heat 2 tablespoons peanut oil in a 10-inch skillet until smoking hot; add beef and sauté until color is gone, about 30 seconds. Heat remaining oil in second skillet; add peppers and onion, and sauté 3 to 5 minutes until heated and well blended. Combine sherry mixture, beef, green peppers and onions; bring to a boil quickly; add molasses and heat thoroughly for about 5 minutes. Serve piping hot with rice or Chinese noodles. Serves 4.

I often serve glossy bean threads, sometimes called Cellophane Noodles, with the beef or other Chinese dishes. Tear off about a 1½-inch hank of an 8-ounce package (about 2 ounces), soak for 5 minutes in cold water in a saucepan; drain; add 1 teaspoon soy sauce and sufficient hot water to cover. Bring to a boil and cook 10 minutes. Drain, then pour into center of beef and green pepper casserole. It is well to cook the Beef and Green Peppers in a serving skillet so that it may be brought to the table piping hot. Serves 3 to 4.

For a complete Chinese menu, try

Cellophane Noodles   *Precious Orange*
Jasmine Tea   *Candied Ginger*

The electric skillet serves an intimate group in intriguing fashion, adding flavor to the contents. Baby Ribs and Egg Roll for appetizers, with steaming towels for sticky fingers and Chinese atmosphere.

CZECH LIVER PÂTÉ

½ pound beef liver
⅛ pound bacon
   (approximately 3 slices)
⅛ pound butter
1 large onion, sliced
½ teaspoon seasoned salt

½ teaspoon monosodium
   glutamate
1 teaspoon mushroom powder
   (optional)
⅛ teaspoon coarsely
   ground pepper

¾ teaspoon salt

Cut the liver into 1-inch squares; dice bacon and place it in large skillet with butter. Heat until butter melts, then add onion and sauté over medium heat until lightly browned; add liver and continue to cook until it has lost all pink, about 10 minutes. Remove from heat and put through grinder, using fine blade. Add all pan drippings to ground ingredients; add seasoned salt, monosodium glutamate, mushroom powder and pepper. Add salt gradually and taste, as bacon varies in salt content. Press through sieve or food mill three times, then pack firmly into a mold or crock; seal with a thin coating of melted butter and refrigerate. Let stand a minimum of 12 hours to "marry" flavors. The pâté keeps for several days. Makes 1½ cups.

Though I have used this pâté as an appetizer, it is a traditional entrée. Served with a spicy salad and a vegetable, the course is complete. Double it for 6 servings.

Buenos Aires is a glimpse of Paris through the small end of binoculars. There is complete recall in the charm and grace of these cultured people. Long established restaurants retain an Old World mien, the cuisine of another day, while a modern façade presents the celebrated Argentine beef, sizzling with outdoor-pit aroma and style.

FILLET OF BEEF ARGENTINE

1 whole 3-pound fillet of beef
¼ cup butter
2 hard-cooked egg yolks, sieved
½ cup chopped mushroom stems
2 tablespoons chopped scallions
    or green onions

2 tablespoons olive or salad oil
½ cup dry red wine
½ cup beef stock or bouillon
½ teaspoon herb blend for meat
1 onion, thinly sliced
2 tablespoons flour

2 tablespoons water

Heat butter in a skillet and brown the fillet evenly, then place it in a shallow roasting pan. Add egg yolks, chopped mushrooms and scallions to butter left in skillet; blend to make a paste; add oil if needed and spread over fillet. Pour in wine, stock; add herbs and onion. Place in 325° oven; roast 20 to 25 minutes per pound for rare, or 140° on meat thermometer. Turn the fillet once during roasting. When done remove to a warm platter. Make a smooth paste of the flour and water; add to drippings in pan, and simmer 5 minutes over direct heat. Slice fillet in 1-inch portions. Serve gravy separately. Serves 6 to 8.

One-half cup boiling water and 1 beef bouillon cube may be used in place of the beef stock.

Here the "on hand" Beurre Manié may conveniently replace the flour and water.

Augment this with a first course and accompaniments such as

Jellied Guacamole with Crabmeat Dressing
Velvet Noodles
Macaroon Torte

FRANKFURTERS IN FROCK COATS

6 frankfurters   ¼ cup melted butter
6 slices fresh bread   6 toothpicks

Place frankfurters in saucepan; add cold water to cover. Bring
to a boil; then remove from heat. Cover pan and let stand 8
minutes. Brush each slice of bread with butter. Place one
frankfurter diagonally on each slice of bread. Enclose by bringing opposite corners together; fasten with toothpicks. Brush
outside of bread with butter and place on a cooky sheet. Broil
6 inches from flame in a preheated broiler until nicely browned,
about 5 minutes. Serve immediately with piccalilli and mustard,
or other desired sauce. Serves 6.

The cooked frankfurters may be dressed in their coats early in
the day. Cover them with towels and refrigerate. Brown under
broiler just before serving.

For a supper plate add

Shiny Potato Salad   Eggplant Towers
Mile High Strawberry Pie

HILLTOP FLANK STEAK

1 flank steak (approximately   1 cup barbecue sauce, prepared,
    2 pounds)   or your favorite recipe
            3 tablespoons steak sauce

Dry steak with paper toweling and place in shallow pan.
Combine barbecue sauce and steak sauce; spread over steak,
covering evenly. Refrigerate and let stand a minimum of one
hour. It may stand overnight. Score steak lightly with a sharp
knife in crisscross lines, forming diamonds; baste with remaining sauce marinade. Place under hot broiler, 3 inches from heat,
and broil 5 minutes, then turn and cook 5 minutes or until of
desired doneness. To serve, cut in thin diagonal slices, and use
pan drippings as sauce. Serves 4 to 5.

Flank steak varies in size and thickness and timing must be
adjusted accordingly. (*It must be cut in thin diagonal slices to
insure tenderness.*)

This sauce can be combined from those ingredients on hand, if additional sauce is needed.

Hilltop Sauce

> ¼ cup steak sauce   ¼ cup French Dressing
> ¼ cup chili sauce   1 tablespoon Worcestershire
>   ½ teaspoon seasoned salt

Combine all ingredients and blend well. Dust beef with hickory smoked salt for an outdoor flavor.

OVEN-BRAISED OXTAILS

2 pounds disjointed oxtails	1 8-ounce can tomato sauce
4 tablespoons salad oil or shortening	½ cup coarsely chopped celery leaves
1 large onion, coarsely chopped	1 tablespoon Worcestershire
¼ cup flour	4 carrots, quartered lengthwise
¼ teaspoon white pepper	1 cup diced celery
1½ teaspoons salt	1 green pepper, diced
1 teaspoon seasoned salt	4 medium potatoes, halved
1 teaspoon sugar	1 10-ounce package frozen peas

Wash oxtails in cold water and dry with paper toweling. Heat oil in large skillet or Dutch oven; add onion and brown lightly. Combine flour, white pepper, salt, seasoned salt, and sugar on wax paper. Dredge oxtails in flour mixture; add to heated oil and brown evenly and well. Add any leftover seasoned flour, tomato sauce, celery leaves, and Worcestershire. Cover tightly and place in 325° oven; bake 3 hours or until meat is fork-tender. Open skillet occasionally while baking and add water if sauce cooks low. Add carrots, celery, green pepper, and potatoes; cover skillet; bake an additional 45 minutes until potatoes are tender. Cook frozen peas according to package directions; do not overcook. To serve, place oxtails and skillet vegetables on platter; drain cooked peas and pour over platter. The fresh green of the peas adds appetizing color. Serves 4.

This is a good preparation for oven serving ware, or an electric skillet.

PINEAPPLE CORNED BEEF

3- to 4-pound corned beef	½ cup brown sugar
1 onion	1 teaspoon mustard
1 carrot	1 cup pineapple juice
3 or 4 bay leaves	cloves

Garnish

6 pineapple slices, heated   6 artichoke hearts, heated and buttered

Place corned beef in a large saucepan; pour in sufficient water to cover; add onion, carrot and bay leaves; cover and simmer about 3 hours or until tender. Combine brown sugar, mustard and pineapple juice in a saucepan and simmer 5 minutes. Remove corned beef from kettle and drain. Score top diagonally with a knife and stick with whole cloves where lines intersect. Place in a shallow roaster; pour sauce over meat and baste frequently with pan juices while roasting. Bake in a 350° oven 1 hour or until glazed. Garnish with heated pineapple slices, drained and centered with buttered artichoke hearts. Serves 6.

The corned beef may be cooked the previous day, with the final baking and glazing just before serving. It will slice more evenly if removed from the oven about 15 minutes before serving.

For a winter dinner serve with

Chinese Sprouts   Bean Pot Argentine
Pumpkin Chiffon Pie

Campaign Cookery

Our good friend, the Hon. Sidney Yates, was a candidate for the House of Representatives while I was compiling this book. Without knowledge of the specific part I might play in the procedure, I hesitatingly offered a hand, and found myself in the role of talking cook in a series of five appearances for Campaign Cookery. With suggestions from Mrs. Yates, there evolved a presentation menu for each performance, with courses named for important campaigners, and a finale of my favorite recipe for "the best Congressman in the House."

One quick, good recipe, which proved especially dear to the heart of the housewife, was Rolled Brisket. When I called my butcher the following day he asked, "Why didn't you give us the word, Mrs. H.? I've had such a run on briskets that we couldn't fill the orders. Please give me the recipe." So I did, and here it is.

ROLLED BRISKET

4 pound single brisket, all fat removed	1 teaspoon seasoned salt
	½ teaspoon savory
1 1½-ounce package onion soup mix	⅓ cup chili sauce

Garnish: beets, horseradish, curly endive

When trimmed, the brisket should weigh about 3¼ pounds. Spread it flat; dry with paper toweling and sprinkle onion soup evenly over surface. Roll tightly as for a jelly roll, and tie in three places with string to hold it firmly. Dust with seasoned salt and savory; spread with chili sauce and place on a large sheet of heavy duty aluminum foil, seam side of meat down. Seal securely but loosely to allow room for air to circulate. Set in baking pan and place in 325° oven; bake about 3 hours or until tender. Serve with the juices which will collect during cooking. Garnish with heated beets scooped out with a melon ball cutter, then filled with horseradish and feathers of curly endive. Serves 8.

I know of no meat which equals the flavor of second-day brisket. Slice leftovers and heat in pan juices; or allow to stand at room temperature for ½ hour, then slice and serve cold.

With it, hot or cold, I suggest Honey Glazed Carrots and Party Potato Pancakes; for dessert — Apple Strips.

Benjamin Green-Field, renowned "Mad Hatter" of Chicago's Magnificent Mile and creator of daring and whimsical Bes-Ben chapeaux, is a consummate culinary artist as well.

Here is his original recipe for porterhouse.

SALUTE TO PORTERHOUSE

3- to 4-pound porterhouse steak, 1-
   1½ inches thick
1 teaspoon paprika
¼ cup dried black mushrooms
4 beef bouillon cubes or 4 teaspoons
   instant beef powder
   (½-ounce envelope)

1 cup hot water
3 onions, sliced
1 4-ounce can water
   chestnuts, drained and
   sliced
¼ teaspoon crushed
   juniper berries

Remove all fat from steak; dry with toweling; place in saucepan and sprinkle with paprika. Wash mushrooms; cover with cold water and let stand. Dissolve bouillon cubes in hot water and pour around meat. Add onions, and mushrooms with liquid. Cover pan and simmer as slowly as possible for one hour; add water chestnuts and juniper berries; adjust seasonings; continue to simmer 1 hour additional. Cut across the grain in ½-inch slices. Serves 6.

With this Mr. Green-Field serves his delectable Chapeau Potatoes, Candied Carrots and Grapes; fresh grape clusters on shiny galax leaves border the platter. For dessert, Grand Marnier Soufflé.

The porterhouse is a delicious but questionable extravagance; thick round steak is my substitution — just as subtly flavored. Use the same method and menu, or a simpler combination of

Fresh Tomato Bouillon
Peas al Dente   Brandy Pears
Coffee Sponge

SAVOY SPROUTS AND MEAT BALLS

A miniature version of stuffed cabbage without the usual cabbage wrappings.

1 pound ground beef
¼ cup dry bread crumbs
¼ cup dry white wine

1 teaspoon salt
2 tablespoons butter or
   margarine

Gingersnap Sauce

½ cup water

2 tablespoons wine vinegar

¼ cup chili sauce

2 tablespoons brown sugar

6 gingersnaps, crumbled

¼ teaspoon dried basil

¼ teaspoon salt

2 10-ounce packages frozen
Brussels sprouts

Blend beef, crumbs, wine and salt together. Shape into balls the size of Brussels sprouts (about the size of walnuts). Heat butter in skillet; add meat balls; brown evenly and lightly. For the Gingersnap Sauce, combine water, vinegar, chili sauce, brown sugar, basil, salt; mix well; pour over meat balls; add gingersnaps; cover and simmer 10 minutes. Add Brussels sprouts; bring to a boil, then cook 5 minutes or to your taste. Serve in casserole or on a platter with parsley bouquets for trimming. Serves 6.

I have served this for a buffet dinner as one of two meat courses; for a three-course dinner, adding

Green Garlic Noodles
Third Hole Chocolate Cake   *Coffee*

STEAK AND KIDNEY PIE

1 recipe English Pastry

1 pound lamb or veal kidneys

2 pounds top sirloin or chuck
steak cut in 1-inch cubes

¼ cup flour

1 teaspoon salt

¼ teaspoon freshly ground pepper

½ teaspoon thyme

½ teaspoon rosemary

¼ cup butter

1 cup chopped onion

1 10-ounce can consommé

1 teaspoon Worcestershire

dash Tabasco

½ teaspoon sugar

1 cup oysters, canned or
fresh, drained

½ pound fresh mushrooms,
sliced

1 egg, well beaten

Prepare English Pastry or your favorite pie crust recipe, and roll into a ball; wrap in wax paper and refrigerate. Soak kidneys in cold, lightly salted water for 20 minutes. Drain and remove fat and membranes; slice thinly. Combine flour, salt, pepper, thyme, rosemary, and toss with beef to dredge it evenly. Heat butter in large skillet and add beef; sauté until golden brown. Add kidneys and onion; sauté 5 minutes. Stir in any remaining seasoned flour, consommé, Worcestershire, Tabasco, sugar; cover skillet and simmer 1½ hours or until meat is tender. Turn into greased 2-quart casserole; stir in oysters and mushrooms.

Cut off a third of the pie crust pastry dough and roll onto floured board to ¼-inch thickness. From it, cut a 1-inch strip long enough to fit rim of casserole. Moisten bottom of strip lightly with water and press dough around rim; now moisten top of strip. Roll out the remaining dough to cover casserole; spread over contents and strip; flute together to seal firmly. Prick top with tines of fork and brush with beaten egg. Place in 450° oven and bake 15 minutes; reduce heat to 375° and bake another 20 minutes. Serves 6.

ENGLISH PASTRY

1½ cups sifted flour	½ cup butter or
½ teaspoon salt	vegetable shortening
1 teaspoon baking powder	1 egg yolk, slightly beaten
5 tablespoons water	

Sift flour, salt, and baking powder together; add butter and cut with knives or pastry cutter until mixture resembles coarse meal. Blend in egg and water; mix with fork until dough holds together. Chill, then roll out when needed. Sufficient for 8-inch two-crust pie, and for 2-quart casserole.

For a beefsteak pie, use 3 pounds beef and omit kidneys.

Either pie is good without the oysters, if that is your preference.

SUNNY SIDE UP MEAT LOAVES

1½ pounds ground beef
1½ teaspoons salt
¼ teaspoon freshly ground
    pepper
1 teaspoon seasoned salt
¼ teaspoon monosodium
    glutamate
1 egg, well beaten
1 small onion, grated
1 tablespoon Worcestershire
1 slice white bread

¼ cup catsup
¼ cup water
6 hard-cooked eggs
1 cup prepared cornflake crumbs
6 tablespoons chili sauce
2 onions, sliced
½ cup water
½ teaspoon seasoned stock base or
    beef bouillon cube
4 tablespoons butter
watercress

Place beef in large bowl; sprinkle with salt, pepper, seasoned salt, and monosodium glutamate. Combine egg, grated onion, Worcestershire, and add to meat mixture. To second bowl add bread, catsup, and water; mix to a paste and add to meat mixture. Blend very well and divide into 6 portions, making each into a flat circle. Place a hard-cooked egg on each; wrap meat around it, conforming to oval of egg; seal well and roll in cornflake crumbs. Place in shallow baking pan; spread with chili sauce and top with sliced onion. Add water and seasoned stock base to pan and dot loaves with butter. Bake in 350° oven 40 to 45 minutes, basting occasionally and adding more liquid if needed. To serve, cut each loaf in half from top to bottom, through the egg yolk, and serve cut side up, sunny eggs facing outward, nestled in a bed of watercress. Serves 6.

The beef mixture makes delicious hamburgers, too.

PAN GRAVY

Add a teaspoon of instantized flour, 1 bouillon cube, 1 teaspoon gravy browner, and ½ cup water; bring to a boil, scraping bits from bottom of pan. Pass separately in gravy boat.

TOMATO GLAZED SIRLOIN TIP

1 4- to 5-pound sirloin tip roast   1 teaspoon seasoned salt
Tomato Basting Sauce

Remove roast from refrigerator; rub with seasoned salt and let stand at room temperature for approximately one hour before roasting. Insert meat thermometer and place roast in 375° oven for 10 minutes to heat through; reduce temperature to 325° and bake, uncovered, allowing 20 minutes per pound for rare and 25 minutes for medium. When figuring roasting time, allow 15 minutes for roast to stand before carving — the meat will cut more smoothly. Baste with half the Tomato Basting Sauce and repeat basting, using pan drippings, every 20 minutes. If meat becomes too brown, cover lightly with foil. Remove roast to platter when done; add balance of sauce to pan drippings, mixing with all the brown bits in the pan; heat and serve separately. Garnish platter with a border of Hot Spiced Pears, stemmed with watercress. Serves 6.

A meat thermometer is really an indispensable item, leaving no doubt as to desired doneness. I do urge its use.

Tomato Basting Sauce

1 8-ounce can tomato sauce   ½ teaspoon chili powder
½ cup dry white wine   1 teaspoon salt
½ cup salad oil   ½ teaspoon basil
1 tablespoon sugar   ½ cup finely chopped onion

Combine ingredients; heat and simmer 5 minutes. The sauce should be hot for basting. It is rather thick, but develops a fine coating for the roast.

With this entrée I served Glazed Cold Trout with Dill Sauce as a first course, and accompanied the beef with

*Broiled Potatoes
and Roasted Onions*

The potatoes are simple and simply delicious; have them sliced and ready to pop into the oven as the roast comes out. While it is "resting" before carving, potatoes and onions can be browning to tenderness.

Use leftover meat to make another delicious entrée such as Russian Salad.

Memorabilia from Noves, France —

TOURNEDOS PETITE AUBERGE

4 beef tournedos (sandwich steaks) 1 inch thick — 2 inches diameter	1 cup sliced mushrooms (about 12 fresh)
½ teaspoon freshly ground pepper	1 beef bouillon cube
2 tablespoons butter	½ cup water
2 tablespoons salad oil	2 teaspoons butter
¼ cup Madeira or dry white wine	1 teaspoon flour
2 tablespoons coarsely chopped or grated onion	2 tablespoons heavy or sour cream

4 slices Fried Bread

Wipe beef with paper toweling and press each with palm of hand to flatten to ½-inch thickness. Sprinkle with pepper; heat 2 tablespoons butter and 2 tablespoons salad oil in skillet and add tournedos. Sauté quickly, 3 to 4 minutes on each side or to desired doneness; remove and keep warm. Add wine to skillet, blending with pan drippings, then add onions and mushrooms; blend quickly. Stir in bouillon cube, water, 2 teaspoons butter and flour; adjust seasonings. Add cream and heat; push mushrooms to one side in pan and add cooked tournedos. Heat quickly; place Fried Bread on platter; top each slice with a tournedo then pour pan sauce over. Serve at once, garnished with crisp watercress and canned red Kieffer pears. Serves 4.

1 tablespoon Beurre Manié may be used instead of the 2 teaspoons butter and 1 teaspoon flour listed in ingredients.

Beurre Manié

Blend 4 tablespoons butter and 4 tablespoons flour to a paste and form into a roll. Wrap in wax paper and keep on hand in refrigerator for thickening of sauces and gravies. It may be prepared in larger quantities and will keep for 2 weeks. In this form it will blend well wherever the addition of butter and flour is indicated.

FRIED BREAD

4 slices bread   1 tablespoon butter
1 tablespoon salad oil

Remove crusts from bread; heat butter and salad oil in skillet and sauté bread until lightly browned on both sides. Add more butter or oil if needed.

Leftovers on Parade

Pot Roast is a homely name and a homely dish. For the first "homely" I quote Webster, "plain"; for the second and preferred definition, "characteristic of home life". Both are true, but creative preparation easily adds a glamorous touch, by which a prosaic dish becomes party fare. I especially like a Boston Cut for Pot Roast, either oven-baked or over the heat; the blade cut is good though it does not slice as well. Brisket is traditional and becomes more and more popular; delicious when sliced cold, and considered a delicacy by many. There are other cuts, too, the round, the rump, the round bone. Any Pot Roast cut must be cooked a long time on low heat, or in the oven at low temperature, about 300°, and almost an hour per pound. Be certain it is cooked until tender.

Leftovers are an infinite delight

Cold sliced beef or veal and potted leg of lamb make delicious sandwiches. Use a thin slice of rye bread and top with a teaspoon of potato salad, open-face.

Slice meat and add to gravy to reheat.

To the gravy, for variety, or to extend amount, add tomato soup, canned or fresh mushrooms with liquid, any cooked vegetables, or a 10-ounce carton of frozen mixed vegetables.

Arrange sliced beef on hamburger buns and serve with plentiful Barbecue Sauce.

Add a consommé and drop in raised dumplings.

Casseroles are simple and convenient

Slice meat, layer with cooked rice or cooked noodles; dust with crumbs or grated cheese and bake at 350° for 30 minutes.
  Top with a layer of mashed potatoes.
  Top with baking powder biscuits.

Hash

Grind the meat; add onions, and other seasonings, and brown in a skillet or in a 375° oven.

Cut the meat in cubes; add raw potatoes, also cubed, and sauté 10 to 15 minutes.

Fill casserole or muffin tins with seasoned ground cooked meat; make indentations and drop a raw egg in each; bake 15 minutes or until eggs are done, in 375° oven.

Lamb

BRAISED LEG OF LAMB

1 4-pound leg of lamb without shank bone	1 cup celery leaves, tied in a bouquet
½ tablespoon salt	¼ teaspoon rosemary
½ tablespoon seasoned salt	¼ teaspoon thyme
1 teaspoon paprika	2 cups water
1 clove garlic (optional)	2 chicken bouillon cubes
2 tablespoons butter	6 cloves
1 bay leaf	6 small onions
5 carrots, quartered lengthwise	

Have the lamb bone removed at the market. Dry lamb and rub

with salt, seasoned salt and paprika. Make slits in the lamb and insert slivers of garlic. Heat butter in deep pan with cover; add lamb and brown evenly on all sides. Add bay leaf, celery leaves, rosemary, thyme, water and bouillon cubes; cover. Bring to a boil; reduce heat and simmer 3 hours. Insert a clove in each onion and add to lamb; add carrots; cover and simmer 1 additional hour, or until tender. Check occasionally and add water if necessary. To serve, remove celery leaves and bay leaf; place lamb on platter, either whole or sliced, and border with carrots and onions. Pour pan gravy over all and garnish with crisp parsley. Serves 6.

EAST INDIAN CURRY D.C.

3 pounds boned lean lamb shoulder
boiling water to cover
3 tablespoons salad oil
1 medium onion, chopped
2 garlic cloves, minced
4 teaspoons curry powder
½ teaspoon powdered coriander
1 teaspoon paprika
2 tablespoons tomato paste

2 tablespoons slivered, blanched almonds
1 cup reserved liquid
1 cup light cream
4 tablespoons sweet pickle relish
1 teaspoon monosodium glutamate
dash cayenne pepper
Curry Accompaniments
Fluffy Rice

Cut lamb in 1″ x 2″ thin slices; place in shallow pan and cover with boiling water; simmer 5 minutes; set aside; reserve 1 cup liquid. Heat oil in large heavy skillet; add onion and garlic; cook over low heat. Stir often until onion is soft but not brown; stir in curry powder, coriander, paprika, tomato paste and almonds; add the cup of reserved liquid in which lamb was simmered, then the cream. Bring to boil and add pickle relish, monosodium glutamate, cayenne pepper, stirring until well blended. Drain lamb slices and place in the skillet; bring to boil, then lower heat; cover, and simmer 45 to 60 minutes or until lamb is fork tender and done. Adjust seasonings, and serve with Curry Accompaniments and Fluffy Rice. Serves 8.

Curry Accompaniments

Your choice of four or more:

almonds	crumbled crisp bacon	pineapple chunks
chopped eggs	grated orange rind	raisins
chutney	flaked coconut	sautéed onion rings
currant jelly	peanuts, chopped	sliced avocado
	pickles	

Shish Kabab has acquired international flavor. Its name is Turkish in origin, "shish" meaning skewer and "kabab" meaning broiled. This Satay is an important Indonesian counterpart; there it appears as an appetizer or main course at special functions and (very much like the "hot dogs" in which we indulge), served from braziers at sports events, the succulent bits are a special delight.

This recipe with a slight American influence is good, a bit different, and adjusts itself comfortably to barbecue pit, brazier or broiler. Being city folk, we broil.

INDONESIAN LAMB SATAY

2 pounds boned leg of lamb, cut into 1-inch cubes
Satay Marinade

Satay Marinade

2 medium onions, finely chopped	3 tablespoons brown sugar
1 clove garlic, minced, or ¼	¼ teaspoon salt
teaspoon garlic powder	¼ teaspoon crushed red pepper
⅓ cup smooth peanut butter	⅓ cup soy sauce
	3 tablespoons lemon juice

Combine all ingredients except lamb; blend well; add lamb and mix until well coated. Place in refrigerator and chill a minimum of 1 hour. Cover a baking sheet with foil; arrange lamb cubes in single layer on it, or string on small skewers, 4 to a serving. Place under preheated broiler, about 4 to 5 inches from heat, and broil 5 minutes, then turn and broil an additional 5 minutes. Baste with any remaining sauce or with drippings. When tender, serve piping hot, with or without Satay Sauce. Serves 4 as a main course, 6 as an appetizer.

Satay Sauce

Prepare double the recipe for Satay Marinade; reserve half and add to it

½ cup tomato sauce   dash or two of Tabasco
¼ cup water

Bring combined ingredients to a boil; mix well, and serve very hot.

Often a whole leg of lamb is too large for a single dinner. Here is one preparation which offers diversity. Have a sufficient amount cut from the shank for a stew and freeze it for another day. Another thrifty maneuver is to slice the desired number of lamb steaks from the larger end, using balance of leg for roasting. The steaks are delicious; prepare as for Potted Lamb Steaks.

LAMB BREAST BARBECUED

4 lamb breasts (about 1½ pounds each)   Marinade Piccante
meat tenderizer   watercress

Sprinkle breasts on both sides with tenderizer, pricking with fork to penetrate (according to directions). Place in a shallow pan; let stand at room temperature 1 hour. Pour Marinade Piccante over the lamb and refrigerate overnight, turning occasionally to season thoroughly.

This versatile cut of meat may be cooked three ways. Remove lamb and reserve marinade (1) Place ribs on a charcoal grill, 4 inches above the coals; cook from 1 to 1½ hours or until tender. (2) Thread on a spit, in a rotisserie, or over coals, timing as directed in (1). (3) For indoor cooking, broil 6 inches from heat, same length of time, turning frequently as it browns. Baste often with reserved marinade in all three methods. Garnish with an abundance of watercress for eating as well as trimming. The flavor "marries" well with the lamb. Have paper napkins available with this juicy bit. Serves 6 to 8.

With this I like

Pilaf Vermicelli   *Zucchini Strips*
Apricot Torte

Marinade Piccante

1 teaspoon dried Italian seasoning	½ cup red wine
1 tablespoon brown sugar	¼ cup chili sauce
1 teaspoon seasoned salt	¼ cup Italian Dressing
2 cloves garlic, minced	½ cup water

Combine Italian seasoning, brown sugar, seasoned salt; blend well. Stir in garlic, then add wine, chili sauce, Italian dressing, water; blend all together well.

LAMB RIBLETS PICCANTE

2 pounds lean lamb ribs, separated   1 cup Marinade Piccante

Remove any fat along edges of ribs but keep the meat intact on the bone. Place ribs in container; pour in ½ cup Marinade Piccante and marinate at room temperature for 1 hour. Turn ribs frequently so each will be well-coated and flavorful. Set heat of electric skillet at 350°; cook about 15 minutes or until well-browned. Pour off grease; baste with additional marinade; reduce heat to 325°. Cook for one hour or until tender, basting frequently; if grease accumulates, remove it before basting. Ribs should be well-browned and glazed. Serves 4.

These delectable bits may be used as appetizer or entrée. For the latter, the quantity had best be doubled.

The oven method of preparing Lamb Riblets Piccante calls for a 350° oven for entire cooking. Proceed as above; do not cover but if ribs brown too quickly, top loosely with foil. If insufficiently browned when done, place under broiler for a minute or two.

LEG OF LAMB MARINARA

1 5- to 6-pound leg of lamb, boned	Spicy Marinade
2 teaspoons seasoned salt	Kidney Dressing or Lamb Stuffing Indy

Dry lamb with paper toweling; rub well with seasoned salt; set aside while preparing marinade and dressing. Spread lamb on flat surface, cut side up and cover with Kidney Dressing; bring sides of meat together, then fold over the piece left at shank end. Truss securely with poultry pins and lacings so that dressing will not seep. Place in bowl and pour over the Spicy Marinade; set in refrigerator a minimum of 2 hours. Turn occasionally so that meat is evenly marinated.

Three to three and one-half hours before serving, remove from refrigerator and let stand at room temperature for one half hour. Remove from marinade and place in roasting pan; reserve marinade for basting. Roast in 325° oven, basting frequently; allow 30 minutes per pound for medium done, 18 minutes for "pinky" rare. To serve, slice vertically through roast to include dressing. Border platter with halved pears, hollow side up and filled with defrosted frozen raspberries; add tufts of fresh watercress. Serves 8.

Spicy Marinade

1 garlic clove, peeled and halved	½ cup finely chopped parsley
1 cup coarsely chopped onion	¼ cup wine vinegar
¼ cup salad or olive oil	

Combine all ingredients and blend well.

Kidney Dressing

6 lamb kidneys	¾ teaspoon salt
4 tablespoons butter	⅛ teaspoon freshly ground pepper
1 clove garlic, minced	
2 tablespoons finely chopped parsley	1 4-ounce can mushroom stems and pieces
1 green onion, thinly sliced	1 tablespoon flour
¼ teaspoon dill weed (optional)	

Wipe lamb with moist toweling, then dry carefully. Sprinkle

with seasoned salt. Set aside while preparing dressing and marinade.

Split kidneys in half lengthwise; remove white membrane and cut in thin slices. Melt butter in saucepan; add garlic, parsley and onion; sauté 2 minutes, then add kidneys and sauté about 5 minutes additional until brown. Make a paste of the flour and 2 tablespoons of mushroom liquid; blend into kidney mixture. Add salt, pepper, drained mushrooms and dill weed. Bring to a boil; simmer 5 minutes; remove from heat and cool.

Lamb Stuffing Indy

1 pound ground lamb	½ cup crushed pineapple
½ teaspoon savory	and juice
4 strips bacon, cooked crisp and crumbled	

Combine lamb, pineapple and juice, and savory; blend well, then fold in bacon lightly. Taste, and add salt if desired.

Though this recipe is for stuffing a boned leg of lamb, it is also a fine entrée when made into patties and sautéed lightly. Serves 4.

I like these recipes with lamb

Spinach Soufflé   *Paprika Potatoes*
Frozen Angel Toffee

Spices of the Old World led Columbus to uncharted waters which dashed him against our shores. Today they guide us on flavorful tours transported by exotic recipes of other lands. Cinnamon was so revered as a love potion by the ancient Greeks that offerings in its honor were made on Mount Olympus. The Persians inherited a predilection for this spice, and their cinnamon-spiced lamb is a modern means of travel fantasy to Iran.

PERSIAN LAMB

2 tablespoons shortening	¼ teaspoon oregano
2 pounds boned shoulder of	½ teaspoon cinnamon
lamb, cubed	1 tablespoon lemon juice
1 large onion, finely chopped	2 apples, peeled, cored
1 cup water	and quartered
1 teaspoon salt	parsley
¼ teaspoon pepper	paprika

Heat shortening in saucepan; add lamb and sauté until lightly browned, then onion and sauté for additional 5 minutes. Add water, salt, pepper, oregano, cinnamon and lemon juice; cover and simmer about 45 minutes or until fork-tender, but not mushy. Add apples and simmer 15 minutes. Serve garnished with parsley, dusted with paprika and bordered with the apples. Serves 4.

Persian Proverb

"Woman is a torment but, oh God, let no home be without it."

Variations

Omit apples and add ¼ cup tomato juice and ½ cup canned, drained kidney beans. Simmer the last 15 minutes.

Instead of kidney beans, substitute eggplant. Cut a large unpeeled eggplant in 1-inch lengthwise slices. Sprinkle lightly with salt and sauté quickly in 2 tablespoons butter; set aside. Just before serving, add to the lamb and simmer until heated through, about 10 minutes. Adjust seasonings.

Try 4 lamb shanks instead of the cubed lamb, 1 to each serving.

With the lamb this menu will complete a typical Persian dinner

Kateh (Crusty Rice)
Fresh Vegetable Salad   Dill Dressing
Fruit in Season

POTTED LAMB STEAKS

We have been serving these Lamb Steaks for lo, these 40 years, and finally I stood at pot-side and measured the ingoing ingredients. Hope you like this homespun combination.

4 lamb steaks (about 2 pounds)
¼ cup Seasoned Flour
½ teaspoon seasoned salt
3 tablespoons salad oil
1 cup onions, diced in ¼-inch squares
1 10-ounce can tomato sauce
½ teaspoon celery seed

1 teaspoon sugar
½ cup water
½ teaspoon monosodium glutamate
1 teaspoon garlic salt or minced garlic clove (optional)
1 green pepper, cut in ¾-inch squares

1 8-ounce package Bohemian noodles, cooked

Dredge lamb steaks with Seasoned Flour; sprinkle with seasoned salt. Heat oil in Dutch oven or heavy skillet; add steaks and brown evenly over medium heat for about 15 minutes. Remove steaks to warm dish; add onions to skillet and brown lightly. Return steaks to skillet with onions; add tomato sauce, celery seed, sugar, water, monosodium glutamate and garlic salt or minced garlic. Simmer about 1 hour or until tender. Check occasionally during cooking to see that steaks do not stick; add water if necessary. When tender add green pepper; cover and cook 5 additional minutes. To serve, heap noodles in center of platter, steaks around the mound, and pour the tomato pan gravy over all. Serves 4.

Rice or broad noodles may be substituted for Bohemian noodles.

RIB CHOP ROAST

2½ pounds lean rib chops, lamb or pork
1 tablespoon lime or lemon juice
½ teaspoon savory

2 tablespoons brown sugar
1 teaspoon salt
1 teaspoon rosemary

Center cut chops are preferable because they are meaty. Have the chops cut about ¾-inch thick. There should be about 10. Tie

them together as a roast, in their original shape. Rub with
lime or lemon juice and place in a shallow roasting pan. Combine sugar, salt, rosemary and savory; spread over meat; insert
thermometer; place in a 325° oven; add ¼ cup water (more if
pan becomes dry). Bake about 2 hours, allowing 35 to 40
minutes per pound, or until thermometer reaches 185°. Baste
frequently with pan drippings. Remove to platter when done
and keep warm while completing Spiced Gravy. Serves 4 to 6.

SPICED GRAVY

1 tablespoon butter	1½ cups boiling water
1 onion, chopped fine	2 cloves
1 teaspoon brown sugar	1 tablespoon flour
2 chicken bouillon cubes	

While meat is roasting melt butter; add onion and brown
lightly; sprinkle with sugar and flour; blend evenly. Stir in 1
cup water; add cloves and chicken bouillon cubes; simmer until
smooth and heated, about 5 minutes. When roast is done add
drippings and ½ cup water to onion mixture; heat and pour
over roast or serve separately. Border with unpeeled orange
slices, centered with artichoke hearts, moisten with French
Dressing; add contrast with watercress sprigs.

Add a tossed salad and cake to complete this easy menu; also
"Mamma Do Like Rice and Peas."

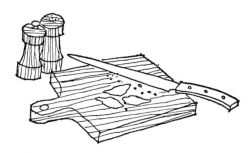

Aromas from grill and garden tantalized the arriving guests.
Every morsel of the barbecue dinner justified our expectations.
Our host-chef, like many good cooks, was thoroughly non-

plussed when I asked for recipes; he had no accurate measurements. The following week, I received explicit detail from his wife; she had watched and measured as he prepared dinner for another fortunate group. The entrée was

SHASHLIK À LA H.B.F.

1 boned leg of lamb, cut in 1½-inch cubes

chopped onions	Hot Sauce

Marinade

1 large onion, sliced thin	1 teaspoon oregano
½ cup red wine	1 teaspoon salt
¼ cup olive oil	⅛ teaspoon cayenne pepper
1 crushed garlic clove	⅛ teaspoon red pepper

¼ teaspoon black pepper

Place lamb in bowl; combine Marinade ingredients and pour over the lamb. Turn meat occasionally so that it is evenly flavored. Remove from marinade ½ hour before grilling and string on skewers. Be certain to separate the cubes as you string them so that heat will penetrate evenly. Place on grill over hot charcoal; roast until pink inside and nicely charred. There are so many variables with outdoor cooking, no chart can be completely dependable so test carefully for doneness.

As an alternate for winter cooking and the inexperienced barbecue cook, the shashlik may be oven roasted indoors for 30 minutes. Serve with chopped onions and Hot Sauce. Serves 8 to 10. The boned leg of lamb will weigh about 4 pounds, ½ pound servings per person.

Hot Sauce

1 cup chili sauce	1 tablespoon Worcestershire
½ cup catsup	¼ cup prepared horseradish

½ teaspoon Tabasco

Blend all ingredients in saucepan; simmer slowly 10 minutes. Serve well heated.

Our first course was Crab Fingers with Sauce Margery and Barbecued Polish Sausage.

With the Shashlik we had

Tossed Salad   Brown Rice Pilaf
Herb Bread
'Lasses Lace Cookies

Pork

BOYLAND SPARERIBS BAKED

6 pounds meaty spareribs
2 to 3 cups Boyland Barbecue Sauce

Place ribs on rack in shallow roaster; bake in 350° oven 1 hour, draining fat frequently. Baste with sauce, continuing to bake an additional ½ hour or until tender. Remove from oven; cover thickly with sauce and set aside a minimum of 1 hour. To serve, place in 350° oven and bake 45 minutes to 1 hour until piping hot. Serves 6.

BOYLAND SPARERIBS BARBECUED

To barbecue the ribs, heat the coals until gray and smoldering. Place ribs on rack, 12 inches above the heat and grill 1½ hours. Keep a filled sprinkling can at hand to put out flames from dripping grease. Remove the ribs and place on rack in shallow roaster; cover with Boyland Barbecue Sauce and set aside. Heat as for baked spareribs.

Boyland Barbecue Sauce

There is a leisurely feeling at Boyland Farm until we hear "Dinner is served." Mattie's barbecue ribs waft an irresistible aroma. The sauce freezes well, and can be kept in the refrig-

erator two or three weeks. I use it for Short Ribs at Home, as a
basting sauce for poultry and as the liquor for stews. In short,
it's long on goodness.

1 8-ounce can tomato sauce	3 cups water
1 6-ounce can tomato paste	1 green pepper, finely chopped
1 onion, grated	1 tablespoon tarragon vinegar
1 tablespoon brown sugar	1 tablespoon olive oil
½ clove garlic, minced	1 tablespoon Worcestershire
dash Tabasco	

Combine all ingredients in saucepan; bring to boil. Cover and
reduce to simmer. Cook 3 to 4 hours. Make this in advance as
the flavor improves with age. Makes about 4 cups.

With this Mattie served

Petite Tomato Zucchini   Slaw Down Under
Blueberry Cantaloupe à la Mold
Coffee — Hot or Iced

Despised by ancient peoples, the pig was legally recognized by
Parisiens in 1476, his specialty butcher shop duly licensed, and
presided over to this day by the "charcutiers." Their variety of
gourmet preparations include the favorite American flight of
fancy, Butterfly Pork Chops.

BUTTERFLY CHOPS CHARCUTIERS

6 pork loin chops, 1 inch thick	1 teaspoon dry mustard
3 tablespoons shortening	1 cup beef stock
1 large onion, coarsely chopped	½ cup dry white wine
1 teaspoon cornstarch	2 tablespoons thinly sliced
2 teaspoons salt	gherkins or sweet pickle
⅛ teaspoon cracked pepper	relish
2 tablespoons chopped parsley	

Have bone removed from chops; split each almost in half, and
spread flat in butterfly fashion. Heat 2 tablespoons shortening

in skillet; spread chops flat and brown on both sides. Remove and set aside. Heat remaining shortening in same skillet; add onion and sauté until lightly browned, about 3 minutes. Sprinkle with cornstarch, salt, pepper and mustard; blend well. Stir in stock carefully until smooth; add wine and gherkins or relish. Cook 5 minutes, then place chops in the sauce, turning until well moistened; cover and cook slowly about 15 minutes or until tender. To serve, cover with pan sauce and sprinkle with parsley. Serves 6.

Use 1 bouillon cube dissolved in 1 cup water if beef stock is not at hand.

CALIFORNIA SPARERIBS

2 sides spareribs	½ cup tomato catsup
6 cups stale bread crumbs	1 cup beef bouillon
2 cups dried fruit, stewed	2 tablespoons Worcestershire
and drained	1 teaspoon dry mustard
1 cup finely chopped celery	1 minced garlic clove
½ cup minced onion	1 tablespoon minced parsley
2 teaspoons salt	8 slices pineapple
½ cup melted butter	
or margarine	

Wipe ribs with paper toweling and place in shallow pan, hollow side up. Combine bread crumbs, stewed fruit, celery, onion, salt and butter. Spread on one side of spareribs and cover with other side placed curved side up; skewer together. Place stuffed spareribs in a 450° oven for 10 minutes, or until browned; lower temperature to 375°. Combine catsup, bouillon, Worcestershire, mustard, garlic, and parsley in saucepan; bring to a boil and pour over the meat. Bake and baste spareribs for 1 hour and 10 minutes, or until tender. Add pineapple slices and bake 10 minutes longer. Serve immediately. Serves 4.

Loin Pork Chops

Use 8 loin chops in two layers instead of spareribs. With either chops or spareribs, vary the flavor by substituting chopped apple for dried fruits.

HAM EN CROÛTE

6- to 7-pound precooked canned ham, drained	2 tablespoons honey
	1 tablespoon lemon juice
½ cup brown sugar	2 tablespoons milk or
2 teaspoons dry mustard	1 egg, beaten
Caraway Biscuit Dough	

Remove ham from can; scrape off gelatine. Blend sugar, mustard, honey and lemon juice together and spread over ham. Place ham on Caraway Biscuit Dough and encase it completely, moistening edges of dough to seal well. Trim edges evenly. For decoration on crust, make leaves or geometric figures from surplus dough; moisten and seal to surface. Bake in 450° oven 10 minutes; reduce to 350°; brush with milk and bake additional 15 minutes. Serve hot or cold. Serves 12.

Caraway Biscuit Dough

3 cups sifted flour	½ teaspoon caraway seeds
4 teaspoons baking powder	⅓ cup shortening
1½ teaspoons salt	⅔ cup ice-cold milk

Sift flour, baking powder and salt together; add caraway seeds. Blend in shortening with two knives or pastry blender until mixture resembles coarse cornmeal. Add milk gradually and mix only enough to form a firm dough. Knead on floured board a minute or two until smooth; chill 30 minutes. Roll out to ¼-inch thickness, and large enough to encase ham.

To secure a better "fit" for crust, cut 2 ovals of dough for top and bottom. Cut another strip wide enough to circle ham, and enclose by moistening edges and sealing them tightly.

Sherried apples are a bright complement to this recipe. Frame them with crisp green watercress.

With this I like to serve

Eggplant Casserole   *Fruit Compote Mayfair*
Chocolate Igloo

PEACHY HAM IN SKILLET
(or oven)

1 cooked center cut ham slice
   (1½ to 2 pounds)
2 dozen whole cloves
   (approximately)
1 tablespoon butter or margarine

3 tablespoons peach syrup
   from can
1 1-pound can home-style
   peaches, drained and sliced
½ cup currant jelly

Stud the ham with cloves around the fat outside edge, about 1 inch apart. Heat skillet to 325°; melt butter or margarine and add ham; sauté 5 minutes. Turn over and sauté reverse side 5 minutes. Pour in peach syrup and arrange peach slices in rows over ham; cover with jelly and cook 10 more minutes, basting continuously with pan drippings. Peaches should be glazed and shiny. Serve from skillet or remove to hot platter. Serves 3 or 4.

The ham slice may be prepared in the oven. Bake at 375° about 20 minutes. Add fruit and jelly as above and bake an additional 10 minutes.

Also use fresh or canned pears or pineapple; vary the jelly (apricot with the pears, or marmalade with the pineapple). Just a secret — use any refrigerator remnants and be creative.

I like to serve this with

Gazpacho   Cinnamon Strips
Bee Hives

ROAST PORK LOIN DIJON

4-pound pork loin or rib roast   syrup from spiced apples
Garnish: hot spiced apples, parsley
Dijon Spread
   3 tablespoons lemon juice
   2 tablespoons prepared mustard
     (Dijon type optional)
   ½ teaspoon powdered ginger
   ½ teaspoon onion salt or
     garlic salt
   1 teaspoon salt

Have backbone of roast loosened for easier carving. Place in open shallow roaster, fat side up. Combine ingredients for

Dijon Spread; spoon over the meat. Roast in 325° oven 40 minutes per pound or until meat thermometer reaches 185°. After 1 hour of roasting, baste frequently with apple syrup. Garnish with hot spiced apples and fresh parsley. Serves 6.

Do not allow meat thermometer to touch bone. Time to remove roast from oven 15 to 20 minutes before serving as it slices more easily after standing.

Be certain pork is well done. There must be no tinge of pink, and for this reason a meat thermometer is indispensible.

Lamb responds to this recipe

> 1 boned, rolled leg of lamb, 4 pounds cooking weight
> 1 garlic clove

Make small slits, 2 inches apart, in lamb and insert slivers of garlic. Cover with the Dijon Spread and roast 30 minutes to the pound in 350° oven, basting with syrup from spiced apples or pears. The meat thermometer will register 172° for medium and 180° for well done.

SOUTH SEAS PORK

1½ tablespoons cornstarch
1½ tablespoons sugar
1½ cups chicken broth or 2 chicken
    bouillon cubes dissolved in
    1½ cups boiling water
1½ tablespoons soy sauce
1 teaspoon salt
3 cups cubed cooked pork

1 cup diced green pepper
½ cup bias-cut celery
2 tablespoons vinegar
1 tablespoon instant minced
    onion
hot cooked rice
2 cantaloupes, room
    temperature

⅛ teaspoon pepper

Combine cornstarch and sugar in a saucepan; add broth and cook, stirring until mixture is clear and thickened. Stir in all remaining ingredients except rice and cantaloupe; heat thoroughly. Taste to adjust seasonings. Cut cantaloupes into thick rings; remove seeds and rind. Arrange cantaloupe rings on bed of rice; spoon meat mixture into centers of the rings. Serve hot. Makes 4 to 6 servings.

A flavorful leftover entrée; good with poultry or other meats.

TIPPED CROWN ROAST OF PORK

7-pound crown roast of pork	1 cup boiling water
3 tablespoons lime or lemon	2 chicken bouillon cubes
juice	15 raw potato cubes or foil
¼ cup brown sugar	wrapping
1½ teaspoons salt	1 1-pound jar preserved
1½ teaspoons rosemary	kumquats
1 teaspoon savory	parsley

Have a loin of pork made into a crown at your market. Place in a shallow roasting pan and pour lime or lemon juice over. Combine the sugar, salt, rosemary, savory; rub into the meat. Wrap tips of bone with foil, or cover each with a potato cube. Insert thermometer and place in a 325° oven; bake 35 to 40 minutes to the pound, or until thermometer reaches 185°. When roast has cooked ½ hour, combine boiling water and bouillon cubes; baste meat with ½ cup of bouillon, then frequently with pan drippings, adding more bouillon as needed. One hour before roast is done, remove from oven; pour off excess fat, leaving the skimmed drippings. Fill center with Corn Pudding Michiana or Wild Rice Dressing, and return to oven until done. Baste with remaining bouillon or kumquat liquid. To serve, remove foil or potatoes; spear each rib with a kumquat, and border with Tomatoes Rockefeller on beds of parsley. Serves 8.

For a larger crown, arrange 2 loins together.

Spiced Gravy for Pork Chop Roast is very good with this recipe, or for a change, substitute dry white wine for basting and/or for the bouillon in the gravy. Instead of Corn Pudding the roast may be centered with Hazel's Mashed Potatoes, Browned Potatoes, or vegetables of your choice, added just before serving. The roasting proceeds uninterrupted until it reaches 185° on meat thermometer.

With this I like a center of Corn Pudding Michiana

Tomatoes Rockefeller
Acorn Squash Compote   *Sundae Ring*

Veal

Les Baux

Leaving the circuitous road which borders the Riviera, we drove north, consulting the hieroglyphics of the *Guide Michelin*. La Baumanière at Les Baux was rated one of eleven luxury restaurants in France, having earned the coveted "five-fork" listing. A winding woodland trail halted suddenly at the edge of a breathtaking canyon and there, nestled in the rocks, was this delightful inn. Perched on a ledge above was a cottage in which Van Gogh was said to have lived.

After apéritifs on the terrace overlooking a pool, we entered the dusky dining room to partake of an unforgettable luncheon. My appreciation must have been evident, for in addition to this recipe and a few extra tidbits just to taste, mine host gifted me with a perfume made of herbs from his own garden, bottled in lovely Limoges.

Here is an American adaptation of his recipe for Sweetbread and Oyster Pie. It is a combination of an 1853 gem and modern accurate convenience; common denominator — gourmet results.

SWEETBREAD AND OYSTER PIE

1 pound prepared sweetbreads, broken in pieces	½ cup hot water and 1 chicken bouillon cube or
1 pint oysters or 2 8-ounce cans oysters	½ cup chicken consommé
2 tablespoons butter or margarine	¼ cup half and half cream
½ pound mushrooms, sliced	¼ cup Madeira or dry sherry
½ teaspoon onion flakes	½ teaspoon salt
2 tablespoons flour	¼ teaspoon paprika
	¼ cup oyster liquor

Poach the sweetbreads; use recipe for simple water and lemon juice method to insure subtlities of flavor. Heat oysters in their liquor about 5 minutes or until edges curl. Add butter to another saucepan; sauté mushrooms 3 minutes; add sweetbreads and onion flakes; simmer an additional 5 minutes, then sprinkle with flour, blending well. Instantized flour does not become lumpy and is excellent for this purpose. Dissolve bouillon cube in hot water and add to sweetbreads; stir in cream, wine, salt, paprika and oyster liquor; cook, stirring lightly so that sweetbreads do not separate. Grease a 4-cup casserole well. Remove oysters from liquid with slotted spoon, or drain and place half in bottom of casserole; add half of sweetbread mixture, then repeat. Cover top with flaky pastry and bake in 425° oven 15 to 20 minutes, or until lightly browned. Serves 6.

Cream Cheese Pastry is excellent for this recipe. A convenient flaky pie crust mix is good, too.

POACHED SWEETBREADS

1 pound sweetbreads	salted water to cover
ice water to cover	¾ tablespoon lemon juice

Soak sweetbreads in ice water 45 minutes to 1 hour. Drain; place in saucepan; cover with salted water (½ teaspoon salt to 1 cup of water). Add lemon juice; bring to a boil and simmer 15 minutes. Remove and plunge into ice water. When cool, remove cartilage and membrane. Sweetbreads are now ready for inclusion in any recipe. Serves 4.

For a distinctly different flavor, poach sweetbreads in Court Bouillon.

SCALOPPINE GYPSY STYLE

1½ pounds veal steak, thinly cut in 3″ x 4″ scallops	3 green peppers, cut in ¼-inch strips
¼ cup flour	1 1-pound can tomatoes, drained
1½ teaspoons salt	2 teaspoons sugar
¼ teaspoon freshly ground pepper	¼ teaspoon savory
¼ teaspoon oregano	⅓ cup juice from drained tomatoes
3 tablespoons salad oil	½ teaspoon onion salt (optional)
½ cup dry white wine	

With a cleaver or edge of saucer, pound steak until ¼-inch thick. Combine flour, salt, pepper and oregano. Dredge veal scallops evenly and well; heat oil in large skillet and sauté over moderately high heat until meat is browned on both sides. Add the wine and cook until it evaporates. Push veal to one side of skillet; add green peppers and cover them with the veal. Sauté 5 minutes; pour drained tomatoes over veal. Add sugar and savory to tomato juice and pour over. Dust meat with onion salt; cover and cook over very low heat 20 minutes. Serve with Butter Dumplings. Serves 4.

The veal may be prepared except for the last 20 minutes of cooking, then refrigerated or frozen. Thaw completely before cooking.

This is a fine skillet recipe.

VEAL CHOPS PAPILLOTTE

2 tablespoons butter	2½ teaspoons salt
¼ pound mushrooms, thinly sliced	½ teaspoon ground pepper
1 cup peeled diced tomatoes	6 veal chops, ¾-inch thick
¼ cup julienne-cut ham	3 tablespoons oil
¼ cup dry white wine	2 tablespoons minced parsley

Melt butter in saucepan; sauté mushrooms 3 minutes. Add tomatoes, ham, wine, 1 teaspoon salt, ¼ teaspoon pepper. Bring to a boil, then simmer 10 minutes. Season chops with remaining salt and pepper. Heat 2 tablespoons of the oil in skillet; brown chops on both sides. Cut 6 pieces of foil or parchment paper, each large enough to enclose a chop; brush foil with remaining oil. Place a chop in center of each piece; cover with sauce and sprinkle with parsley. Fold sides of foil inward, sealing edges well. Place on baking sheet and bake at 375° for 30 to 45 minutes, until tender. Serve in the foil wrap. Serves 6.

Good with a green salad, buttered spaghetti, and Parmesan cheese.

VEAL PARMIGIANA

For the very thin veal specified, slice while partially frozen, or buy it at your market already frozen and sliced.

3 pounds thin-sliced veal	1 medium onion, minced
½ cup Seasoned Flour	2 cloves garlic, minced
2 eggs, slightly beaten	(optional)
1 cup dried bread crumbs	1 1-pound 13-ounce can
¼ cup salad oil or olive	tomatoes
oil	1½ teaspoons salt
6 slices Swiss cheese	⅛ teaspoon pepper
⅓ cup grated Parmesan cheese	

The veal should be in pieces about 4" x 2". Dredge with Seasoned Flour; dip in egg, then coat with bread crumbs and refrigerate 30 minutes to set. Heat 1 tablespoon of oil in skillet and add only sufficient slices of veal to cover pan in single layer; sauté until golden brown on both sides; turning once. Repeat until all have been sautéed, arranging slices in large shallow baking pan (12" x 8" x 2" is good). Place cheese slices over veal and set aside. To make sauce, heat remaining oil in the skillet; add onion and garlic; sauté until golden. Pour in tomatoes, salt and pepper; simmer 10 minutes uncovered. Pour over sautéed veal; sprinkle with grated cheese; place in 350° oven and bake 30 to 45 minutes or until nicely browned. Serves 6.

VEAL VERONESE

2 pounds thin veal steak cut	6 tablespoons butter or margarine
in 2-inch square scallops	1 clove garlic, minced (optional)
¼ cup flour	½ pound fresh mushrooms
¾ teaspoon salt	¾ cup white wine
⅛ teaspoon white pepper	1 teaspoon chopped parsley

Pound veal with back of cleaver or edge of saucer until ¼-inch thick, and scallop has spread to larger size; dredge with flour; sprinkle with salt and pepper. Heat butter in skillet until it sizzles; add veal and garlic; brown lightly on both sides. Reduce

heat; add mushrooms and wine, mixing well with pan juices.
Simmer 5 minutes; adjust seasonings and sprinkle with parsley.
Arrange on platter garnished with lemon wedges and serve with
Gnocchi. Serves 6.

With the Veal Veronese I like an Italian-style menu

Antipasto Pomodori   *Gnocchi alla Romano*
Garlic Bread   *Crema di Fragoli*

Though this combination may seem to have an extra aroma
of garlic, the veal has but a suggestion and that optional.
Substitute a dash of basil for garlic if you prefer.

Dinner-in-a-Dish

Fɪsʜ in Newfoundland, smoked foods of Denmark, the spices in Spain, the rice of China — since time immemorial menus have been arranged with such foods as are indigenous to their locales.

The expanse of our own land, and its diverse characteristics, offer us endless regional combinations, which are reflected in great detail and prolific array, on our pantry shelves.

As you will see, delicious dishes may have a fresh start or a head start with leftovers. In either instance they will tie as winners at the finish line.

CORNED BEEF MUFFINS

½ pound freshly cooked corned beef
1 small green pepper
1 small onion
1 15½-ounce can corned beef hash
2 stalks celery, finely diced
¼ teaspoon freshly ground pepper
1 tablespoon Worcestershire
⅛ teaspoon oregano
¼ cup bouillon or tomato juice
2 tablespoons butter
seasoned salt
parsley sprigs
tomato wedges

Grind freshly cooked corned beef, green pepper and onion together. Add prepared corned beef hash, celery, pepper, Worcestershire, oregano and bouillon; mix well. Turn into 6 well-greased muffin-pan cups; dot with butter and sprinkle with seasoned salt. Bake in 350° oven 30 minutes or until nicely browned. Remove from pan to individual plates or to platter and garnish with parsley and tomato wedges. Serves 6.

For a delightful brunch dish

Make an indentation in each unbaked hash muffin, using the bottom of a custard cup. Bake 25 minutes and remove from oven; break a whole egg into each indentation; reduce heat to 325° and return to oven to bake an additional 12 minutes or until eggs are set. Serves 4 to 6.

The hostess performs a challenging role, and she seeks constant diversification. That delectable tidbit balanced on a skewer may require the juggling skill of a veteran of the stage. The respite of a "homey" preparation is a welcome alternate to palates and cooks.

BOILED DINNER NEW ENGLAND STYLE

1 4- to 5-pound corned beef brisket	1 clove garlic, split (optional)
water to cover brisket	6 whole carrots, pared
1 bay leaf	6 whole turnips or parsnips, pared
4 whole peppercorns	6 medium potatoes, pared
½ teaspoon ground cinnamon	1 head green cabbage, cut in 6ths

Rinse the beef with cold water; place in deep kettle and add water to cover. Add bay leaf, peppercorns, cinnamon and garlic; bring to a boil, then skim foam from top. Reduce heat to simmer; cover and cook about 4 to 5 hours until fork-tender, Turn off heat and skim fat from surface of liquid. Add carrots. turnips, and potatoes; simmer about 30 minutes or until vegetables are almost done; add cabbage and simmer an additional 15 minutes. Remove beef; slice and arrange on platter with vegetables surrounding attractively. Serves 6.

The vegetables may be of your choice. Subtract what you will and add 12 small peeled onions with the carrots, or add and heat a drained 1-pound can of whole onions just before serving.

A salad and dessert complete the dinner

Cucumber Salad Coupe
Toffee Bar Cake

BURGUNDY POT PIE

1 teaspoon salt
¼ teaspoon white pepper
4 tablespoons flour
2 pounds lean beef or veal, round
   or stewing beef, diced in
   1-inch cubes
2 tablespoons salad oil
2 tablespoons butter or margarine
1 clove garlic, peeled and
   split
¼ teaspoon marjoram
½ teaspoon dill weed

1 cup Burgundy or other red
   wine
1½ cups water
2 beef bouillon cubes
2 teaspoons wine vinegar
1 10-ounce package frozen
   artichokes
1 1-pound can small boiled
   onions, drained
2 tablespoons butter or
   margarine
½ pound fresh mushrooms

Parmesan Biscuit Ring

Combine salt, pepper, and flour. Dry beef and dredge it in flour mixture. Heat oil and butter in saucepan; add garlic and meat and brown meat evenly. Remove garlic, add marjoram, dill weed, wine, water, bouillon cubes and vinegar. Cover tightly and simmer slowly about 1½ hours or until tender. Cook artichokes one minute less than package directions and add to meat with onions. Heat butter, add mushrooms and sauté 5 minutes. Pour into meat mixture. Mix contents gently and pour into 2-quart greased serving casserole. Crown with Parmesan Biscuit Ring; bake 15 to 20 minutes in 425° oven. Prepare in advance, except for biscuits, and refrigerate until baking time. Serves 6.

Parmesan Biscuit Ring

1 8-ounce package refrigerated biscuits
¼ cup melted butter or margarine
¼ cup grated Parmesan or Cheddar cheese

Separate biscuits; dip in butter, then in cheese and place around rim of casserole. Bake a second package on a cooky sheet for gravy "dunking."

CHILI MAC

1 pound ground beef
2 onions, diced
1 1-pound 12-ounce can tomatoes
1 10-ounce can tomato soup
1 1-pound can kidney beans
salt and pepper to taste

2 ounces thin spaghetti, broken in small pieces (¼ of 8-ounce package)
½ teaspoon chili powder (more if preferred)

Heat skillet; add meat and sear until brown. Add onions and sauté over moderate heat until beef is tender (approximately ½ hour). Add tomatoes, tomato soup, kidney beans, salt and pepper; cover and simmer slowly about 2 hours. Stir occasionally. Add uncooked spaghetti and when spaghetti is tender (about 10 minutes) add chili powder. Blend well. Serve very hot. Serves 4 to 6.

CHOWDER DINNER

2 tablespoons butter or margarine
1 large onion, thinly sliced
5 stalks celery, ½-inch slices
1 pound lean ground beef chuck
2 quarts water
½ teaspoon garlic powder

1 tablespoon seasoned salt
2 teaspoons salt
3 onion bouillon cubes
1 7-ounce cellophane tube vegetable soup mix
½ cup white raisins (optional)
1 teaspoon gravy browner

Heat butter in large kettle and add onions and celery. Sauté until onions are golden, then add ground beef; stir with vegetables until meat is broken into small pieces and has lost pink color. Add water, garlic powder, seasoned salt, salt, and bouillon cubes; stir in vegetables from soup mix. Bring to boil, then reduce heat and simmer 1 hour. Plump the raisins by soaking in boiling water for 15 minutes; drain and add to boiling soup. Add noodles remaining from soup mix in cellophane, and gravy browner. Cook 10 minutes and adjust seasoning; serve in bowls. Makes about 2½ quarts.

This sumptuous soup needs but a simple salad and a light dessert for a satisfying dinner; add a crusty bread.

If made in advance, the chowder thickens as it stands. To dilute, dissolve 1 onion bouillon cube in 1 cup of boiling water. Blend in and heat thoroughly; serve piping hot.

Pasties are travelers from another era; they come from Cornwall where miners' wives have long nourished their men with this hearty turnover, via the mountains of Pennsylvania, with a stop in Michigan, to settle in Montana where they are regional favorites with the copper-mining men. International in flavor and appeal, in England it is the Pasty; to the Russians, a Knish; the Spanish call it an Empanada and the Poles, a Pierogi.

ENGLISH PASTY

2 tablespoons butter or margarine	⅛ teaspoon savory
½ medium onion, finely chopped	1 teaspoon Worcestershire
½ pound lean beef, cut in ¼-inch cubes	½ cup raw potatoes, cut in ¼-inch cubes
½ teaspoon salt	½ cup carrots, cut in ¼-inch dice
1 teaspoon minced parsley	1 egg yolk, slightly beaten.
½ teaspoon seasoned salt	Pasty Pastry

1 egg white, slightly beaten

Heat butter in skillet and add onion; sauté until very lightly browned, then add meat and sauté quickly. Add salt, parsley, seasoned salt, savory, and Worcestershire. Mix in potatoes, carrots, and egg yolk. Divide pastry into sixths, and roll each into a 6-inch circle. Place one-sixth of filling on each; fold in half and seal by pressing ends together with tines of a fork. Place on ungreased cooky sheet. Make 2 or 3 gashes across the top of each; brush with egg white and place in 450° oven. Bake 10 minutes to set crust, then reduce heat to 325° and bake an additional 45 minutes or until nicely browned. Makes 6.

Pasty Pastry

2 cups sifted flour	½ cup margarine
1 teaspoon salt	4 to 6 tablespoons ice water

Pour flour and salt into mixing bowl; add margarine and cut with pastry blender or knives until consistency of small peas. Sprinkle water on dough and knead with fingers until dough holds firmly together; it must be well blended. Pat between 2 sheets of wax paper, lightly floured; roll to desired thickness.

GEORGIAN MEAT AND CABBAGE
(Russian)

1½ pounds beef, cut in 1-inch cubes	1 apple, peeled and coarsely
1 whole onion	chopped
1 1-pound can tomatoes	¼ cup lemon juice
4 cups beef stock or 3 10-ounce	¼ cup brown sugar
cans beef bouillon	1 teaspoon caraway
2½ teaspoons salt	⅛ teaspoon powdered
3 cups coarsely shredded cabbage	ginger
(about 2 pounds)	

Place beef and onion in large saucepan. Add tomatoes, bouillon and salt; cover and simmer slowly about 1½ to 2 hours or until beef is almost tender. Add cabbage, apple, lemon juice, sugar, caraway and ginger. Simmer 25 minutes longer, or until beef is tender. Adjust seasoning, adding more lemon and/or sugar to please your palate. Serve in bowls with crisp hot rye bread. Serves 6 for entrée; 8 for first course.

LASAGNE À LA STEFFI

6 quarts water	2 eggs
1 teaspoon salad oil	salt and pepper
1 pound lasagne noodles	1 pound Mozzarella or Scamorza
1 pound ricotta cheese or	cheese, sliced very thin
creamed cottage cheese	Mushroom Meat Sauce

Bring water to boil; add oil, then noodles; cook 10 minutes.

When done, pour cold water into the pot until noodles are cold enough to be handled. Do not drain. Mix cheese with eggs, salt and pepper. Butter a large oblong baking dish and place a layer of noodles in long strips on bottom; next a layer of creamed cheese mixture, then slices of Mozzarella, then Meat Sauce. Repeat these layers until dish is filled, ending with noodles, meat sauce, and topping with sliced cheese. Bake in 325° oven 1½ hours. Serves 8 to 10.

Mushroom Meat Sauce

3 tablespoons olive oil	⅛ teaspoon pepper
¼ cup onion, chopped fine	¼ cup grated Parmesan cheese
1 small clove garlic, minced	2 teaspoons chopped parsley
¼ cup celery, chopped fine	1½ teaspoons salt
1 1-pound 12-ounce can Italian	½ teaspoon oregano
peeled tomatoes	2 4-ounce cans mushrooms
2 6-ounce cans tomato paste	(optional)
¼ teaspoon nutmeg	1½ pounds ground beef
1 teaspoon sugar	1 teaspoon salt

½ teaspoon baking soda

Heat 2 tablespoons olive oil in skillet; add onion, garlic, and celery; mix and sauté 5 minutes. Strain tomatoes into large bowl and discard seeds; mix tomatoes with tomato paste. Add onion mixture and all other ingredients except baking soda. Heat 1 tablespoon olive oil; add meat and salt; sauté until it loses red color, then add to tomato mixture. Cover and simmer 1½ hours. Add baking soda during last 5 minutes of cooking and blend well. Makes about 5 cups.

The Way to Flavor

The chameleon change of a recipe can be likened to the hilarious result of the parlor game "Telephone." A whispered phrase repeatedly transmitted to several waiting ears emerges delightfully unrecognizable.

Remote and unlikely places turn up heritage recipes, believed lost, of different kinds but basically similar; sometimes even including a fortunate mistake, a new flavor. A bit of herb is added, a dash of wine, cream for thickening, and a stew has been whispered into a Ragoût de Maison. By word of mouth, many recipes have traveled, in one form or another, from family to family and from one country to many others. Here is a perfect example.

RAGOÛT DE MAISON

2-inch strip of beef fat	¼ cup white wine (optional)
3 onions, cut in ½-inch dice	1 slice rye bread
4 pounds lean beef, cut in	¼ teaspoon garlic salt
2-inch cubes	6 small carrots, cooked
1 tablespoon paprika	6 small potatoes, cooked
¼ teaspoon white pepper	2 cups diced celery, cooked
1½ teaspoons salt	Spaetzle
1 cup consommé	¼ cup chopped parsley

Remove a 2-inch piece of fat from beef; dice and place in large skillet or Dutch oven. Add onions and sauté until yellow, then add meat and brown evenly and slowly. Add paprika, pepper and salt; cook 5 minutes. Stir in consommé, wine, rye bread and garlic salt. Cover; reduce heat to a simmer and cook very slowly 2 to 3 hours or until meat is fork-tender. Stir occasionally to prevent sticking to pan. Add cooked vegetables, and simmer briefly. Place meat on platter; sprinkle with parsley, border with Spaetzle and vegetables; dress with gravy. Serves 6 to 8.

Vegetables for Ragoût

Pour 1 inch of salted water into a saucepan (½ teaspoon salt for each cup); add carrots and potatoes; cook 10 minutes, then add celery and cook 10 to 15 minutes or until tender. Do not allow them to become mushy. Add carefully to beef and heat quickly.

I like to remove the meat to the platter first; the vegetables can then be arranged colorfully with the Spaetzle.

The Ragoût may be baked in a 325° oven. Cover it tightly, using foil if necessary to close it well.

If a smoother gravy is preferred, pour through a sieve and reheat before serving.

Serve with a simple dessert such as the compatible Apple Sauce, and add cookies from the kitchen jar.

For first course glamour, serve Egg Roll with the Ragoût

Spaetzle   Tomato Onion Platter
Spiced Apple Sauce   Cookies

SPAGHETTI CASSEROLE

2 tablespoons butter or margarine	2 large green peppers, diced
2 pounds ground beef	1 8-ounce package spaghetti,
1 6-ounce can mushrooms or	cooked and drained
1 pound fresh mushrooms	1 teaspoon chili powder
2 large onions, thinly sliced	½ teaspoon salt
1 1-pound 14-ounce can tomatoes	¼ teaspoon pepper
1 1-pound can small peas	1 cup grated cheese

Heat butter in saucepan; add beef and brown lightly. Add all ingredients except cheese; mix well; pour into greased 6-cup casserole. Place in 325° oven and bake one hour. Remove from oven and sprinkle with grated cheese; return to oven and bake an additional 30 minutes. Serves 6 to 8.

STREETERVILLE FRANKS AND 'TATERS

4 cups sliced cooked potatoes (about 6 medium)	1 cup water
2 tablespoons butter	2 tablespoons white vinegar
1 pound frankfurters, sliced diagonally in 1-inch pieces	1 tablespoon brown sugar
1 package (1⅝-ounce) dry onion soup mix	⅛ teaspoon white pepper
1 tablespoon flour, all-purpose or instantized	¼ cup dairy sour cream
	1 tablespoon chopped parsley
	½ teaspoon celery seed

Pare potatoes and cook whole; slice while warm and set aside. Heat butter in saucepan; add frankfurters and sauté until browned, about 5 minutes. Remove from heat, blend in soup mix and flour. Add water gradually; stir in vinegar, brown sugar, and pepper. Return to heat; bring to a boil, stir until thickened. Cover, reduce to a simmer and cook 10 minutes. Blend in sour cream, parsley, and celery seed, then fold in potatoes lightly. Heat to serve. Serves 4 to 6.

Potatoes vary in texture, and while a whole potato will cook in 35 to 40 minutes, the rule has exceptions. In this recipe, if the potatoes are too soft they will become mushy; time them carefully.

A dinner party boasted a large turkey as the main attraction. The following day, surfeited with leftovers, we improvised this casserole.

CASSEROLE TOMORROW

4 ounces broad noodles	¼ cup grated Parmesan cheese
8 large slices breast of turkey	2 tablespoons slivered
1 cup cooked green beans	almonds (optional)

Cheddar Sauce

Cook the noodles according to package directions. Rinse in hot water; drain well. Pour half the noodles into well-greased 4-cup casserole. Layer with 4 slices of turkey, remainder of noodles, and repeat turkey. Make a border with green beans. Pour sauce over all and dust with Parmesan cheese; sprinkle with almonds. Bake in a 400° oven 25 to 30 minutes, or until brown. Serves 4.

Cheddar Sauce

2 tablespoons butter or margarine	1 teaspoon boullion powder or J chicken bouillon cube
2 tablespoons instantized flour	½ teaspoon salt
2 cups milk	1 tablespoon steak sauce
2 egg yolks, beaten	¼ cup grated Cheddar or
dash Tabasco	American Cheese

Heat butter in saucepan; add flour, stirring until smooth and lightly browned. Add milk slowly, stirring constantly until blended; stir a small amount into egg yolks, then return to milk mixture. Heat; add remaining ingredients; simmer until well blended and thickened. Makes about 1 cup.

CHICKEN TETRAZZINI CASSEROLE

1 8-ounce package spaghetti, cooked	¼ teaspoon celery salt
1 tablespoon salad oil	dash Tabasco
3 tablespoons butter	2 tablespoons sherry
½ pound fresh mushrooms, sliced	1 cup sour cream
½ cup water	2 10-ounce cans cream of celery soup
¼ teaspoon salt	¼ pound Herkimer cheese, diced
	2 cups diced, cooked chicken

Topping

2 tablespoons bread crumbs	2 tablespoons butter

Cook spaghetti according to package directions; add 1 tablespoon salad oil to water to prevent sticking. Cook tender, but not too soft; blanch in hot water, then drain. Heat butter in large skillet; add mushrooms; sauté 5 minutes. Stir in water, salt, celery salt and Tabasco; add sherry. Blend in sour cream and celery soup; toss with spaghetti, cheese and chicken; turn into well-greased 6-cup casserole. Top with bread crumbs and dot with butter; bake in 350° oven 45 minutes or until well heated and browned. Serves 6.

PETITE MARMITE

2 pounds short ribs	4 cups diced mixed vegetables
10 cups water	(onions, turnips, carrots,
1 teaspoon salt	potatoes, parsnips)
6 chicken legs and thighs	4 ounces fine noodles, cooked
6 chicken wings	salt
2 cups canned tomatoes	½ teaspoon sugar

Combine short ribs, water and salt in large saucepan; cover and simmer about 2 hours or until meat is tender. Remove meat and allow liquid to stand until fat rises to the top, then skim.

Save fat to use for shortening. Add chicken to soup; cover and simmer ½ hour. Then add tomatoes and vegetables and simmer additional ½ hour or until chicken and vegetables are tender. Remove beef from bone, cutting into 1-inch cubes; discard fat; add beef to chicken and vegetables. Just before serving, bring to a full boil; then add noodles and boil gently, uncovered, about 10 minutes. Chicken may be served in the soup, disjointed or with bones removed. Adjust seasoning, adding salt to taste, and sugar. Serves 8 to 10.

Rice, Bohemian noodles, egg barley, or other pasta of your choice may be added or substituted.

This is a hearty soup, with good flavor, and it freezes well. I have added beef frankfurters to a defrosted quart for a main course. As a first course it hones the fine edge of appetites. Serve with a side dish of toasted bread and grated cheese.

SAVORY BAKED CHICKEN

2 chicken breasts, split
4 legs and thighs, disjointed
2 teaspoons seasoned salt
1½ cups long grain rice
1 10-ounce can cream of
    mushroom soup
1 10-ounce can cream of
    celery soup

1 4-ounce can mushrooms,
    with liquid, stems and
    pieces
1 1⅜-ounce package dry onion
    soup mix
1 teaspoon savory
2 cups chicken broth
parsley sprigs

Sprinkle chicken pieces with seasoned salt and let stand at room temperature ½ hour. Grease a 3-quart casserole well and spread rice over bottom; layer with mushrooms, then place chicken on mushrooms in one layer and pour over the cream of celery and cream of mushroom soups. Sprinkle with onion soup mix and savory. Pour broth around sides to moisten rice. Cover tightly with foil and place in a 350° oven. Bake about 1½ hours or until fork-tender. May be served direct from baking dish. If removed to platter, scoop rice from the pan so that it remains covered with the brown chicken pieces. Garnish with crisp parsley. Serves 6.

This is one of the few dishes we like cooked to softness. It is a wonderful blend of flavors. Any variety of chicken parts may be used, and fresh sautéed mushrooms may be substituted for the canned.

With it we had

Iceberg Salad Parmesan
Top Banana

CRABMEAT TUREEN

1 10-ounce can cream of tomato soup
1 10-ounce can beef bouillon
1 cup half and half cream
1 tablespoon lemon juice
½ teaspoon salt

1 pound fresh lump crabmeat or 2 8-ounce packages frozen, defrosted
4 tablespoons sherry
French bread, thickly sliced, toasted and buttered

⅛ teaspoon freshly ground pepper

In a 6-cup saucepan combine tomato soup, bouillon, cream, lemon juice, salt and pepper. Heat and simmer 10 minutes. Separate crabmeat, remove cartilage and add to soup mixture. Heat again and add sherry; heat but do not boil. Serve in deep bowls with French bread. Serves 6 for first course; 4 for entrée.
   Add 1 10-ounce can split pea soup for change of flavor.

This is delicious with

Pimiento Hearts of Palm Salad
Rainbow Ice Cream   *Punch Cookies*

Deep South Gumbo

Being an early riser, I often enjoy the first glow of dawn. One Sunday morning, the compulsive thought of an untried recipe propelled me into the kitchen and Deep South Gumbo emerged with the daylight. That success brought on a coffee cake and soon my larder was full.

Guests came for cocktails, and the freezer produced

Roquefort Pie Sardine Anchovy Turnovers

It was pleasant visiting, and rather than have my friends leave, I impulsively said, "Please stay and chance the testing," and they did. We were nine people. We had

Deep South Gumbo   Croutons
Cold Pickled Tongue   Swiss Cheese
Wild Noodle Rice
Tossed Salad
Royal Cream Cheese Coffee Cake

The chicken was in the freezer, the tongue and cheese in the refrigerator.

The canned wild rice was not in itself enough, but sufficient mixed with buttered boiled noodles.

Tossed salad was one of those "on hand" things, Parmesan sprinkled.

I recount this episode as reassurance in an emergency. You may not have these items on hand, but your pantry and imagination can produce other ingredients for informality, good eating and gaiety.

DEEP SOUTH GUMBO

¾ cup green pepper, seeded
and diced
1 large onion, coarsely chopped
3 stalks celery, cut in ½-inch
slices
1 tablespoon flour
¼ cup bacon or chicken fat
2 tomatoes, diced
½ pound okra or 1 10-ounce
package frozen okra
salt and pepper to taste
dash cayenne pepper
1 tablespoon Worcestershire
1 teaspoon seafood seasoning or
1 teaspoon poultry seasoning

liquor from drained oysters
2 bay leaves
1 clove garlic, minced
6 cups soup stock or canned
beef bouillon
1 8-ounce can or ½ pound
crabmeat
1 pound cleaned fresh or frozen
shrimp
1 cup diced, cooked chicken
1 8-ounce can oysters or 1 cup
fresh oysters
2 teaspoons gumbo filé
2 cups cooked fluffy rice

Dredge peppers, onion and celery, with flour, then heat fat in large kettle; add dredged vegetables and sauté 5 minutes. Add tomatoes and okra; sauté an additional 5 minutes, stirring constantly to avoid sticking. Blend in salt and pepper to taste, cayenne, Worcestershire, seafood seasoning, oyster liquor, bay leaves, garlic, and stock.* Bring to boil, cover, reduce heat and simmer 2 hours. Add crabmeat, shrimp, and chicken; simmer 10 minutes; add oysters and simmer until edges curl, about 5 minutes. To serve, remove bay leaves; heat briefly and thoroughly. Add gumbo filé; stir well and remove from heat. Serve from tureen with fluffy rice, placing 2 tablespoons rice in each bowl; ladle soup over it. Serves 10 to 12.

Stock made from the bone of a baked ham or from a fresh ham bone is very good.

Stock made from chicken is excellent, as chicken may then be used in gumbo. The simple method is canned bouillon, or water and bouillon cubes.

* See Index for chicken or beef soups.

SEAFOOD TETRAZZINI

1 8-ounce package shell macaroni
1 tablespoon butter
1 10-ounce can cream of celery
    soup
½ pound fresh mushrooms,
    sliced and sautéed
1 cup dairy sour cream
½ cup grated sharp Cheddar
    cheese

2 tablespoons sherry
½ pound cooked shrimp,
    fresh, frozen or canned
½ pound crabmeat, fresh,
    frozen or canned
½ pound lobster, fresh,
    frozen or canned
3 tablespoons slivered almonds
    (approximately)

In the morning prepare casserole for baking. Cook macaroni according to package directions. (Add 1 tablespoon of butter to boiling water to prevent sticking.) Drain. Combine celery soup and mushrooms with pan juices, sour cream, cheese and sherry. If frozen seafood is used, defrost early in the day; separate and remove bone and cartilage. Clean and devein shrimp, and if large, split in half, lengthwise. Grease a 6-cup casserole very well; make 3 layers, using ⅓ macaroni, ⅓ seafood, and ⅓ celery soup mixture for each. Sprinkle top with almonds. Place in 350° oven and bake 1 hour. Serves 10.

Use 4 cups diced cooked chicken or turkey instead of seafood. A delicious way to utilize leftovers.

With this I like

Broad Bean Salad
Tangerine Mousse   Cookies
Coffee

SPANISH-AMERICAN PAELLA

Paella is the famous Spanish national dish, and à la Valencia is the ultimate in regional preparation. In Palma, Majorca, the ceremony of presentation in the indigenous skillet, the "paellera," was memorable. In this adaptation, the American convenience foods, the freezer "treasures," and electric or stove skillet, combine to present a dish worthy of comparison. I suggest that in the recipe for cooked chicken, an additional quantity be prepared at the same time and frozen. Here you can proceed with those bonus chicken portions, for just such a need as this.

1⅓ cups boiling water
1 13-ounce package prepared rice with Valencia sauce or Toreador Rice
6 chicken joints
4 frankfurters, cut in ½-inch slices

3 medium tomatoes, cut in 6ths
½ teaspoon sugar
¼ teaspoon curry powder
1 8-ounce can mushrooms
1 5-ounce can shrimp
1 24-ounce can steamed clams
1 cup canned peas, drained
liquid from peas

Pour water into 10-cup skillet; add rice and its enclosed can of Valencia sauce; bring to a boil; simmer 5 minutes. Arrange chicken joints, frankfurter slices, and tomatoes on rice; dust with sugar and curry powder, then pour over the mushrooms and liquid; simmer 10 minutes. Mix in shrimp gently; arrange clams over top; cover and simmer 15 minutes or until clams open. Distribute peas over top; continue heating, slowly, until liquid in the paella is absorbed, and the rice soft. However, if the mixture sticks or seems too thick, add a small amount of the liquid from the peas. It need not be served at once; the flavor "sets" as it stands. It may be kept warm over low heat. Serve from skillet, piping hot. Serves 6.

For added Spanish flavor serve

Sangria   Salad Casa Botin
Peaches and Cream Cake

This is a versatile recipe. So many ingredients may be added or substituted, and leftovers are a bounty.

Lobster, crawfish, eels or mussels are used.

Diced ham, other smoked meats or sausages are good.

Leftover veal or pork are delicious substitutions for chicken or may be added.

If you are partial to garlic, add a bit, minced.
Artichoke hearts added with the peas are a gourmet touch.

If you do not have the prepared rice on hand, you may start "from scratch" with

TOREADOR RICE

2 tablespoons oil	1 10-ounce can tomato sauce
1 cup rice	pinch of saffron
1 onion, finely chopped	2 cups liquid (from shrimp,
1 clove garlic, minced	mushrooms and peas)

Heat the oil; add rice and brown lightly. Blend in onion and garlic, sauté until golden brown. Mix in tomato sauce, saffron, and liquid (if not sufficient for 2 cups, add water). Cook 20 minutes, stirring occasionally. Makes 3 cups.

Ode to
the Vegetable

Cauliflower is nothing but cabbage with a college education.

MARK TWAIN

My garden will never make me famous,
I am a horticultural ignoramus,
I can't tell a string bean from a soybean,
Or even a girl bean from a boy bean.

OGDEN NASH

ACORN SQUASH COMPOTE

3 medium acorn squash, halved
water
4 tablespoons dark brown sugar
1 1-pound 5-ounce can apple pie
    filling

1½ teaspoons cinnamon
salt
2 tablespoons butter

Place halved squash, cut sides down on baking pan; add ½-inch
water to the pan. Bake in 450° oven 45 minutes or until tender,
then turn cut sides up. Sprinkle each center with 1 teaspoon
brown sugar and fill with apple pie filling. Sprinkle each again
with a second teaspoon of sugar for each; dust with ¼ teaspoon
cinnamon and dash of salt; top with butter. Bake in 350° oven
15 to 20 minutes. Serves 6.

May be prepared in advance and reheated to serve.

Use the same method without the apple pie filling. Fill each half with 1 teaspoon brown sugar and ½ teaspoon butter, then bake in 350° oven the additional 15 to 20 minutes.

Cutting the squash crosswise reveals a scalloped edge; be sure to cut a small slice from either end so that it will stand evenly.

APRICOT CARROT RING

½ cup brown sugar, firmly packed
½ cup butter, softened
1½ cups grated cooked carrots
2 egg yolks, beaten

2 tablespoons lemon juice
1½ cups flour
1 teaspoon baking powder
grated rind of 1 lemon
¼ cup raisins (optional)

2 egg whites, stiffly beaten

Cream butter and sugar; add carrots. Beat egg yolks with lemon juice and add to carrot mixture. Blend in flour, baking powder and lemon rind; stir in raisins if desired, then fold in egg whites. Pour into 6-cup form cake mold or ring mold and bake at 350° for 45 minutes or until firm to the touch. Turn out on platter and cover with Apricot Sauce.

Apricot Sauce

1 pound dried apricots
4 cups water
1 cup brown sugar, firmly packed

1 10-ounce can concentrated frozen orange juice, defrosted

3 ounces brandy

Wash apricots; place in saucepan with water. Cook 35 minutes; press, with liquids, through coarse sieve or food mill. Combine brown sugar and orange juice in top of double boiler and heat until well blended. Add puréed apricots; blend and heat until smooth. Just before serving, add brandy to heated sauce. Serves 8.

Note: Instead of adding brandy to sauce, it may be warmed to pour over ring, and flamed as it is being served. A modest bit of glamour.

This recipe merits the contrast of a simple preparation, such as Fillet of Beef or broiled poultry. The Apricot Carrot Ring may be served without the sauce and centered with a vegetable of contrasting color — Italian or green beans, or peas.

ARTICHOKES
(Preparation)

6 artichokes	2 tablespoons lemon juice
water for boiling	1 teaspoon salt
½ teaspoon garlic powder (optional)	¼ cup salad oil

With proper grooming artichokes have a tidy, stylized look. First slice about 1 inch off the top, then cut off stem close to base. With a scissors snip off the end of each petal. Place artichokes in a saucepan, close together, stem side down, so they can stand erect. Add water to about 1½ inches in depth; add garlic powder, lemon juice, salt and oil. Bring to a boil, then cover and simmer 30 minutes. Turn stem side up and simmer 15 additional minutes or until petals pull away easily from stem. Remove; tap trimmed petals sharply so they open flowerlike; reach inside and remove chokes with fingers or small prongs. The choke is a spiny growth which clings to the heart. If necessary tie artichoke with a string to hold shape. Turn upside down to drain. Serve hot or cold.

Artichokes may be used as salad or vegetable and this basic recipe is preparation for either.

ARTICHOKE BOTTOMS GRATINÉS

1 14-ounce can artichoke bottoms, drained	½ cup chopped mushrooms
2 tablespoons butter	4 tablespoons grated Gruyère or Swiss cheese

Sauté artichoke bottoms in butter; remove from skillet and keep warm. Add mushrooms to skillet and sauté in remaining butter 5 minutes. Divide evenly and mound on each artichoke; cover with grated cheese and place under broiler until cheese melts. Serve at once. Serves 6 to 8.

ASPARAGUS RING

1 1-pound 10-ounce can green asparagus tips, drained	3 tablespoons flour
3 tablespoons butter or margarine	1 cup half and half cream or 1 cup milk
½ teaspoon salt	4 egg yolks, well beaten
¼ teaspoon pepper	½ teaspoon baking powder
	4 egg whites, stiffly beaten

Cut asparagus into small pieces. Heat butter in saucepan; add salt, pepper and flour; stir until well blended; add cream and cool. Pour into egg yolks and add asparagus tips. Fold baking powder into egg whites, then fold into asparagus mixture. Turn into a well buttered 6-cup mold; set in a pan of hot water and place in 475° oven; bake 30 to 40 minutes or until set. Center with bowl of Hollandaise Sauce. Serves 6 to 8.

BEAN POT ARGENTINE

6 strips bacon	2 teaspoons dry mustard
2 1-pound 10-ounce jars prepared baked beans	1 tablespoon brown sugar
1 medium onion, coarsely chopped	¼ cup Curaçao
	1 orange, sliced thin

Sauté 3 strips of bacon until crisp; crumble and set aside. Dice 3 remaining raw strips and combine with beans, onion, mustard, sugar and Curaçao. Mix gently but well; pour into greased casserole. Arrange orange slices over top. Cover and bake in a 325° oven for one hour, or until piping hot. Sprinkle with reserved crumbled bacon. Serves 6 to 8.

BRAISED CELERY HEARTS

1 1-pound can celery hearts	1 cup reserved celery liquid
4 tablespoons butter	¼ cup Madeira or sherry
2 tablespoons minced onion	½ teaspoon salt
1 teaspoon beef paste extract	⅛ teaspoon coarsely ground pepper
1 tablespoon instantized flour	

Drain celery hearts; reserve liquid. Heat butter in large skillet and add onion; brown lightly. Stir in beef extract and flour, then gradually add celery liquid, wine, salt and pepper. Add celery hearts and heat gently but thoroughly. Serves 6.

BROCCOLI ORIENTALE

¼ cup butter or margarine	½ teaspoon curry powder
¼ pound mushrooms	¼ teaspoon garlic powder
2 10-ounce packages frozen broc-coli, cooked and drained	1 teaspoon soy sauce
1 10-ounce can cream of mushroom soup, undiluted	3 tablespoons grated Parmesan cheese

Heat butter in a large saucepan and sauté mushrooms 5 minutes. Cook broccoli 1 minute less than package directions and add to mushrooms. Place in casserole; combine soup with curry powder, garlic powder and soy sauce; pour over broccoli; sprinkle cheese over top. Bake in 350° oven for 20 minutes until very hot. Brown under broiler if more color is needed. Serves 8.

To prepare over direct heat, add cheese to soup mixture, blending well. Pour sauce over broccoli and mushrooms in the saucepan; simmer gently about 10 minutes, until heated thoroughly.

Substitute spinach, Brussels sprouts or string beans for variation. For string beans, sprinkle with ¼ cup slivered buttered almonds.

BRUSSELS SPROUTS BACCHUS

2 10-ounce packages frozen Brussels sprouts	2 tablespoons melted butter
	paprika
Chablis or other white table wine	½ teaspoon salt

Cook Brussels sprouts according to package directions, substituting wine for water. Do not use salt in cooking. Drain; place on serving plate; dot with butter and sprinkle with salt and paprika. Serves 6.

These become Brussels Sprouts Véronique by simple addition; when sprouts first come to a boil, add 1 cup seedless white grapes, and proceed as above.

CHINESE SPROUTS

1 cup water	1 5-ounce can water chestnuts
½ teaspoon salt	drained and thinly sliced
⅛ pound butter or margarine	⅛ teaspoon ginger
2 10-ounce packages frozen	½ teaspoon soy sauce
Brussels sprouts	3 tablespoons toasted onions

Combine water, salt and 1 tablespoon butter in saucepan; bring to a boil; add sprouts and cook one minute less than package directions. Drain and turn into serving dish. Combine chestnuts in same saucepan with remaining butter, ginger and soy sauce. Heat and pour over sprouts; sprinkle with toasted onions. Serves 6.

CANDIED CARROTS AND GRAPES

3 cups cooked sliced carrots   2 cups green grapes, seedless or seeded

Wash grapes and add with carrots to Brown Sugar Glaze; toss lightly until well-coated and serve very hot. Serves 6.

Brown Sugar Glaze

⅓ cup brown sugar	¼ teaspoon cinnamon
¼ cup butter or margarine	⅛ teaspoon chopped juniper
1 teaspoon lemon juice	berries (optional)

Combine sugar, butter, lemon juice, cinnamon and juniper berries in saucepan; heat until blended.

CARROT FAROFA
(Brazilian)

4 tablespoons butter or margarine	¼ cup dried bread crumbs
6 medium carrots, grated	1 teaspoon salt
¼ cup raisins	1 tablespoon finely sliced
⅛ teaspoon nutmeg	green onion tops

Heat 2 tablespoons butter in saucepan; add carrots and sauté 15 minutes. Soak raisins in hot water for 15 minutes while carrots are cooking; then stir in with carrots. Add 2 tablespoons butter and remaining ingredients; combine well and cook, stirring, for 2 minutes. Serve very hot. Serves 4.

CAULIFLOWER SMÉTANE

Select a white solid head of cauliflower; clean, leaving a few fresh leaves at the base. Place in saucepan with salted water to cover. Bring to a boil and cook 15 minutes, until tender but firm enough to remain whole; drain; place on serving platter, and cover with Sauce Smétane; dust with paprika. Serves 4 to 6.

Sauce Smétane

2 egg yolks, beaten	⅛ teaspoon salt
1½ cups sour cream	¼ teaspoon sugar
1½ teaspoons lemon juice	dash pepper

Combine all ingredients in top of double boiler and stir constantly over boiling water until thickened. Makes 1¾ cups.
Dress broccoli, asparagus or fish with this sauce.

CHESTNUTS MADEIRA

1 pound chestnuts	2 tablespoons water
1 tablespoon salad oil	1 tablespoon beef paste extract
Sauce Madeira	

With a sharp knife, make two crisscross gashes on flat side of chestnuts. Place in baking pan with oil and toss to coat them evenly. Bake in 375° oven for 15 minutes and cool. Remove shells and inner skins. Combine water and beef extract in skillet; add chestnuts and cook very slowly for 10 minutes until liquid is reduced and chestnuts are glazed. To serve, add ½ cup Sauce Madeira, then heat quickly. Serves 4.
Prepare another combination by adding 1 10-ounce package frozen Brussels sprouts, cooked, or ½ pound sautéed mushrooms.

Sauce Madeira

2 tablespoons butter or margarine	2 cups consommé
1 small onion, grated	½ teaspoon salt
2 tablespoons flour	2 tablespoons tomato purée
½ cup Madeira	

Heat butter in skillet; add onion and sautée slowly 5 minutes, then add flour, stirring until lightly browned. Pour in consommé; simmer until sauce is reduced about half. To serve, add Madeira and heat quickly. Makes about 1½ cups.

Without Madeira, this is a Brown Sauce, used as the base for other sauces and gravies to dress a variety of vegetables.

CORN RING

1 1-pound can cream style corn	⅛ teaspoon white pepper
4 egg yolks, well beaten	⅛ teaspoon paprika
1 teaspoon salt	1 cup half and half cream
4 egg whites, stiffly beaten	

Press corn through colander or food mill and add well-beaten egg yolks, salt, pepper and paprika; adjust seasonings to taste. Add cream and blend well. Fold in beaten egg whites and pour into well-buttered 6-cup ring mold. Set in a pan of hot water and bake in a 350° oven 45 minutes or until set. Turn out on hot platter. Center with bright green buttered peas or green beans. Add a border of tiny beets for a colorful party platter. Serves 6.

DILLED CUCUMBERS

6 small cucumbers, peeled	2 teaspoons chopped fresh or
boiling salted water	frozen dill, or dill weed
⅓ cup butter	¼ teaspoon salt

With a French cutter, slice cucumbers in ½-inch slices. Bring 3 cups water with 1½ teaspoons salt to a boil; add cucumbers. There should be sufficient water to cover them. Remove from heat; blanch in cold water; drain. Heat butter in skillet; add cucumbers and sauté until well covered with butter and heated through; sprinkle with dill and salt. Serve piping hot. Add a dash of paprika for color. Serves 6.

The very small cucumbers, available in season, are delicately delicious. Three large cucumbers may be substituted. Quarter in length and slice off center with seeds. Cut in 1-inch slices and trim corners to give them a "football" look. The method is the same.

Try freshly ground pepper instead of dill.

EGGPLANT CASSEROLE

2 eggplants, peeled	½ pound sliced mushrooms
2 tablespoons butter	salt
1 10-ounce can tomatoes	pepper
1 10-ounce can tomato soup	1 teaspoon oregano
1 1½-ounce package spaghetti	½ pound Mozzarella cheese slices
sauce mix	¼ cup grated Parmesan cheese

Cut eggplants into thin slices. Heat butter in a skillet; add eggplant slices and sauté lightly. Combine tomatoes, soup, spaghetti sauce mix and mushrooms; add salt, pepper and oregano. Grease a 6-cup casserole; layer eggplant slices alternately with sauce mixture. Top with Mozzarella cheese cut into 1-inch strips, then sprinkle with grated Parmesan. Bake in 350° oven 45 to 50 minutes. Serves 6 to 8.

EGGPLANT ENTRÉE

2 small eggplants, about 7 inches long	½ cup grated Parmesan cheese
1 1-pound can tomatoes	2 tablespoons butter
1 teaspoon oregano	¼ pound mushrooms
1 teaspoon salt	8 chicken livers
1 egg	1 clove garlic, minced
1 tablespoon olive oil or salad oil	2 cups fresh, coarsely crumbled bread, about 4 slices

Cut eggplants evenly in halves lengthwise. Place in large saucepan; cover with water; bring to a boil and cook 5 minutes; they should be firm. Drain and cool; remove pulp leaving shells intact (a grapefruit knife is efficient), then chop pulp coarsely. Combine with tomatoes, oregano, salt, egg, oil and cheese. Heat butter in skillet; add mushrooms, livers and garlic; sauté 5 minutes. Cut livers in small pieces and add with mushrooms to tomato mixture. This sauce may be made in advance. To bake, combine sauce with bread crumbs; fill eggplant shells and bake in 325° oven one hour. Serves 4.

This flavorful dish is excellent with the chicken livers, both as an entrée or as an accompaniment to roast meat or poultry.

A good substitute for the chicken livers is 1 cup of diced cooked shrimp.

EGGPLANT TOWER

1 large eggplant	¼ cup salad oil or shortening
⅓ cup flour (approximately)	2 large tomatoes
¼ teaspoon salt	6 slices Cheddar cheese
¼ teaspoon pepper	1 8-ounce can artichoke hearts
2 tablespoons snipped parsley	

Cut eggplant into ½-inch slices; there should be at least six; coat with flour; dust with salt and pepper. Heat oil in skillet; add eggplant slices and sauté about 3 minutes on each side until golden brown; remove to buttered cooky sheet. Cut tomatoes into 6 thick slices; top each eggplant slice with a tomato slice, then with cheese. Heat artichoke hearts in saucepan and keep warm. Place cooky sheet in broiler 6 inches below heat until cheese is well-melted and "tower" well covered, about 10 minutes. The cheese will run; as you remove the vegetables to a serving platter, scoop the extra cheese up and spoon over tomato slices; top each with a drained artichoke heart. Sprinkle with snipped parsley. Serves 6.

During a cooking interview, a charming young reporter gave me this recipe.

FOURTH ESTATE SAUERKRAUT

2 tablespoons chicken fat or butter	1 10-ounce can tomato soup
1 1-pound can sauerkraut, drained	2 tablespoons brown sugar
	1 tablespoon caraway seed

Heat butter in saucepan; add sauerkraut and toss lightly; stir in soup, sugar and caraway seed. Bring to a boil; cover and simmer 30 minutes. Serves 4 to 6.

This original was my contribution.

RED APPLE CABBAGE

3 strips bacon	1 1-pound 5-ounce can
2 tablespoons bacon fat or butter	apple pie filling
1 onion, chopped fine	½ teaspoon tarragon
1 1-pound jar sweet-sour red cabbage	½ cup red wine

Sauté bacon until crisp; drain on paper toweling, then crumble and reserve. Heat 2 tablespoons of the bacon fat or butter in a saucepan; add onion and sauté until light brown. Stir in cabbage and apple filling gently; add salt and tarragon; blend in wine. Simmer 10 minutes; turn into serving bowl and sprinkle with crumbled bacon. Serves 6.
We like this with duck.

GREEN BEANS MIMI

1½ pounds green beans	1 teaspoon salt
6 tablespoons butter	¼ teaspoon white pepper
2 tablespoons flour	¼ teaspoon monosodium glutamate
½ cup shredded Swiss cheese	1 cup sour cream
2 tablespoons instant onions	1 teaspoon Dijon type mustard
¼ cup fine dry bread crumbs	

Wash beans and cut diagonally in 1-inch pieces. Place in saucepan and add water to 1-inch in depth (salted with ½ teaspoon per cup of water). Add 1 tablespoon butter and cook beans 15 minutes or until "al dente" (almost tender) then drain. Heat 2 tablespoons butter and blend in flour until smooth and bubbly. Add cheese, onions, salt, pepper and monosodium glutamate; combine with sour cream and mustard. Pour over the beans and heat but do not boil. Turn into greased casserole; top with bread crumbs, browned in the remaining 3 tablespoons of butter. Bake in 350° oven 10 minutes. Serves 4 to 6.

GREEN BROILED TOMATOES

3 green tomatoes, medium to large	2 tablespoons flour
	½ teaspoon seasoned salt
2 tablespoons butter or margarine	½ teaspoon oregano
	paprika

Cut off stem ends of tomatoes, then slice ½-inch thick. Each tomato should make 4 slices. Spread each slice with butter. Combine flour, seasoned salt and oregano; then spread over each slice. Place under broiler, 3 inches from heat, for 5 minutes or bake in a 375° oven 10 minutes. Sprinkle with paprika and use as a border for meat, or with other vegetables. Serves 4.

We picked tomatoes in a luscious garden, where the plants bowed low with the weight of their fruit. The glossy firmness of the green beauties tempted me to pluck them. I remembered having eaten them when "marching through Georgia" one winter, so I asked a Southern friend for this recipe. The tartness of green tomatoes is fine contrast to any bland entrée.

GREEN TOMATOES SAUTÉED

½-inch slices firm green tomatoes (2 to 3 tomatoes)	¼ teaspoon salt
¼ cup dry bread crumbs	¼ teaspoon seasoned salt
¼ teaspoon oregano	2 tablespoons butter or margarine
	paprika

Remove a slice from each end of tomatoes. Combine crumbs,

oregano, salt and seasoned salt. Dip each slice of tomato in mixture, coating well. Set aside for 5 minutes, and dip again if necessary. Heat butter; add tomato slices, sauté until lightly browned and tender, about 5 minutes on each side. Garnish with a dusting of paprika. Serves 4.

ITALIAN BEANS DILLED

1 10-ounce package frozen Italian green beans
1 small onion, finely chopped
½ teaspoon dill weed
2 tablespoons butter or margarine
¼ teaspoon salt

Cook beans according to package directions. Sauté onion in butter; add beans and salt. Mix in dill weed thoroughly but quickly. Be careful not to break beans, or overcook. Serve very hot. Serves 4.

Mushrooms

Divine food, believed by the Pharaohs to possess magic.

To sauté

Melt 2 tablespoons butter in skillet; add mushrooms and heat gently about 5 minutes, tossing occasionally to cook evenly.

To steam

Add ¼ cup water and 2 tablespoons butter, then cover and cook over medium heat for 5 minutes. Mushrooms will be soft and juicy. Or, cook in top of double boiler about 20 minutes.

For button mushrooms

Use small variety and cut stems even with caps. Use mushroom caps as toppers or with fillings. Utilize the removed stems in fillings, sauces, stuffings and marinades.

For a large slice

Cut mushrooms thinly through stems and caps.

For a larger bite

Quarter mushrooms.

MUSHROOMS AND WATER CHESTNUTS

2 4-ounce cans mushroom stems and pieces, drained	$\frac{1}{2}$ cup liquid from mushrooms
	$\frac{1}{2}$ teaspoon seasoned salt
1 4-ounce can water chestnuts, sliced	1 teaspoon A-1 sauce
	2 teaspoons soy sauce
2 tablespoons butter	$\frac{1}{4}$ teaspoon sugar
2 tablespoons flour	2 teaspoons claret (optional)

Drain mushrooms and reserve liquid; drain water chestnuts and slice. Heat butter in skillet; add flour and blend until smooth and lightly browned. Stir in mushroom liquid, seasoned salt, A-1 sauce, soy sauce, sugar and claret. Heat, stirring until blended and thickened. Add mushrooms and water chestnuts; heat thoroughly. Serve on toast points as a poultry or roast accompaniment. Serves 4.

Double recipe and use as an entrée.

MUSHROOM SOUFFLÉ

3 tablespoons butter	$\frac{1}{4}$ pound butter
3 tablespoons flour	1 pound fresh mushrooms, ground
1 cup half and half cream	4 egg yolks, beaten
$\frac{1}{2}$ teaspoon salt	4 egg whites, beaten stiff
$\frac{1}{8}$ teaspoon pepper	2 10-ounce packages
1 teaspoon minced shallot or green onion (optional)	frozen peas and onions, cooked

Garnish: kumquats or other bright fruit

Place 3 tablespoons butter in skillet and heat; add flour, stirring until well blended. Pour in cream gradually, stirring until thick

and smooth. Add salt, pepper, shallots and set aside to cool.
Heat ¼ pound butter in another skillet; add mushrooms and
sauté about 5 minutes. Add egg yolks to the cooled white sauce,
blending well. Stir in mushrooms evenly, then fold in beaten
whites carefully. Pour into well-greased 6-cup ring mold.
Place mold in pan of hot water and bake in 325° oven 40 minutes
or until set. Turn out on platter and fill center with peas and
onions; garnish with kumquats or other bright fruit. Serve with
fresh mushrooms or seafood dish of your choice. Serves 8.

I like to purchase 1½ pounds mushrooms, using the stems for
grinding, adding sufficient caps to make 1 pound for the recipe,
and remaining caps to mix with peas and onions for the center.

PETITE TOMATO ZUCCHINI

½ cup lightly salted water	2 teaspoons lemon juice
1 pound zucchini, cut in ½-inch slices	⅛ teaspoon basil
⅔ pint cherry tomatoes (about 2 dozen), halved	½ teaspoon salt
2 tablespoons butter or margarine	⅛ teaspoon freshly ground pepper
¼ teaspoon sugar	

Bring water to a boil; add zucchini; cover and simmer slowly 8
minutes. Drain and add tomatoes. Heat butter in a saucepan.
Add lemon juice, basil, salt, pepper and sugar.   Pour over
vegetables; toss lightly and cook 3 minutes or just until heated
thoroughly and tomatoes begin to pop open. Serve in a casserole. Serves 4 to 6. A good skillet dish.

PIMIENTO LIMAS

1 10-ounce package frozen lima beans	2 teaspoons dill seed
½ cup water chestnuts, sliced and drained	½ teaspoon salt
¼ cup butter	¼ teaspoon ground pepper
2 tablespoons red wine vinegar	¼ teaspoon monosodium glutamate
	¼ cup coarsely chopped pimiento

Cook lima beans according to package directions and drain; mix
with water chestnuts and keep warm. Melt butter in saucepan

and add vinegar, dill seed, salt, pepper and monosodium glutamate. Heat and pour over beans in serving dish. Sprinkle with pimiento and serve at once. Serves 4.

RATATOUILLE NIÇOISE

8 green peppers
8 zucchini
2 large Bermuda onions
3 bay leaves
2 1-pound cans Italian tomatoes

1 teaspoon salt
⅛ teaspoon freshly ground pepper
1 teaspoon basil
2 10-ounce cans beef consommé
6 tablespoons butter

2 tablespoons olive oil

Wash peppers; scrub zucchini; strip onions. Quarter peppers and arrange a layer in bottom of Dutch oven; quarter the zucchini lengthwise and layer over the peppers. Cut onions in chunks (approximately eighths), and arrange over zucchini; add bay leaves and pour tomatoes over all. Sprinkle with salt, pepper and basil. Pour the consommé over all; dot with butter and drizzle olive oil on top. Bake 2 hours in a 350° oven. If vegetables become too dry, add water. Serves 6 to 8.

ROASTED ONIONS

1 pound whole small onions
2 teaspoons brown sugar
½ teaspoon salt
⅛ teaspoon pepper

3 tablespoons butter or margarine
1 cup beef consommé or bouillon
1 teaspoon lemon juice
2 tablespoons finely chopped parsley

Remove loose outer leaves; wash and arrange onions in well-buttered baking dish. Sprinkle with brown sugar, salt and pepper; dot with butter. Pour consommé around onions. Bake in a 325° oven 1 hour and 15 minutes, or until tender. To serve, add lemon juice, and sprinkle with parsley. Serves 6.

SPINACH SOUFFLÉ

6 tablespoons butter or margarine
6 tablespoons flour
1½ cups hot milk
4 egg yolks, beaten

1 tablespoon grated onion
¼ teaspoon black pepper
1 cup firmly packed chopped spinach, fresh or frozen
1½ teaspoons salt

6 egg whites, stiffly beaten

Melt butter in a saucepan; add flour and blend well until smooth and bubbly. Add milk and cook, stirring constantly, until mixture thickens. Slowly blend in egg yolks, onion, pepper and spinach. Add salt to egg whites before beating; do not allow them to become too dry. Fold into spinach mixture, ¼ at a time. Spoon into buttered 1-quart soufflé dish or casserole; with a spatula make a groove around soufflé about 1 inch deep and 1 inch from the edge of casserole to form a "high hat." Place casserole in a pan of boiling water, then in oven and bake at 325° for 1 hour or until a knife inserted halfway between center and outside edge comes out clean; serve at once. Serves 4 to 6.

SWEET SOUR GREEN BEANS

1 1-pound can green beans or 1 10-ounce package, frozen and defrosted
½ onion, chopped fine
2 tablespoons butter or margarine
1 tablespoon sugar

2 tablespoons instantized flour
1 tablespoon lemon juice
1 tablespoon vinegar
½ teaspoon salt
2 cloves
1 bay leaf

Cook frozen beans according to directions on package; drain. Heat butter in skillet and add onions; sauté until golden. Sprinkle sugar and flour over onions, stirring until smooth and blended. Add lemon juice, vinegar, salt, cloves and bay leaf. Simmer 8 to 10 minutes, then remove bay leaf and cloves. Add beans and toss carefully; heat thoroughly. Serves 4.

SWISS GREEN BEANS

1 10-ounce package frozen green beans
2 tablespoons butter
2 tablespoons instantized flour
1 teaspoon salt
⅛ teaspoon ground pepper
¼ teaspoon monosodium glutamate

1 cup sour cream
½ cup grated Swiss cheese (2 ounces)
2 tablespoons instant onion flakes
2 tablespoons butter
¼ cup dry bread crumbs

Cook beans 1 minute less than package directions; drain and set aside. Heat 2 tablespoons butter in saucepan and add flour, salt, pepper and monosodium glutamate; cook until bubbly and blended. Stir in sour cream, cheese and onion flakes; toss with beans and turn into 4-cup greased casserole. Combine 2 tablespoons butter with bread crumbs in a small skillet and heat until lightly browned; spread over beans and bake 10 minutes in 350° oven, just until heated. Serves 4 to 6.

Use 1 pound fresh green beans if preferred.

CURRIED TOMATOES

6 medium tomatoes
½ teaspoon salt
⅛ teaspoon pepper
½ teaspoon curry powder

1¾ cups dried bread crumbs
¼ cup butter or margarine, melted
2 tablespoons snipped parsley

Cut a thin slice from each end of tomatoes so they will stand firmly; cut in half, crosswise. Place tomatoes in a baking dish. Make a paste of salt, pepper, curry powder, crumbs and butter. Spread over tomatoes. Place in a 450° oven until very hot and crumbs are lightly browned, about 15 minutes. Sprinkle with parsley. Serves 6.

TOMATOES POLONAISE

6 medium tomatoes
4 tablespoons butter, melted
½ teaspoon dry mustard

6 tablespoons dry cread crumbs
1 teaspoon salt
1 teaspoon Worcestershire

Cut a slice from the top of each tomato, about ½-inch thick.

Combine remaining ingredients into a paste and spread equally on cut top of each tomato. Arrange in shallow baking pan and broil 10 minutes or until heated and browned. Serves 6.

You may prefer three large tomatoes, cut in half and spread on cut side with this mixture.

TOMATOES ROCKEFELLER

6 medium sized tomatoes, halved

Rockefeller Topping

4 tablespoons butter	½ teaspoon salt
1 tablespoon finely minced shallot or onion	1 cup cooked, chopped spinach
	2 tablespoons minced parsley
½ clove garlic, minced	⅓ cup dry bread crumbs

1 tablespoon anisette (optional)

Place tomatoes on baking sheet cut side up. Heat butter in skillet; add onion and garlic; sauté until lightly browned. Remove from heat; blend in salt, spinach, parsley and bread crumbs (anisette if desired). Spread over tomato halves and bake in a 400° oven 15 minutes. Serves 6.

When used with a roast in lower oven temperature, wait until meat is removed, then place tomatoes under broiler until browned, about 5 minutes, and watch them closely.

WHITE TURNIP BAKE

6 white turnips	½ teaspoon dried basil
3 cups water	¼ teaspoon salt
1½ teaspoons salt	¼ cup sour cream
12 caraway seeds	⅛ teaspoon paprika
¼ teaspoon lemon juice	

Peel turnips and cut into 8ths (I use the apple corer-cutter). Heat water to boiling; add salt, caraway seeds and turnips. Cook 10 minutes until parboiled; drain and place in well-buttered baking dish; sprinkle with basil and salt. Spread sour cream over top and bake in 375° oven 20 minutes or until tender. Dust with paprika and sprinkle with lemon juice.

You may add ¼ teaspoon dried sautéed onions before adding sour cream. Or, instead of sour cream, sprinkle with ¼ cup grated Parmesan cheese and pour ¼ cup half and half cream in bottom of casserole. Serves 2 to 3.

ZESTY ZUCCHINI

4 zucchini, about 6 inch size	½ teaspoon seasoned salt
2 tablespoons butter	½ cup water
2 tablespoons minced shallots	1 teaspoon soy sauce
or onion	⅛ teaspoon ground pepper
8 sprigs watercress	

Cut ends from zucchini, then cut into ¾-inch slices. Heat butter in skillet; add shallots and zucchini. Do not place zucchini on the shallots as they may burn. Push shallots to center; sauté zucchini on both sides quickly until lightly browned. Sprinkle with seasoned salt; add water, soy sauce and pepper. Cover and steam 10 to 12 minutes or until tender; turn once while steaming. When piping hot, arrange on platter; serve with pan drippings. Give it dash with sprigs of watercress. Serves 3 to 4.

Figure 1 zucchini per person.

May be topped with chopped pimiento or sprinkled with grated cheese and paprika.

An adaptable: omit water and add 1 cup chopped fresh tomatoes instead.

The Peripatetic
Potato

An attachment à la Plato for a bashful young potato,
or a not too French French Bean!   W. S. GILBERT

ANCHOVY SCALLOPED POTATOES

4 large baking potatoes   ¼ teaspoon rosemary (optional)
1 cup minced onion   1 2-ounce can anchovies
2 tablespoons flour   ¼ cup butter or margarine
½ cup minced parsley   2½ cups half and half cream

Garnish: pimiento strips, anchovies

Wash and peel potatoes; slice thin as possible. Soak in ice
water in refrigerator at least 1 hour; drain and dry. Grease a
6-cup casserole very well; combine onions, flour, parsley, rosemary, and anchovies. Arrange potatoes in 4 layers; dot each
layer with butter and sprinkle evenly with onion mixture. Pour
cream over all. Bake in 450° oven 10 minutes; then reduce heat
to 350°, and bake 1½ hours or until tender. Garnish with strips
of pimiento and anchovies, crisscrossed. Serves 6.

BROILED POTATOES

4 medium potatoes, thinly sliced   ½ teaspoon paprika
4 tablespoons butter   ½ teaspoon salt

Line broiler pan with foil and spread potatoes evenly; dot with butter and dust with paprika and salt. Place under broiler, about 3 inches from heat for 5 minutes. Turn over and broil 5 minutes more or until browned to taste. Serves 6.

FLAMING YAMS

grated rind of 2 oranges	6 cooked yams, sliced
¾ cup dark brown sugar	1 teaspoon cinnamon
¼ cup dark rum	½ teaspoon cloves
2 tablespoons butter	

Grease a 1½-quart casserole well with butter. Sprinkle with half the orange rind, ¼ cup brown sugar and 2 tablespoons rum. Layer half the sliced yams; sprinkle with ¼ cup brown sugar, ½ teaspoon cinnamon, ¼ teaspoon clove. Add another layer of yams and sprinkle with remaining brown sugar, orange rind, cinnamon and cloves. Dot with butter; bake in 350° oven 45 minutes or until brown. Heat remaining 2 tablespoons rum; pour over hot casserole, and set aflame. Serve to 6 glowing guests.

CHAPEAU POTATOES

So called, as the recipe is that of a famous designer of bewitching hats, Mr. Green-Field of Bes-Ben.

6 medium potatoes, sliced very thin	1 teaspoon salt
¼ cup butter or margarine	½ teaspoon paprika

Place sliced potatoes in water and refrigerate overnight. Dry with paper towels, then layer in shallow buttered pan. Dot each layer with butter and sprinkle with salt and paprika. Bake in 325° oven 2½ hours, basting frequently. If butter dries out, add more. Keep turning and separating slices so each one is crisp and brown. Serves 6.

CRISP POTATO DISK

2 cups grated raw potatoes	2 tablespoons butter
1 tablespoon vegetable shortening	½ teaspoon salt

1 teaspoon snipped chives (optional)

Pare, and shred potatoes using large cutter of flat grater. Do not grate in advance as the potato discolors. Heat shortening in skillet until it sputters, tilting skillet to coat well; add potatoes and dot with butter. Cover until butter melts, then remove cover and sauté at moderate heat. Sprinkle with salt and chives; sauté about 15 minutes or until very brown and crisp. Turn over with broad spatula or pancake turner. If necessary cut "cake" in thirds and brown reverse side about 15 minutes. Serve piping hot. Serves 3.

Increase the quantities as needed. If you are "potato eaters," this will serve two. Try 2 skillets for easier manipulation.

DANISH DILL POTATOES

12 new potatoes ¼ cup melted butter
½ teaspoon dill salt or weed

Scrub the potatoes and cook in boiling water about 35 minutes or until tender. Place in serving bowl; cover with melted butter and dust with dill salt or dill weed and salt. Serves 4 to 6.

You may peel larger matured potatoes; halve them and serve as above.

DUCHESS POTATO PUFF

1 cup mashed potatoes	2 tablespoons melted butter
1 cup small curd cottage cheese	1 tablespoon snipped chives
1 teaspoon salt	or grated onion
1 cup sour cream	1 teaspoon sesame seeds

Combine potatoes, cottage cheese, salt, sour cream, 1 tablespoon butter and chives in bowl of electric mixer. Beat until smooth and fluffy; pour into greased 4-cup casserole. Sprinkle with sesame seeds and drizzle with remaining tablespoon butter. Bake in 350° oven one hour. Serves 6.

EARLY AMERICAN POTATOES

6 medium baking potatoes	2 tablespoons salad oil
2 tablespoons butter	1 teaspoon paprika

1 teaspoon salt

Peel potatoes and slice thinly in disks. Soak in ice water 1 hour, then dry thoroughly. Heat butter and oil in 12-inch skillet. Add potatoes; sprinkle with paprika and salt. Cover tightly. If skillet does not have a secure cover, seal pan with aluminum foil. Cook over low heat 10 minutes; uncover; turn potatoes on reverse side; seal and cook 10 additional minutes. They will be tender and brown. If a browner crust is desired, turn up heat and cook another minute or two until of desired crispness. Serves 6 to 8.

HAZEL'S WHIPPED POTATOES

6 large potatoes, pared and cut in 8ths	⅓ cup hot milk
4 tablespoons butter or margarine	¾ teaspoon salt
	⅛ teaspoon whitepepper

Cook potatoes in boiling salted water (½ teaspoon salt per cup of water) for 30 minutes or until done. Drain, then shake gently in pan over heat to dry. Mash and force through coarse sieve to remove lumps; add butter to hot milk, then beat in potatoes, a small amount at a time with salt and pepper. Heat over low heat, mixing carefully so they do not stick. When heated and fluffy, place pan with potatoes into a pan of simmering water to keep hot for serving. Fluff into a bowl or heap on platter with roast or baked chicken. Sprinkle with paprika and chopped parsley. Serves 6.

For a more distinct flavor, when serving as an accompaniment for beef or veal goulash, add the following Herb Seasoning.

Herb Seasoning

1 clove minced garlic	⅛ teaspoon paprika
1 teaspoon salad or olive oil	¼ teaspoon celery seeds

Sauté garlic in oil 5 minutes. Combine with paprika and celery seeds, then add to hot milk before combining with mashed potatoes. Serves 6.

HOLLYWOOD SWEETS

1 1-pound 13-ounce can sweet potatoes; reserve liquid	¼ cup maple-flavored syrup
	¼ cup brown sugar
½ 6-ounce can orange juice concentrate, defrosted	2 tablespoons butter
	½ teaspoon salt

Drain sweet potatoes. If potatoes are large, halve or quarter to serving portions. Pour liquid into saucepan; boil until reduced one-half. Add orange juice, syrup, and brown sugar; heat and blend. Melt butter in skillet until heated; add potatoes and sauté until browned. Place in greased 4-cup casserole; sprinkle with salt and pour syrup over. Bake in 350° oven 45 minutes. Serves 6.

This is a good casserole to prepare on the previous day. Heat to serve.

PAPRIKA POTATOES

6 medium potatoes, cooked	½ teaspoon salt
1½ teaspoons paprika	½ teaspoon seasoned salt
½ cup vegetable shortening	

Boil potatoes in salted water (½ teaspoon salt to each cup water) about 35 minutes. They should be tender but not mushy. Drain; return to pot and shake over heat to dry. Combine paprika, salt, and seasoned salt. Shake paprika-salt mixture through a sieve over potatoes to coat them well and evenly. Use more salt mixture if needed; heat shortening in skillet; add potatoes and sauté, turning on all sides to brown evenly. Remove to paper toweling to drain for a minute. Serve piping hot, crisp on the outside and mellow within. Serves 6.

Potatoes may be boiled and coated an hour in advance.

They may be sautéed a half hour in advance and kept heated in medium oven. Increase amounts as needed. The proportions remain the same.

PARTY POTATO PANCAKES

5 medium potatoes, peeled and grated | 2 eggs, well beaten
1 small onion, grated | 3 tablespoons sour cream
3 tablespoons flour | 1 teaspoon salt
chicken fat or salad oil

Drain grated potatoes very well, pouring off as much liquid as possible. Add remaining ingredients except oil and mix very well. Pour fat or oil into skillet to a depth of ½ inch, and heat. Drop batter from tablespoon into very hot fat and fry until well browned on both sides. Serves 4 to 6.

Applesauce is the perfect accompaniment to pancakes and the combination a perfect accompaniment to beef.

The recipe of a Swiss Missus.

ROASTED BEEF POTATOES

6 medium-size potatoes | 2 tablespoons chili sauce
½ pound ground beef | 1 tablespoon water
⅛ teaspoon Worcestershire | ⅛ teaspoon oregano
⅛ teaspoon garlic powder | ¼ cup butter or margarine,
1 egg yolk | melted
½ teaspoon salt | dash salt
2 tablespoons fine bread | dash paprika
crumbs | 6 sprigs parsley

Try to select potatoes of uniform size. Peel; slice a small amount from one end so potato will stand upright; from opposite end hollow the potato by removing a cone-shaped piece with an apple corer, leaving ¼-inch shell. Combine beef, Worcestershire, garlic powder, egg yolk, salt, bread crumbs, chili sauce, water, and oregano; mix well. Fill each potato with 2 tablespoons prepared beef. Stand the potatoes in a greased, flat baking dish; pour melted shortening over each, and dust with salt and paprika. Baste frequently while baking in 400° oven about 45 minutes or until soft and brown. Top with a sprig of parsley. Serve as an entrée, or with a buffet which includes poultry. Serves 6.

POTATO PUDDINGS

5 large red potatoes	1 teaspoon salt
1 medium-size onion	¼ teaspoon pepper
4 eggs, separated	¼ cup chicken fat

Grate potatoes; place in sieve and rinse under cold running water, then press out water. Remove to bowl. Grate onion and add to potatoes. Season with salt and pepper. Add beaten egg yolks to potatoes, then fold in stiffly beaten whites. Place ½ teaspoon chicken fat in each 3-inch cup of muffin pan and heat thoroughly in 450° oven. When fat is very hot, pour in potato batter; reduce heat to 375°; bake 30 minutes. Remove from muffin pans and serve hot as border for entrée. Especially good with beef and poultry. Makes 24 small puddings.

SHINY HOT POTATO SALAD

12 large potatoes	¾ cup vinegar
6 green onions, sliced thin	1 cup water
2 stalks celery, sliced thin	½ teaspoon salt
2 tablespoons finely snipped parsley	¼ teaspoon pepper
	¼ teaspoon paprika
6 slices bacon	2 teaspoons sugar
1 teaspoon dry mustard	

Scrub potatoes and cook in skins until tender but not soft. Drain thoroughly; peel and slice thin while still hot. Sprinkle onions, celery, and parsley on top of sliced potatoes. Sauté bacon in skillet until crisp, then remove and drain; crumble and set aside. Add all other ingredients to bacon fat in skillet; simmer 5 minutes to heat thoroughly. Adjust seasonings; pour while hot over potatoes and other vegetables. Toss gently with rubber spatula, being careful not to break potatoes. Salad will be moist and glossy. Serve immediately. Serves 12.

For earlier preparation, refrigerate, then allow salad to stand at room temperature a maximum of 1 hour.

SLASHED BROWNED POTATOES
(White and Sweet)

6 medium sized potatoes, peeled ¼ teaspoon paprika
¼ cup (approximately) softened ½ teaspoon salt
   butter or margarine

Slice potatoes to within ¼ inch of bottom across length, making slices as close together as possible. Brush liberally with butter; sprinkle with paprika and salt. Place on baking sheet in 450° oven and bake about 45 minutes or until done when pressed with fingers, or fork-tested. Use a pot holder to protect your digits.

Sweet potatoes may be pared and prepared in the same fashion. Serve both for a flavor choice. Serves 6.

Pastas and Rice

THE LIFE of Thomas Jefferson, one of the greatest of our statesmen, was a succession of "firsts," but surely one of the least suspected was his introduction of spaghetti to the United States from Naples in 1790.

Looked upon with condescension for generations, pastas have now reached celebrity status. Their popularity has grown by leaps and into boundless distances. The earliest origins are nebulous, attributed to Marco Polo as a discovery in China, and yet earlier in the twelfth century, mentioned in Italy.

Italy may well be the origin of the many shapely noodles, but it is no longer the largest producer or consumer. Scotland and the United States vie for this honor. Rice is inevitably identified with China and other far eastern lands.

Both pastas and rice need observant cooking. The variety is rewardingly extensive and adaptable.

BUTTER DUMPLINGS

3 tablespoons butter, softened	¼ teaspoon salt
½ cup flour	⅛ teaspoon savory or nutmeg
1 egg, beaten	½ teaspoon snipped parsley

Cream butter and flour until smooth, then beat in egg, salt, savory and parsley. Beat until well blended. Remove batter with a wet tablespoon and cut off almond-shaped pieces with a wet teaspoon and drop into boiling soup or salted water (about

½ teaspoon to a cup). Use a large kettle since they rise as they boil; cook 10 minutes. Drain and serve with soup or gravies. When cooking in salted water, remove and drain before serving. Place in one layer to prevent sticking together. These are tender and delicious. Makes about 40 small dumplings. Serves 4 to 6.

CANNELLONI

2 12-ounce packages cannelloni or	Spinach-Cheese Filling
rigatoni	Sherry Sauce

Cook cannelloni or rigatoni according to package directions. Each contains about 16 pieces. Stuff the pastas with Spinach-Cheese Filling, using a pastry tube with a large opening, or a small spoon. Grease a large flat casserole; place filled pasta in a single layer, cover with Sherry Sauce and bake in 350° oven 40 minutes. Place under broiler about one minute to brown nicely before serving. Makes about 32 pieces. Serves 8 to 10.

Spinach-Cheese Filling

1 10-ounce package frozen chopped spinach, cooked and drained	⅛ teaspoon pepper
	1 13-ounce package ricotta or dry cottage cheese
⅓ cup melted butter or margarine	2 tablespoons Parmesan cheese, grated
⅛ teaspoon garlic powder, or to taste	2 tablespoons Romano cheese, grated
½ teaspoon salt	

Combine all ingredients, and blend well.

Sherry Sauce

1 tablespoon butter or margarine	½ cup grated Parmesan cheese
1 tablespoon flour	2 tablespoons dry sherry
1 10-ounce can chicken broth, heated	

Heat butter in skillet; add flour and blend well, heating until bubbly. Stir in hot broth and cheese; simmer until cheese melts, then add sherry. Makes about 2 cups.

The number and size of the rigatoni vary with each brand; therefore, it is difficult to give exact quantities; if cannelloni squares are used, allow 2 tablespoons filling for each 4-inch square.

CANNELLONI FOR A CROWD

2 10-ounce packages frozen
    chopped spinach, cooked
    and drained
¾ cup melted butter or
    margarine
½ teaspoon garlic powder or
    to taste

2 13-ounce packages ricotta or
    dry cottage cheese
¼ cup grated Parmesan cheese
¼ cup grated Romano cheese
1 teaspoon salt
¼ teaspoon white pepper
5 12-ounce packages cannelloni

Combine all ingredients except cannelloni; blend well. Triple quantity in Sherry Sauce recipe. Fill and prepare as for smaller recipe. This one makes about 80 pieces; serves 20 to 25.

Cannelloni freeze exceptionally well, and double for both appetizer and entrée. Prepare for baking as above. Remove from freezer; cover with sauce; cover pan tightly with foil, and place in 400° oven for about one hour. If desired, brown under broiler just before serving.

FRUITED NOODLE PUDDING

1 cup apricots, prunes, or
    mixed dried fruits
1 8-ounce package broad noodles
1 cup sour cream
4 eggs, well beaten

1 cup creamed cottage cheese
6 tablespoons butter, melted
½ cup sugar
1 teaspoon cinnamon
½ teaspoon salt

Soak dried fruit several hours; drain and chop coarsely. Cook noodles in salted water about 7 minutes (½ teaspoon salt to 1 cup water). Combine sour cream with eggs, cottage cheese, butter, sugar, cinnamon and salt; mix together well. Fold in noodles, then fruit; pour into 6-cup buttered casserole. Place in a 375° oven and bake 45 minutes, or until very brown on top. Serves 8.

Fresh sliced apples and/or raisins may be added or substituted for the mixed dried fruit.

To border a roast or a poultry platter, pour mixture into 12 well-greased 3-inch muffin-pan cups. Bake 30 to 45 minutes in 375° oven until very crusty and brown.

GREEN GARLIC NOODLES

2 quarts water   1 8-ounce package green noodles
1 teaspoon salt   ¼ cup butter or margarine
                1 clove garlic, peeled and split

Bring water to boiling; add salt and noodles and cook about 8 minutes or until tender but not mushy; blanch with hot water and drain. Heat butter in large skillet, add garlic and sauté until browned, then remove from butter. Add noodles; toss well and serve at once. Serves 6.

Add 1 tablespoon salad oil to boiling water. It will prevent noodles from sticking together.

MACARONI MOZZARELLA

1 8-ounce package elbow mararoni   ⅛ teaspoon freshly ground
3 tablespoons butter   black pepper
3 tablespoons flour   1 cup diced Mozzarella cheese
2 cups milk   1 1-pound can Italian style
1 teaspoon salt   tomatoes, drained
                ½ cup grated Parmesan cheese

Cook macaroni in boiling salted water for 8 minutes. Drain and blanch with hot water; drain again. Prepare a roux: melt butter in saucepan over low heat and add flour; stir in milk, continuing to mix until smooth and thickened. Combine with salt, pepper and Mozzarella; cook until cheese has melted and sauce is smooth. Pour half of macaroni in shallow greased 2-quart casserole; cover with half the sauce and half the tomatoes; add ¼ cup grated Parmesan cheese. Repeat layers, then top with remaining ¼ cup grated Parmesan cheese. Place under broiler, 4 inches from heat, for 10 minutes or until browned. Serves 6 to 8.

Four sliced fresh tomatoes may be substituted for the canned.

NOODLES IN PECAN CRUST

Crust

¼ cup butter or margarine, melted   ½ cup brown sugar, firmly packed

1 cup coarsely chopped pecans

Pour butter into 6-cup casserole; spread with sugar and sprinkle with pecans. Set aside.

Pudding

1 8-ounce package medium noodles

2 tablespoons melted butter or margarine

2 eggs, slightly beaten

¼ cup light or dark raisins

8 dried apricots, coarsely chopped

1 apple, peeled and thinly sliced

¼ cup sugar

¼ teaspoon cinnamon

1 teaspoon salt (approximately)

Boil noodles according to package directions, or boil in salted water, using 2½ quarts water to 1 tablespoon salt; cook 10 minutes. Drain well; rinse in hot water; toss with melted butter. Combine noodles with remaining ingredients and mix well. Place in refrigerator. About 1 hour and 45 minutes before serving, turn into prepared crust; sprinkle with Topping; bake in 350° oven 1½ hours or until browned. Serve from casserole, piping hot. Serves 6 to 8.

Topping

¼ cup cornflake crumbs   2 tablespoons butter or margarine

Melt butter in saucepan; add coarsely crushed cornflakes and mix well.

UPSIDE DOWN NOODLE RING

Prepare as for Noodles in Pecan Crust; turn into 6-cup buttered ring mold. Turn out on platter for a nut-glazed ring. Center with peas and carrots as a vegetable accompaniment. Serve with Hot Poached Fruits for dessert.

ORANGE NOODLE SOUFFLÉ

¼ pound butter or margarine
⅓ cup sugar
3 egg yolks, beaten
1 cup sour cream
½ teaspoon vanilla

1 orange, rind and juice
½ pound creamed cottage cheese
1 8-ounce package broad
    noodles, cooked
3 egg whites, stiffly beaten

Cream butter and sugar as for cake; add yolks, then remaining ingredients, except whites. Add to noodles and blend very well; fold in stiffly beaten whites. Pour into well-buttered 6-cup casserole and bake in a 400° oven 15 minutes. Reduce heat to 350° and bake an additional hour. Serves 6.

SPAETZLE

1 egg, well beaten
½ teaspoon salt

½ cup half and half cream
1½ cups flour

Combine egg, salt, and cream; mix well. Add flour gradually, beating until well blended. Drop off the tip of a spoon into boiling, lightly salted water. Dip spoon in water each time and drop about ½ teaspoon from spoon tip, or to save time fill wet spoon and cut off about ¼ into water with small knife.

There is a gadget, a Spaetzler Maker, which sends the mixture through openings, slicing the dough in even lengths.

SPINACH NOODLE RING

1 8-ounce package broad noodles,
    cooked
2 10-ounce packages chopped
    spinach, defrosted and drained
1 onion, chopped fine

½ cup butter or margarine
3 eggs, slightly beaten
1 cup sour cream
1 teaspoon salt or to taste
⅛ teaspoon white pepper

Cook noodles until barely tender; drain. Mix noodles and spinach. Sauté onion in butter until slightly browned, then add to noodle-spinach mixture; add eggs, sour cream, salt, and pepper. Blend well and pour into well-greased casserole or ring mold. Bake in 350° oven 30 to 45 minutes or until set. Turn out on serving platter and center with carrots or other bright vegetable. Serves 6.

When done, a silver knife inserted in noodles will be clear when withdrawn.

TORTELLINI

Noodle Dough
- 2 eggs
- 2 teaspoons salad oil
- ¼ teaspoon salt

- 1½ to 2 cups sifted flour
- Meat Filling or Spinach-Cheese Filling
- ¼ cup melted butter

Beat eggs slightly; combine with oil; add salt and flour and blend thoroughly. Dough should be stiff; add more flour if necessary. Knead well for about 5 minutes, then cover and let stand for 30 minutes to rest dough. Place on floured board and roll to ¼-inch thickness. Cut into 2-inch squares; place a heaping half teaspoon of Meat Filling on each. Fold into oblong or triangle shape and curve slightly; moisten between edges and, using tines of fork, seal firmly. Drop into slightly boiling water and cook 20 minutes or until dough is tender. Drain; pour melted butter over to keep from sticking together. Arrange on heated platter and serve with Spiced Cream Sauce or Tomato Sauce. To serve, sprinkle with grated cheese. Makes 35 to 40 pieces. Serves 6 to 8.

Tortellini and Ravioli are first cousins. The former is a curved morsel, the latter round. Both are delicious appetizers or entrées. Here they are selected for main billing. To make them in advance, arrange on ovenware platter, cover with sauce and refrigerate. To serve, place in 400° oven for 15 minutes, or reheat in butter before dressing with sauce.

With Tortellini I like such accompaniments as

Ratatouille Niçoise	*Artichokes Vinaigrette*
Tortoni Glacés	*Espresso*

Meat Filling for Tortellini,
Creplach or Pierogi

1 cup cooked beef, veal, or pork	⅛ teaspoon thyme
½ slice dry white bread	1 egg, slightly beaten
1 tablespoon butter or margarine	⅛ teaspoon Italian seasoning
2 teaspoons chopped onion	⅛ teaspoon salt
1½ teaspoons Worcestershire	

Put meat through grinder, adding bread as last of meat goes through. (The bread is a binder and prevents waste, as all the meat is utilized and none remains in grinder.) Heat butter in saucepan; add onion and brown lightly. Add to meat in a bowl. Combine with remaining ingredients and mix well. Makes about 1 cup.

Tortellini Tomato Sauce

1 tablespoon salad or olive oil	¼ teaspoon salt
2 tablespoons flour	⅛ teaspoon basil
1 1-pound can stewed tomatoes	dash thyme

Heat oil in saucepan; add flour and cook while stirring until smooth and browned. Add ½ cup of tomatoes and mix until well blended. Add remaining tomatoes, gradually stirring to avoid lumps. Blend in basil, salt and thyme. Simmer until smooth and slightly thickened.

Spiced Cream Sauce

1 cup milk	2 tablespoons butter or margarine
½ bay leaf	2 tablespoons flour
3 peppercorns	½ teaspoon salt
1 teaspoon onion flakes	⅛ teaspoon pepper
1 sprig parsley	1 egg yolk, slightly beaten
1 whole clove	½ teaspoon paprika
1 tablespoon snipped parsley	

Combine milk with bay leaf, peppercorns, onion flakes, parsley, and clove in saucepan. Bring just to a boil; remove from heat and set aside. Melt butter in another saucepan; add flour; blend well. Strain scalded milk into the roux (butter and flour mixture) and cook until smooth and thickened. Add salt and pepper; adjust to taste. Pour a small amount into egg yolk while stirring and return to pan. Heat (do not boil) and pour over Tortellini. Sprinkle with paprika and minced parsley.

VELVET NOODLES

1 8-ounce package medium noodles, cooked and drained	1 8-ounce package cream cheese, softened to room temperature
2 cups sour cream	2 eggs, well beaten

Blanch cooked noodles in hot water and drain again. Blend sour cream and cream cheese together; add eggs and noodles; mix well. Pour into well-greased 6-cup casserole and bake in 350° oven one hour or until golden brown and set. Serve hot with entrée, or sliced cold as dessert. If you like a crisp crust, allow an additional 10 minutes. Don't let it burn! Serves 6.

Any fruit sauce is a delicious addition to the dessert version.

BAKED BROWN RICE

3 tablespoons butter	2½ cups hot water
1½ cups raw brown rice	3 beef bouillon cubes
½ teaspoon salt	½ cup slivered almonds

Heat butter in saucepan; add rice and sauté until a rich brown, about 10 minutes. Add salt, water, and bouillon cubes; stir until dissolved. Pour into well-greased casserole and bake in 350° oven ½ hour; sprinkle with almonds and bake an additional ½ hour or until liquid is absorbed. Serves 4.

BROWN RICE PILAF

4 tablespoons butter	½ pound fresh mushrooms
½ cup chopped green onions or	½ cup slivered almonds
½ cup chopped dry onions	1 cup brown rice, cooked

Heat butter; add onions and mushrooms, and sauté 5 minutes;

add almonds. Heat quickly and toss with cooked rice; blend well. Heat to serve. Serves 4.

May be prepared in advance.

To cook Brown Rice

Add 1 cup brown rice to 2½ cups boiling water very slowly; do not disturb boiling point. Add 1 teaspoon salt, cover lightly and cook over very low heat for 45 minutes until water is absorbed and rice is tender. Do not stir while cooking.

My Chinese friend gave me this recipe and it is infallible.

CHINESE FLUFFY RICE

1 cup long grain rice
water   ½ teaspoon salt

Wash rice in 4 changes of water and place in saucepan. Rest palm of hand on top of rice and add sufficient water to cover hand; add salt. Bring to boiling; cover and reduce heat. Simmer about 30 minutes or until water is absorbed. Let stand covered 10 more minutes. Do not uncover or stir while cooking. Makes 3 cups.

Hands being of various sizes, to be more accurate, add 1½ cups water, cooking as above.

KATEH
(Crusty Rice)

2 cups raw rice	¼ teaspoon turmeric
4 cups water	4 tablespoons butter or
1½ teaspoons salt	4 tablespoons margarine
	watercress

Wash rice very well; drain. Place in saucepan with water and salt; cook covered on medium heat until water is absorbed; stir in turmeric. Heat butter in a skillet and add rice; cover and sauté slowly about 35 minutes. Rice should be brown and

crusty.   Loosen with a spatula and invert on serving plate.
Garnish with watercress.   Makes about 5 cups.

Long years ago, we disembarked from a Cunard liner at the
island of Nassau.   A group of singing, dancing natives, circling
like whirling dervishes, greeted us.   The words they chanted
finally came through as "Mama don't want no rice, no peas, no
coconut oil —"   This recipe brings back the tune with happy
recollection and this Mama *do* like rice and peas.

"MAMA *DO* LIKE RICE AND PEAS"
(Risi Bisi)

1½ cups raw long grain rice
  3 tablespoons butter or margarine
½ teaspoon seasoned salt
  3 cups boiling water
  3 chicken bouillon cubes

1 10-ounce package frozen
  peas
2 tablespoons chopped
  pimiento

Do not wash rice.   Heat butter in heavy skillet; add rice and
sauté slowly about 3 minutes.   (It should have milky color.)
Combine salt, water, and bouillon cubes; stir until cubes dissolve, then add to rice.   Cover tightly; cook over moderate heat
about 20 minutes, or until liquid is completely absorbed.   Do
not uncover or stir the rice.   Take a look after 15 minutes of
cooking, and tilt the pan so that liquid may appear.   From the
amount you can judge the additional length of time.   Cook peas
according to package directions; drain and toss with rice.   Turn
onto serving plate and sprinkle with pimiento.   Serves 6.

With a bland entrée you may like to add other flavors.

One-fourth cup minced onions, and/or ¼ cup chopped green
pepper may be added with the rice and butter.

Or, toss ½ cup sliced ripe olives, and/or ¼ cup slivered
toasted almonds with the peas.

PILAF VERMICELLI

¼ cup butter   ¼ cup white wine (optional)
¼ pound vermicelli noodles   1 10-ounce can chicken broth
1 cup unwashed rice   ¼ teaspoon powdered saffron
1 teaspoon salt   1 chicken bouillon cube
                1 cup hot water

Melt butter in saucepan; add noodles and sauté until golden brown. Stir constantly to prevent scorching. Blend in rice, salt, wine and broth; let come to a boil and stir in saffron, then add bouillon cube in hot water, bring to a boil, cover and simmer 35 minutes, or until liquid has been absorbed and rice is tender. Serves 6.

May be made early in the day and reheated slowly. Add broth if necessary.

Add 12 sliced water chestnuts (approximately the contents of a 6-ounce can). Or, add a 4-ounce can of mushroom stems and pieces, drained, or ¼ cup toasted slivered almonds.

RICE MOUNDS

1 cup long grain rice   1 tablespoon butter
2 cups boiling water   ½ cup grated American cheese
1 teaspoon salt   paprika

Add rice to boiling water, then salt; cover and cook 20 to 25 minutes until water is absorbed and rice is tender. Add butter and cheese; mix lightly and well. Pack into 6 buttered cups and let stand 1 minute. Turn out mounds to border meat or vegetable platter. Dust with paprika. Serves 6.

Use the Rice Mounds as a border for roasts or with gravied entrées. The cheese may be omitted; add 1 tablespoon chopped parsley.

RAISIN RICE RING

⅓ cup butter   3 cups cooked rice (1 cup raw)
½ cup chopped onion   ½ cup seedless raisins
¾ teaspoon salt

Heat butter in skillet, add onion; cook until soft but not browned; combine with rice, raisins and salt. Pack into hot buttered 4-cup mold; let stand 5 minutes and unmold in center of platter. Border with entrée or vegetables. Serves 4 to 6.

Very good with curry dishes. If served with other than curry recipes, such as fried chicken or steak, add ½ teaspoon curry powder or more if desired.

BOILED WILD RICE

1 cup raw wild rice   4 cups water
3½ teaspoons salt

Wash rice thoroughly. Bring water to a rolling boil in large kettle; add salt and then add rice slowly so water does not stop boiling. Shake pan occasionally to prevent sticking but do not stir. Cook 30 to 40 minutes or until tender and water has been absorbed. Makes 3 to 4 cups.

In Canada, where a great deal of wild rice is grown, one is advised to soak it overnight before cooking.

WILD RICE SORRENTO

1 cup raw wild rice   5½-ounce can chopped ripe olives
1½ cups grated Cheddar cheese   1 cup hot water
1 cup fresh mushrooms,   1 cup canned tomatoes
    sautéed, or 2 4-ounce cans   ½ cup salad oil
    mushrooms, drained   salt and pepper to taste

Wash rice very well, changing water several times. Add 1 teaspoon salt to 1 quart boiling water and add rice slowly so water continues to boil. Do not stir; shake pan to keep rice from sticking. Cook until tender and water is absorbed, 30 to 35 minutes. Combine with remaining ingredients and toss lightly and thoroughly to blend well. Turn into well buttered 6-cup casserole and bake in 375° oven one hour or until liquid is absorbed. Top should be crusty and browned. Delicious with beef or chicken. Serves 6 to 8.

Necessity, the mother of invention, produced this one, which proved a worthwhile "quickie" recording.

WILD NOODLE RICE

4 tablespoons butter	1 10-ounce can prepared wild rice
1 8-ounce package medium noodles, cooked	2 tablespoons chopped chives or green onions

Heat butter in skillet and add remaining ingredients; toss lightly and heat thoroughly. For buffet service, a chafing dish is fine. Serves 6.

EGG BARLEY DELUXE

6 tablespoons butter	1 1⅜-ounce package onion soup mix
½ pound mushrooms	
½ pound chicken livers, diced	4 cups water
1 8-ounce package toasted egg barley	¼ cup slivered almonds

Heat 4 tablespoons butter in saucepan, add mushrooms and sauté 5 minutes; add livers and sauté 5 more minutes; add egg barley and onion soup mix. Turn into greased 6-cup casserole and add water. Top with almonds, dot with remaining 2 tablespoons butter and bake in 350° oven 45 minutes. Serves 6 to 8.
A hot or cold assortment of meats or poultry is companionable.

GNOCCHI ALLA ROMANA

4 cups milk	6 tablespoons butter or margarine, melted
1 teaspoon salt	
⅛ teaspoon nutmeg	2 eggs, beaten
1 cup farina	1 cup grated Parmesan or Romano cheese

Pour milk into a saucepan and bring to a boil; add salt and nutmeg; reduce heat and pour in farina gradually, stirring until thickened. Blend in 2 tablespoons butter; remove from heat and beat in eggs and ¼ cup cheese. Pour on a buttered flat dish and spread to ½-inch thickness. Chill a minimum of one hour. Cut with a wet knife into 1-inch diamond shapes. Layer them on an ovenproof baking dish, sprinkling each layer with remaining cheese and moistening with 4 tablespoons melted butter. Place in 350° oven and bake 20 minutes or until slightly browned. Serves 6.

We served them with baked ham slice and found it a good combination.

For an attractive pattern, pile the Gnocchi in pyramid fashion, on an ovenproof platter and bake in 350° oven until edges are browned, about 15 to 20 minutes.

One day, influenced by a recipe for Couscous, I shaped each diamond into a ball and rolled all in the melted butter; sprinkled thickly with the cheese, they were then baked for 20 minutes until brown. Both forms were equally appetizing.

Couscous sounds like another of these imaginative exotics, but is, prosaically, a mideastern version of farina, eaten almost daily to replace rice. In Morocco it is steamed with a variety of vegetables, then formed into balls that look like tiny dumplings, and are considered a choice morsel.

KASHA KASSEROLE

2 cups buckwheat groats	⅛ teaspoon pepper
1 egg, beaten	3 tablespoons chicken fat
1 teaspoon salt	4 cups boiling water
½ teaspoon garlic powder (optional)	

Pour groats into saucepan, blend in egg, salt, and pepper; place in 350° oven and toast for 10 to 15 minutes; watch that it becomes crunchy but does not burn. Stir and remove from oven; add chicken fat, then replace in oven and bake additional 10 to 15 minutes or until browned. Pour boiling water over groats mixture, cover and bake 30 to 45 minutes until nicely browned. Serves 6 to 8.

KASHA KASSEROLE II
(with Noodle Shells)

Add 1 cup cooked noodle shells to above recipe before replacing in oven with boiling water. Then bake 30 to 45 minutes as above.

Prepare casserole in the morning. Reheat to serve. A natural with beef.

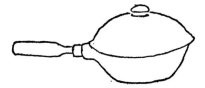

Centuries of
Sauce

•♡•♡•♡•♡•♡•

FROM A FIFTEENTH CENTURY COOKRY BOKE

Sauce for Shulder of Moton

"Take percely, and oynons, and mynce þem and þe rostyde shulder of Moton; and take vynegre, and poudre gingere, salt and cast a-pon þe mynced shulder, and ete hym so."

TWENTIETH CENTURY INTERPRETATION

Sauce for Shoulder of Mutton

Take parsley, and onions, and mince them and the roasted shoulder of mutton; and take vinegar, and powdered ginger, salt and cast upon the minced shoulder, and eat him so.

AVOCADO SAUCE
(for fish)

1 cup sour cream	½ teaspoon sugar
2 tablespoons tarragon vinegar	1 teaspoon chopped parsley
1 tablespoon chopped chives or onion	½ teaspoon celery seed (optional)
1½ teaspoons seasoned salt	1 ripe medium avocado

Combine and blend all ingredients, except avocado. Peel avocado; cut in halves and separate them, removing seed. Cut into ½-inch dice. Fold carefully into blended mixture. Delicious with a simple broiled, boiled or poached fish, pike or trout, or your selection. Makes about 1½ cups.

BLACK BUTTER
(Beurre Noir)

Hardly a recipe, but so good over vegetables or broiled fish.

Heat ⅓ cup butter (or needed quantity) until very dark brown, but not burned. Pour over prepared recipe.

For another flavor, add 2 tablespoons white vinegar to pan after removing butter. Bring to a boil and reduce quantity for 1 minute. Pour over Black Butter–sauced food.

BLENDER BÉARNAISE SAUCE

1 tablespoon tarragon vinegar
3 tablespoons dry white wine
1 teaspoon dried tarragon or 2 teaspoons chopped fresh tarragon
2 teaspoons minced shallots or green onions

¼ teaspoon freshly ground pepper
3 egg yolks
1 tablespoon lime juice
dash cayenne
¼ teaspoon salt
6 tablespoons butter

Combine vinegar, wine, tarragon, shallots, and pepper in saucepan; cook until liquid is reduced by half; cool. Pour egg yolks, lime juice, cayenne, and salt into blender, then add reduced liquid. Cover blender; turn to high speed and whirl for one minute, flicking the switch on and off several times. Turn off the motor, let stand. Heat butter until foamy, but do not allow it to brown. Turn blender on high, pour butter in gradually, then whirl for one minute. Serve warm at room temperature. Makes ¾ cup (approximately).

BORDELAISE SAUCE

2 tablespoons butter
2 tablespoons minced shallots or
   2 tablespoons green onion
½ cup dry red wine
1 tablespoon lemon juice

1 cup brown sauce (without
   wine) or 10-ounce can beef
   gravy, with or without
   mushrooms
1 tablespoon snipped parsley

salt and cayenne to taste

Heat butter in saucepan, add shallots and cook 5 minutes; add wine and simmer 10 minutes, then add remaining ingredients and heat well. Makes about 2 cups.

The traditional recipe includes 4 ounces beef marrow, cut in rounds, heated in boiling water and added with remaining ingredients. Or, you may add ¼ pound sliced fresh mushrooms sautéed with the shallots. Do not brown shallots; they become bitter.

BROWN SAUCE

2 tablespoons butter or
   margarine
1 ¼-inch slice onion
2 tablespoons flour

1 cup undiluted canned beef
   consommé
2 tablespoons tomato paste
1 teaspoon Worcestershire

salt and pepper to taste

Heat butter in saucepan, add onion and sauté until golden brown. Remove onion and add flour, stirring until evenly browned. Add remaining ingredients; cook until smooth and thickened. Makes about 1 cup.

A minced clove of garlic may be added with the onion, and sherry or Madeira, 2 tablespoons of either, may be added.

CASHEW CAPER SAUCE

1 cup mayonnaise
2 tablespoons capers,
   coarsely chopped

1 tablespoon grated onion
¼ cup coarsely chopped
   cashews

Heat mayonnaise in double boiler over simmering heat, stirring constantly. Add capers, onion and nuts. Stir until heated and serve. Makes approximately 1 cup.

CHEESE SAUCE PROVENÇALE

2 tablespoons butter or
 margarine
⅓ cup coarsely chopped onion
⅓ cup diced green pepper
1 clove garlic, minced
1 teaspoon Worcestershire

1 10-ounce can Cheddar cheese
 soup, undiluted
¼ teaspoon celery salt
3 tablespoons catsup
½ cup half and half cream or
 milk

Heat butter in saucepan; add onion, pepper, and garlic; sauté about 10 minutes or until softened. Mix in Worcestershire, cheese soup, celery salt, catsup, and cream; blend well and simmer 10 minutes. Makes about 2 cups.

Use as sauce for sautéed fish or as sauce for leftover fish casserole.

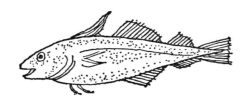

TOMATO SAUCE PROVENÇALE

1½ tablespoons butter
1 medium onion, coarsely
 chopped
1 small clove garlic, minced
1 1-pound can tomatoes or 6
 medium fresh tomatoes,
 peeled

½ teaspoon salt
¼ teaspoon white pepper
pinch of saffron
1 teaspoon sweet pickle relish
1 hard-cooked egg, finely
 chopped (optional)
2 tablespoons chopped parsley

Heat butter in skillet, add onion and garlic; sauté until soft but not browned. Cut tomatoes into coarse pieces and add with salt and pepper; simmer about 15 minutes until liquid has reduced and sauce is thickened. Blend in saffron, relish, egg, and parsley. To serve, heat thoroughly. Makes about 2 cups
    The sauce may be made well in advance and reheated before serving.

COCKTAIL SAUCE
(for seafood)

¼ cup mayonnaise	½ teaspoon prepared mustard
½ cup catsup	1 tablespoon chopped chives or
⅓ cup dry sherry	1 teaspoon onion juice
1 tablespoon Worcestershire	½ teaspoon salt

Blend all ingredients well and refrigerate. Makes about 1¼ cups.

GARLIC BUTTER

½ cup softened butter or margarine	dash salt
2 cloves garlic, mashed	dash freshly ground pepper

Combine all ingredients and beat well until fluffy. Spoon onto wax paper; shape into a 1-inch roll and refrigerate until firm. To serve, cut ¼-inch slices as topping for steaks, vegetables or noodles.

HOLLAND-EASE SAUCE

4 tablespoons butter or margarine	¼ teaspoon salt
	dash cayenne
1 tablespoon flour	¼ teaspoon paprika
½ cup hot milk	¾ tablespoon lemon juice
2 egg yolks, unbeaten	

Heat 1 tablespoon butter in saucepan. Add flour, blending until smooth. Slowly add hot milk to make a white sauce; add salt. Stir in remaining butter, a little at a time, stirring constantly; add remaining ingredients. Cook over hot water until smooth and thickened, stirring constantly. May be made ahead of time and then reheated. Makes ¾ cup.

If you prefer a more tart sauce, add more lemon juice, tasting as you mix.

NEVER-FAIL HOLLANDAISE SAUCE

An accomplished cook gave me this recipe and her secret of its success — that the ingredients must stand at room temperature as directed below.

¼ pound butter	1½ tablespoons lemon juice
3 egg yolks	dash cayenne pepper

Cut butter into 4 pieces and place in top of double boiler; add egg yolks, lemon juice, and cayenne. LET STAND AT ROOM TEMPERATURE A MINIMUM OF ½ HOUR. Just before serving, place over gently boiling water; do not allow top to touch water, and stir briskly with wooden spoon, about 1½ minutes or until thickened and mixture coats spoon. Do not overcook. Serve at once. Makes approximately 1 cup.

No curdling problems with this recipe.

SOUR CREAM HOLLANDAISE

1 cup sour cream	2 egg yolks
1½ tablespoons lemon juice	½ teaspoon salt
¼ teaspoon paprika or dash cayenne	

Pour ingredients into top of double boiler over boiling water; the top should not touch the water. Whip with wire whisk until thickened. Makes about 1¼ cups.

HORSERADISH CREAM

4 tablespoons prepared horseradish, drained	½ teaspoon sugar
1 cup sour cream or 1¼ cups whipped cream	⅛ teaspoon salt
	dash coarsely ground pepper
	paprika

Combine horseradish, cream, sugar and salt. Fill Cucumber Cups, or whole Beet Cups or serve separately with fish or beef. Dust with pepper and paprika. Makes ¾ cup.

Check the amount of horseradish as it is added to the recipe because there is marked difference in the strength of various preparations.

JEZEBEL SAUCE

1 cup apple jelly	1 to 2 tablespoons prepared
¼ cup pineapple preserves	horseradish
¼ cup prepared mustard	salt
freshly ground pepper	

Melt the apple jelly over direct heat while stirring; blend in preserves and mustard, then horseradish. Add salt and pepper to taste. Makes 2 cups.

Delicious with baked ham or cold cuts.

LEMON SAUCE
(for fish or meat)

1 tablespoon butter	¼ teaspoon dry mustard
1 tablespoon flour	2 egg yolks, beaten
¾ cup hot water	1½ tablespoons lemon juice
¼ teaspoon salt	¼ cup dry white wine

Heat butter in top of double boiler over direct heat; add flour and stir until smooth and heated. Pour in water gradually and blend until smooth; add salt and mustard. Place over hot, simmering water; stir in eggs very gradually, continuing to stir until thickened. Add lemon juice and wine; mix and serve piping hot. Makes about 1 cup.

MAYONNAISE

2 egg yolks, slightly beaten	1 cup salad or olive oil
⅛ teaspoon salt	1 tablespoon wine vinegar or
⅛ teaspoon paprika	lemon juice

Pour egg yolks into bowl; add salt and paprika. Beat with rotary or electric mixer, adding oil in a slow trickle; blend in vinegar gradually. Makes approximately 1 cup.

SAUCE VERTE

½ cup chopped cooked spinach
1 tablespoon chopped chives
¼ cup chopped parsley or watercress
1 teaspoon dried dill weed
1 teaspoon tarragon leaves
1 cup mayonnaise

Mix spinach, parsley, chives, dill weed and tarragon together. Add to mayonnaise and blend well. Chill thoroughly for 2 or 3 hours so flavors marry. It is an excellent recipe for a fish accompaniment.

MUSTARD SAUCE

½ cup sugar
2 teaspoons dry mustard
2 eggs, well beaten
½ cup cream
½ cup vinegar
2 tablespoons butter or margarine

Mix sugar with mustard in saucepan. Add eggs and mix well. Add remaining ingredients and cook over low heat, stirring constantly until it bubbles. Remove from heat, beat slightly and cool. Refrigerate until just before serving.

MUSTARD SAUCE MARGERY
(for cold seafood)

½ cup mayonnaise or salad dressing
½ cup sour cream
2 teaspoons dry mustard
2 tablespoons prepared mustard
1 tablespoon prepared horseradish

Blend all ingredients together until smooth; refrigerate and serve cold.

PLUM SAUCE
(Chinese Duk Sauce)

1½ cups plum jelly
¾ cup chutney, chopped fine
4 teaspoons sugar
5 teaspoons white vinegar

Combine all ingredients in bowl and blend well. Makes about 2½ cups.

Plum sauce enhances varied preparations; an exotic sauce requirement for many Chinese dishes. It stores very well, is a delicious basting sauce for meats and, used with discretion, adds interest to salad dressings. Makes about 2½ cups.

It is comparable to Chinese Sweet Sauce available at most markets.

RAVIGOTE MAYONNAISE

½ cup mayonnaise   6 minced capers
⅛ teaspoon onion powder   1 teaspoon snipped parsley
                     dash cayenne

Combine all ingredients and blend well.

SAN JUAN SAUCE
(for beef roasts)

½ cup butter, melted   1 tablespoon steak sauce
1 clove garlic, minced   2 tablespoons snipped parsley
¾ cup catsup   juice of 2 oranges

Combine all ingredients in saucepan and bring to a boil; reduce heat; cover and simmer slowly ½ hour. Serve very hot. Makes about 1½ cups.

SEAFOOD SAUCE MAGENTA

¾ cup catsup   2 teaspoons Worcestershire
⅓ cup chili sauce   2 teaspoons prepared red
1½ tablespoons lemon juice   horseradish
        (½ lemon)   dash tabasco

Combine all ingredients and chill. A zesty sauce for oysters, other seafood and fish. Makes about 1 cup.

White Sauce and Variations

MEDIUM WHITE SAUCE

2 tablespoons butter or margarine   dash paprika
2 tablespoons flour   1 cup milk or 1 cup half
⅛ teaspoon pepper   and half cream
½ teaspoon salt

Your selection of additional seasonings:

½ teaspoon Worcestershire   ½ teaspoon celery seed
½ teaspoon grated onion   1 teaspoon sherry

For *thick* sauce, increase to 4 tablespoons each butter and flour.

For *thin* sauce, reduce to 1 tablespoon butter, 1 tablespoon flour.

Melt butter in saucepan over low heat; add flour and seasonings and stir until blended, but not browned. Add milk slowly, stirring constantly, and continue to stir until smooth and thickened.

Béchamel Sauce

Substitute ½ cup chicken broth for ½ cup milk in Medium White Sauce recipe.

Cheese Sauce

Add ½ cup grated sharp Cheddar cheese to Medium White Sauce. Simmer and stir until cheese melts.

Curry Sauce

To butter, add

2 teaspoons chopped onion   ¾ teaspoon sugar
½ peeled apple, chopped   ⅛ teaspoon powdered ginger
½ bay leaf

Simmer until onion and apple are soft, but not browned. Proceed as for Medium White Sauce.

Supreme Sauce

To butter, add:

1 teaspoon minced onion   1 whole pepper
½ bay leaf

Simmer onion, bay leaf and pepper about 5 minutes. Proceed as for Medium White Sauce. Strain and reheat to serve.

Velouté Sauce

Substitute chicken stock or fish stock for milk in recipe for Medium White Sauce.

Sauce Mornay

2 cups Béchamel sauce   ¼ cup grated Swiss cheese
¼ cup grated Parmesan cheese   2 tablespoons heavy cream

Combine Béchamel sauce, Parmesan and Swiss cheeses in a saucepan and simmer until cheese melts. If very thick, add a small amount of milk and stir in cream; then reheat slowly.

Sauce Suprême

1 cup chopped fresh mushrooms   1 cup Velouté Sauce
1 cup chicken broth   1 cup half and half cream

Combine mushrooms and broth in saucepan and simmer 20 minutes; stir in Velouté Sauce and simmer 10 minutes. Stir in cream; continue to simmer for 5 minutes. Add salt, if needed.

Glazes (for ham, roasts, or poultry)

Currant Jelly Glaze

2 tablespoons currant jelly   ½ cup melted butter
¼ cup white wine

Combine; heat, and use for ham; also especially good for chicken. Apple or any clear fruit jelly may be used.

Orange Honey Glaze

　　　½ cup orange marmalade　　dash cayenne
　　　　　　　1 cup honey

Blend very well.

Cumberland Sauce

　　　1 10-ounce jar currant jelly　　1 tablespoon horseradish
　　　½ teaspoon dry mustard　　　¼ cup orange juice
　　　　　1 teaspoon grated orange rind

Melt jelly over low heat while stirring; blend in remaining
ingredients mixing well.

Cranberry Glaze

Combine 1 cup canned whole cranberry sauce with ½ cup maple
sugar for ham or poultry.

Pineapple Glaze

　　　1 cup brown sugar　　　　¼ cup pineapple juice or
　　　2 tablespoons flour　　　　　gingerale
　　　1 teaspoon dry mustard　　¼ cup corn syrup

Mix all ingredients to a paste and spread over ham.

Melted currant jelly alone makes an excellent glaze.

Cumberland Sauce is fine as a dip for cocktail frankfurters,
ramaki, broiled steak cubes, or other tidbits served hot.

Kumquat Glaze

　　　¾ cup chopped preserved　　1 tablespoon lemon juice
　　　　kumquats　　　　　　　½ teaspoon ground ginger
　　　¼ cup syrup from kumquats　1 tablespoon Curaçao
　　　¼ cup chopped raisins　　　　(optional)

Drain kumquats reserving syrup; remove seeds and chop sufficient kumquats to make ¾ cup. Combine with raisins, syrup,
lemon juice, ginger and Curaçao and blend well. The kumquat

mixture should be spread on roast 30 minutes before completed roasting time. Makes about 1½ cups.

Brown Sugar Glaze

    ⅓ cup brown sugar   ¼ teaspoon cinnamon
    ¼ cup butter or margarine   ⅛ teaspoon chopped juniper
    1 teaspoon lemon juice   berries (optional)

Combine sugar, butter and lemon juice in saucepan; heat until blended; add cinnamon, and juniper berries if desired.

Juniper berries have an unusual pungent flavor, well worth trying.

How Green
Is My Salad

Salad Bar

Oʜᴇ ʜᴏꜱᴛᴇꜱꜱ of distinction gains the title with her imaginative salad arrays. The salad bar always bears a variety of ingredients and a bevy of dressings. The service is a dramatic ritual. Ingredients are seasonal and ever-changing. Chilled bowls contain assorted greens, and for individual combinations an abundant choice from the following:

fresh mushrooms	artichoke hearts	crumbled bacon
hearts of palm	cauliflowerets	anchovy fillets
cucumber slices	grated cheese	sliced olives
	tomato slices or wedges	

A conversational icebreaker! A stunning cruet set holds oil and vinegar. Add any number of other dressings.

Cheese served with salad is good mating.

An imperative suggestion: don't permit the salad to drown. There must be only enough dressing to make the leaves glisten.

Greens must be crisp and dry.

Do not cut, but tear them easily unless a recipe specifically states a slice of lettuce, or a bed of finely shredded greens.

Serve salads icy cold. Have plates chilled.

Do not mix greens with dressing until serving time, unless salads are the marinated kind and are purposely dressed and chilled in advance.

Salad Assortments

Make a choice of the following

With these as basis	*Use these as garnish*
lettuce	curly endive
tomatoes	salad olives
green onions	hard-cooked eggs
spinach	Parmesan cheese
cucumbers	bacon, crumbled
zucchini slices	navy beans
mushrooms, fresh or canned	julienne-sliced salami
French endive	julienne-sliced chicken
watercress	julienne-sliced ham
hearts of palm	julienne-sliced cheese
green pepper	julienne-sliced beets
cooked artichokes	pimiento
asparagus, white or green	anchovy filets

Suggested Combinations

On a bed of lettuce:
  tomatoes, green onions
    Italian Mayonnaise Dressing

On iceberg lettuce wedges:
  sliced tomatoes
  grated Parmesan
    Creamy French Dressing

On white asparagus in green
  pepper rings:
  anchovy filets
    Vinaigrette Dressing

On raw crisp spinach:
  salad olives
  chopped green onions
    Sesame Seed Dressing

On French endive stalks:
  watercress, chopped pimiento
    Garlic French Dressing

On hearts of palm in ¾-inch pieces:
  green pepper rings
  pimiento strips
    Herb French Dressing

On Bibb lettuce:
  raw crisp spinach, navy beans,
  sliced cucumbers, button mushrooms, diced salami
    Wine French Dressing

On raw crisp spinach:
  minced garlic clove, hard-cooked
  eggs, crumbled bacon
    Red Wine Dressing

On iceberg lettuce, torn:
    hard-cooked eggs, sliced Swiss
    cheese strips, crumbled bacon
        French dressing

On Bibb lettuce:
    tomato
    hearts of palm, 3-inch lengths,.
    julienne-cut cooked beets
        Bouquet Dressing

On Boston lettuce:
    grapes, Mandarin oranges
    watercress
        Celestina Dressing

On Bibb lettuce:
    artichoke hearts, diced
    cucumbers, green onions
        Lorenzo Dressing

On assorted lettuce:
Oil and Vinegar Dressing

Use sliced egg whites, sieved yolks for garnish and interchange parsley, watercress, or sprigs of curly endive.

Garlands of Salad Greens

HEAD OR ICEBERG LETTUCE — the crisp sweet leaves make a lovely cup.

LEAF LETTUCE — its flat ruffled leaves make a doily-like base.

CURLY ENDIVE OR CHICORY — lacy leaves give an airy look.

FRENCH ENDIVE — a gourmet ingredient, cut in lengths or crosswise in ½-inch morsels.

CELERY CABBAGE — tastes like its name; dice or slice as an ingredient.

WATERCRESS — sharp flavor and mates well with other greens.

ROMAINE LETTUCE — a lovely border for a bowl and a good mixer when torn.

SPINACH — the fresh tender leaves mix with other greens or succeed alone.

ESCAROLE — attractive, slightly bitter.

BOSTON LETTUCE — soft, tender, delicious.

BIBB LETTUCE — A small version of Boston lettuce and a true delicacy in the field.

RED LETTUCE — A variety of leaf lettuce with a frilled edge of burgundy red.

SUMMER SALAD PLATE

Sandwich

1 slice fresh white bread, halved	1 large or 2 small slices breast of chicken
mustard-mayonnaise	1 slice ham, baked or boiled

1 slice Swiss cheese

Fruit Assortment

1 head Bibb lettuce or your choice	3 large strawberries
2 3-inch wedges watermelon	3 small bunches frosted grapes
6 melon balls	1 Cherry Wine Cup (mold)

4 grapefruit segments

Make a bed of lettuce leaves on a large (dinner size) plate. Spread bread with mustard-mayonnaise and place to one side of plate. On one half of bread lay the chicken slices; on the other half the ham, and cover with cheese. Unmold Cherry Wine Cup in center, a wedge of watermelon on either side. Place grapefruit next to watermelon, a strawberry on either side for contrast, then melon balls with grapes tucked in as needed. Serve with Honey Dressing. Serves one.

Multiply amounts for the number needed.

Omit Swiss cheese in the sandwich, and serve instead with a wheel of assorted cheeses.

Let your imagination soar with the color and beauty of summer bounty; use other varieties, such as a sprinkling of blueberries or clusters of raspberries, or halved peaches filled with berries. Be sure to moisten peeled peaches with lemon juice to prevent discoloration.

Serve Coffee Cooler and avoid the protests of the calorie-conscious.

Lest you say "What of the dressing?" we can honestly answer, "Truly, no need — but, oh, so very good."

Appropriate here: Basic French or Dressing Celestina.

ALMOND CHEESE SALAD

1 3-ounce package lime-flavored gelatine
¾ cup boiling water
1 teaspoon lemon juice
¼ teaspoon salt
¾ teaspoon celery salt
½ cup salad dressing
1 cup coarsely chopped cucumber, large, peeled, diced, seeded
1 tablespoon grated onion (optional)
1 cup creamed small curd cottage cheese
¼ cup Toasted Almonds
leaf lettuce

Add gelatine to boiling water; stir until dissolved; blend in lemon juice, salt, and celery salt. Add salad dressing; beat with wire whisk or beater until completely combined. Place in refrigerator and chill until of jellylike consistency. Mix cucumber, onion, cottage cheese, and nuts together, then blend with gelatine mixture. Pour into greased 4-cup mold; refrigerate until firm. Unmold on lettuce-bordered platter. Serves 4 to 6.

This recipe may be doubled, except for the grated onion, as the flavor is subtle and should not be increased. If you are not onion prone, it may well be omitted; the salad remains delectable.

Trimmings in great variety lend themselves delightfully.

Fruit

1 pint strawberries, unhulled.
½ cantaloupe, in ½-inch slices with French cutter, or shaped with ball cutter.
8 ½-inch slices watermelon, cut in 3-inch triangles.
½ cup blueberries

Mound strawberries; overlap the melon slices; sprinkle berries over arranged fruit and scatter the melon balls. Serve with Honey Dressing.

Vegetable

> Butterfly cucumber slices, radish roses,
>   cherry tomatoes, asparagus spears
> hard-cooked eggs

Seafood

Intersperse 1 pound cooked shrimp with vegetables. Serve cocktail sauce separately.

The Celery Seafood Mold lends itself to these suggestions equally well.

Wondrous Popovers are rightly named. Try them with this salad and apricot preserves. For dessert, Chocolate Cake with Fluffy Ice Cream Frosting.

ANTIPASTO SALAD

1 head Boston lettuce	2 zucchini, thinly sliced
6 ½-inch slices tomato	½ teaspoon salt
10 large mushrooms, thinly sliced	

Italian Dressing

Arrange lettuce cups on 6 salad plates. Place tomato slice in center; top with mushrooms; border tomato slices with overlapping zucchini; sprinkle with salt. Before serving, moisten with Italian Dressing or Dressing Mattée. Serves 6.

Italian Dressing

6 tablespoons olive oil	2 tablespoons wine vinegar
2 tablespoons lemon juice	½ teaspoon coarsely ground pepper
¼ teaspoon oregano	

Combine oil, lemon juice, wine vinegar, pepper, and oregano; blend well. When using this dressing with other salads, add salt to taste.

Dressing Mattée
(Sweet Italian Dressing)

1 cup olive oil	1 small clove garlic, minced
½ cup white vinegar	2 teaspoons salt
2 teaspoons sugar	¼ teaspoon oregano

Combine all ingredients and blend very well. For convenience prepare in Mason jar in advance. Shake well to blend, and store in refrigerator. Keeps well about one week. Shake again before using.

AVOCADO MOUSSE

1 avocado	½ tablespoon chicken-seasoned
1 tablespoon lemon juice	stock base or 2 chicken
½ teaspoon unflavored gelatine	bouillon cubes
¼ cup cold water	1 teaspoon dehydrated onions or
½ cup boiling water	1½ teaspoons grated dry
2 drops Tabasco	onion

Garnish
Bibb lettuce	1 pound shrimp, cooked,
3 hard-cooked eggs, quartered	shelled, and deveined
10 olives	

Peel avocado, split in half, remove pit, mash and blend with lemon juice. Sprinkle gelatine on cold water; let stand 5 minutes; stir in boiling water, Tabasco, stock base, onions. Fold avocado into gelatine mixture; pour into 2-cup well greased mold. Refrigerate several hours until set. Turn out on lettuce-lined platter, border with egg quarters, olives, shrimp, or other relishes of your choice. Serve dressing separately. Serves 6 as an appetizer.

For an entrée, double the recipe and pour into a 5-cup ring mold. Center with shrimp or crabmeat salad. Other seafood may be substituted.

BROAD BEAN SALAD

1 10-ounce package frozen Italian beans	½ cup garbanzos, drained
½ cup water	Italian Dressing
½ teaspoon salt	1 head crisped iceberg lettuce

½-ounce jar pimiento strips, drained

Cook beans in boiling salted water for 5 minutes. They should be as the Italians say, "al dente." Drain, cool, and refrigerate. To serve, toss with garbanzos and Italian dressing. Chill for about one hour. Turn into lettuce cups; sprinkle with pimiento strips for color.

CAULIFLOWER SALAD

1 head cauliflower, broken into flowerets	3 green onions, finely chopped
boiling salted water	½ cup salad oil
6 anchovy fillets	½ cup vinegar
12 stuffed green olives, sliced, or salad olives	1 bunch watercress
	12 cherry tomatoes or 2 small tomatoes cut in 6ths

1 head Boston lettuce

Cook cauliflower in boiling water (½ teaspoon salt to 1 cup water) for 6 minutes. Flowerets should still be firm, but tender. Drain, blanch with cold water and place in bowl. Cut anchovies in ½-inch pieces and add to cauliflower with sliced olives and green onions. Combine oil and vinegar, pour over salad mixture and toss lightly. Cover and refrigerate several hours. Remove from refrigerator ½ hour before serving, to return to room temperature. To serve, pour into lettuce-lined bowl; top with watercress and small tomatoes or tomato wedges. Serves 6.

CELERY ROOT SALAD VIENNA

4 celery roots	2 teaspoons salt
4 cups water	4 tablespoons lemon juice

Boston lettuce

Vienna Vinaigrette Dressing

¼ cup salad oil	¼ teaspoon crushed, dried tarragon
¼ cup wine vinegar	1 tablespoon sugar
¼ teaspoon dry mustard	

Cut celery roots from leaves; remove knobs and peel. Cut into ¼-inch slices, then into ¼-inch julienne strips. Combine water, salt, and lemon juice in saucepan and add celery root strips; bring to boil then reduce to simmer. Cook 20 minutes, until tender but not soft; drain and place in bowl. Combine dressing ingredients; blend well and pour over celery root strips. Let stand in refrigerator several hours, stirring occasionally to marinate evenly. An especially good salad with roasts or cold cuts. Serve on luxuriant beds of lettuce. Serves 4.

Here is another delicious version of a celery root salad so named because it includes apples.

CELERY ROOT SALAD EVE

2 unpeeled red apples, cored
and thinly sliced

1 recipe Celery Root Salad Vienna   2 tablespoons mayonnaise

Stir celery root in the marinade, then remove, lifting the strips to another bowl. Add apples and mayonnaise; blend well. Arrange portions in crisp lettuce cups. Serves 5 or 6.

Another good combination with celery root is julienne-cut beets. Omit apples.

CELERY SEAFOOD MOLD

1 3-ounce package celery-flavored gelatine	½ teaspoon seafood seasoning or seasoned salt
1 cup boiling water	½ teaspoon celery salt
½ teaspoon dill weed	½ cup mayonnaise
2 or 3 drops green coloring	½ cup sour cream
1 teaspoon Worcestershire	1 cup flaked crabmeat or other seafood
1 teaspoon lemon juice	
1 cup finely sliced celery	

Garnish

1 bunch curly endive   2 hard cooked eggs
2 tomatoes cut in 6ths   ripe olives

Dressing Rica

Add the gelatine to boiling water in a bowl and stir until
dissolved; set aside to cool. Mix in dill weed, green coloring,
Worcestershire, lemon juice, seafood seasoning and celery salt.
Combine with mayonnaise and sour cream; beat with rotary
beater until smooth. Blend in crabmeat and celery; place in
refrigerator until of jellylike consistency. Pour into greased
4-cup mold or eight 4-ounce greased molds and refrigerate until
set. Turn out onto a bed of curly endive and garnish with
tomatoes, sliced eggs and ripe olives. Serve with Dressing Rica
if desired. Serves 4 as entrée; 8 as appetizer.

A good entrée; see suggestions following Almond Cheese
Salad.

CHERRY WINE CUPS

1 1-pound 4-ounce can   1 tablespoon lemon juice
  black cherries, drained   ¾ cup domestic cherry or
water sufficient to make   Malaga wine
  1 cup with cherry liquid   1 11-ounce can Mandarin
1 3-inch stick cinnamon   oranges, drained
1 3-ounce package tart,   ¼ cup slivered almonds
  cherry-flavored gelatine   (optional)

8 maraschino cherries for garnish

In a saucepan combine cherry juice and sufficient water to make
1 cup liquid; add cinnamon and bring to a boil. Pour over
gelatine and stir until dissolved, then add lemon juice and wine.
Place in refrigerator and chill until of jellylike consistency.
Remove cinnamon stick and fold in cherries, Mandarin oranges
and almonds. Grease 8 4-ounce molds or cups; cover bottom
with a thin film of gelatine and place Maraschino Blossoms, cut
side down, in it. Return cups to refrigerator and chill until
almost firm. Fill cups with remaining cherry gelatine and chill
again until firm. To serve, turn out on lettuce-lined salad
plates. Serves 8.

To use for a "take out" dinner, fill 6-ounce wax paper cups with cherry gelatine mixture; sprinkle top with almonds and center with Maraschino Blossom.

MARASCHINO BLOSSOMS

Cut the cherry in 6 "petals" from stem and almost to bottom and spread open as a flower.

Motion Saving

With so much action about us today, we must be resourceful and ingenious. Multiple chicken cooking can simplify meal planning. To the chicken breasts indicated in the recipe for Chicken Salad Chin Chin, I added 6 chicken legs. They were removed when done and became Chicken Curry another day. If you find no immediate use for them, put them in the freezer. See suggestion in Spanish-American Paella. We added legs because we like dark meat; add other parts if you prefer. There will be about 6 cups of delicious chicken stock — another bonus. Freeze it in 2-cup containers as a base for soups or sauces. It congeals and makes wonderful Jellied Consommé for a hot day.

CHICKEN SALAD CHIN CHIN

To cook chickens for salad

10 chicken breasts
(approximately ½ pound each)

2 quarts water	2 onions
3 stalks celery, with leaves	1 teaspoon seasoned salt
1 small bunch parsley	2 chicken bouillon cubes

Place chicken in large kettle; add water. It should just cover chicken pieces. Add remaining ingredients; bring to a boil, cover and lower heat. Simmer 40 minutes to 1 hour or until tender. Do not allow fowl to become soft. Remove chicken to platter, drain and cool. Refrigerate. Strain broth into bowl, cool and refrigerate.

The broth will jell. It is a delicious cold consommé and a fine stock for sauces.

To prepare salad

10 cooked chicken breasts, boned, cut in ¾-inch pieces

1½ cups Italian Mayonnaise Dressing

½ cup sour cream

1 tablespoon honey

2 4-ounce cans water chestnuts sliced thin

½ cup coarsely chopped pecans

leaf lettuce

strawberries

12 melon rings ½-inch thick, halved

3 heads Bibb lettuce

Toss chicken with 1 cup dressing; let stand 1 hour to marinate. Combine remaining ½ cup dressing with sour cream and honey; add to chicken and blend well. Mix lightly with water chestnuts and pecans. Mound on beds of leaf lettuce; encircle with melon rings and strawberries and/or Frosted Grapes. Tuck Bibb lettuce about for a curly contour. Add the Cool as a Cucumber individual mold to each plate for a more elaborate entrée.

For luncheon

With this I first served, in tall wineglasses

Claret Cherry Soup or Sherry

The tall glasses for Claret Cherry Soup were in readiness on a tray; the soup in a pitcher.

One half hour in advance the salad plates were "dressed" and in readiness.

The Cinnamon Twists were waiting on a doily lined platter.

COOL AS A CUCUMBER MOLD

1 tablespoon unflavored gelatine

½ cup lemon juice

2 tablespoons cold water

½ cup boiling water

⅔ teaspoon salt

2 tablespoons sugar

6 medium cucumbers, pared

1 8-ounce package cream cheese

1 cup mayonnaise

¼ cup minced onion

¼ cup minced parsley

leaf lettuce

Soften gelatine in lemon juice and cold water; add to boiling water and dissolve. Add salt, sugar, and refrigerate until cold. Cut cucumbers in halves and scrape out seeds; chop finely. Soften cream cheese and add to mayonnaise; beat until fluffy. Add cucumbers, onion, parsley, and chilled gelatine; blend very well. Turn into greased 6-cup ring mold. Refrigerate until set, then unmold on lettuce-lined platter. Center with tossed salad or bowl of simple dressing. Serves 6 to 8.

Very good with a fish course.

CUCUMBER SALAD CUPS

6 Cucumber Cups (see Index)	1 teaspoon sugar
1 small cucumber, peeled and chopped	1 tablespoon tarragon vinegar
6 radishes, trimmed and sliced	1 tablespoon salad oil or 1 tablespoon olive oil
½ teaspoon salt	freshly ground pepper
½ teaspoon snipped chives	paprika

Combine chopped cucumber, radishes in bowl; sprinkle with salt and mix. Refrigerate ½ to 1 hour; drain well; add chives. Combine sugar, vinegar and oil; toss with vegetables. Fill cups and dust with ground pepper and paprika. Serves 6.

An edible and pretty garnish for a cold platter.

CRANBERRY VALENCIA MOLD

3 cups water	2 oranges, peeled, seeded, and cut in small pieces
3 cups sugar	1 cup coarsely chopped walnuts
1 pound raw cranberries	Cucumber Cups
2 3-ounce packages cherry gelatine	Horseradish Cream

paprika

Combine water and sugar in saucepan; bring to a boil; reduce heat and simmer 3 minutes. Cut each cranberry in half; add to sugar mixture and simmer 5 minutes. Add gelatine, stirring until dissolved; add oranges and walnuts. Pour into greased 8-cup mold and refrigerate 4 to 5 hours, or until set. Turn out on curly endive base. Border with Cucumber Cups filled wth Horseradish Cream and dusted with paprika. Serves 12.

Use 2 cranberry molds if the recipe is too large. It keeps well and is a fine accompaniment to meat or poultry.

CRÈME DE MENTHE PLUMS

1 1-pound can greengage plums,
    drained
½ cup drained plum syrup
1 tablespoon unflavored
    gelatine
¼ cup cold water

¾ cup boiling water
3 tablespoons sugar
3 tablespoons green crème
    de menthe
1 large grapefruit, sectioned
    and drained

Garnish: curly endive and persimmon wedges

Set plums in refrigerator; if there is not sufficient syrup for ½ cup, add water to make needed liquid. Sprinkle gelatine over water in bowl; let stand 5 minutes to soften, then add boiling water, stirring until dissolved. Add sugar and dissolve; stir in plum syrup and crème de menthe. Set in refrigerator until of jellylike consistency; pour half into a 4-cup well-greased mold. Arrange half the plums in gelatine and set in refrigerator until almost firm. Add remaining gelatine and plums; border the mold by placing grapefruit segments, curved side out, against the mold. They will stand vertically from base of mold when turned out. Garnish with curly endive and persimmon wedges. Serves 4 to 6.

A salad good with cottage cheese or a meat accompaniment.

If your preference is for more mint flavor, add another tablespoon crème de menthe.

EMERALD PINEAPPLE MOLD

2 envelopes unflavored gelatine
¾ cup cold water
2 cups liquid (pineapple juice
    and sufficient water)
1½ tablespoons lemon juice
2 or 3 drops green vegetable
    coloring

⅛ teaspoon salt
½ cup sugar
2 tablespoons vinegar
1 13½-ounce can crushed
    pineapple, drained
1½ cups chopped cucumbers,
    drained

Sprinkle gelatine on cold water; let stand 5 minutes. Heat 1 cup pineapple liquid; add to gelatine. Stir until dissolved, then add remaining cup of liquid, lemon juice, coloring, salt, sugar, and vinegar. Place in refrigerator; chill until of jellylike consistency. Fold in pineapple and cucumber and pour into well-greased 6-cup mold and return to refrigerator until set. To serve, turn out on bed of leaf lettuce; center with Chili May Dressing. Serves 8 to 10.

This is an adjustable recipe. May be cut in half without a qualm and poured into six 4-ounce molds.

Browsing in Madrid, I chanced upon a beautiful publication, *Cocina y Hogar* (*Kitchen and Home*), on the cover a fine reproduction called "Ensalada Japonesa." Because I found it in Madrid, I endow it here with the appropriate appellation of Ensalada Matador.

ENSALADA MATADOR

1 honey dew melon	4 tomatoes
3 large oranges	1 quart strawberries
2 bunches watercress	

Cut melon in half lengthwise from stem end; form melon balls with ball cutter or use measuring teaspoon. Reserve trimmed peel for garnish; remove excess melon smoothly — eat it up!

Peel oranges, removing all white pulp and cut crosswise in ¼-inch circular slices.

To peel tomatoes

Dip in boiling water to loosen skins, or spear on cooking fork at stem end, rotating over heat until peel cracks; then peel and refrigerate.

One hour before serving, wash and hull berries, saving several large ones with stems for garnish. Wash watercress; drain and refrigerate. Slice reserved melon peel in 1½-inch strips.

This arrangement is especially attractive on a long oval platter. The composition is interesting in its gradation of color. There are the greens on one side and the orange shading to deeper tones of red on the other; a variation from our usual quest for contrast.

On one side of the platter place melon peel strips at right angles, 1 inch apart, extending beyond sides of platter like the ribs of a boat. Tuck bunches of watercress between them. Down the center, arrange a single row of overlapping orange slices. Next, slice tomatoes ¼ inch thick and overlap them in the adjoining row. A line of strawberries next to the tomatoes will border this side of the platter. The melon balls will make a row between the orange slices and the ribs of melon peel. Serve with Dressing Celestina. Serves 10.

This salad enhances a buffet table. Use it as a centerpiece.

For cosmopolitan flair, accompany the Spanish Salad with

French Vichyssoise
Filipino Ensaimada (Golden Muffins)
Viennese Macaroon Torte

FROZEN TOMATO FRAPPÉ

4 or 5 large tomatoes
1 cup tomato juice
½ teaspoon salt
1 teaspoon celery salt
1 3-ounce package lemon-flavored gelatine

1 3-ounce package Italian Salad gelatine
½ cup water
¼ cup mayonnaise
½ cup heavy cream, whipped

Garnish

1 1-pound can whole green beans
pimiento strips

1 cucumber, unpeeled and sliced

Cut tomatoes in small cubes and force sufficient amount through sieve or food mill to make 2 cups purée. Heat tomato juice to boiling; add salt, celery salt, both packages of gelatine and mix until dissolved. Blend in water and tomato purée; place in refrigerator and chill until of jellylike consistency. Mix in mayonnaise, until well blended, using a rotary beater, if necessary, then fold in whipped cream. Turn into greased 1-quart mold and place in refrigerator until thoroughly set and firm; it is well to prepare the mold the previous day. Unmold on platter;

border with bundles of green beans, separated by slices of cucumber and crisscrossed with pimiento strips. Serves 6 to 8.

For a complete entrée, or a hearty first course, turn the salad into a ring mold; unmold and garnish as suggested and center with your choice of seafood and compatible dressing.

HARLEQUIN SALAD

1 3-ounce package lemon-flavored gelatine	5 hard-cooked eggs, chopped
¾ cup hot water	¼ cup diced green pepper
3 tablespoons lemon juice	½ cup thinly sliced celery
1 tablespoon prepared horseradish	¼ cup minced onion
½ cup mayonnaise	5 drops Tabasco
1 cup sour cream	2 tablespoons diced pimiento
	2 tablespoons chopped ripe olives

1 hard-cooked egg, cut in 8 lengthwise sections

Garnish: salad greens, tomato wedges, olives, quartered eggs

Dissolve gelatine in hot water; add lemon juice and horseradish, then beat in mayonnaise and sour cream. Pour a thin layer of mixture into bottom of greased 5- or 6-cup mold, and arrange 8 sections of hard-cooked egg in it. Refrigerate to set; but do not allow gelatine to become too firm as the following layer will not adhere. Combine remaining gelatine mixture with chopped eggs, green pepper, celery, onion, Tabasco, pimiento, and olives. Mix evenly and pour over congealed layer in mold. Place in refrigerator for several hours, or until well set. To serve, turn out on greens and garnish with tomato wedges, olives, and quartered hard-cooked eggs. Serves 6 to 8.

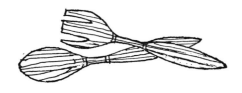

One morning in Paris I went marketing with my friend Susie on the Left Bank. Standing before the array of prepared foods, the creative beauty of French cuisine caught my eye. We returned with marinated artichoke hearts, mushrooms Italienne, pâté de foie gras Périgueux and Iced Ratatouille. The hot vegetable mélange is a favorite and I couldn't wait to try the cold. We weren't disappointed.

ICED RATATOUILLE

¼ cup salad or olive oil
1 small eggplant, peeled,
   cut in 1-inch dice
2 tablespoons salad or olive oil
1 onion, finely chopped
1 clove garlic, minced
1 1-pound can Italian tomatoes
   or 4 fresh tomatoes, peeled
   and chopped

4 zucchini, sliced
4 green peppers, cut in
   thin strips
1 teaspoon crushed tarragon
1 teaspoon basil
1 teaspoon salt
6 large firm tomatoes
Oil and Vinegar Dressing
romaine lettuce

Garnish: lemon wedges, cucumber sandwiches

Heat ¼ cup oil, add eggplant and sauté until lightly brown. Do not let them overlap; rather, do less at one time. They absorb the oil and it may be necessary to add more. Set aside. Heat 2 tablespoons oil in another skillet, add onion and garlic, sauté until golden. Combine onion and eggplant in the large saucepan, add tomatoes, zucchini, green peppers, tarragon, basil and salt. Cover and simmer very gently 30 minutes, or until quite thick. If too liquid, remove cover and allow it to reduce. Cool and chill. Blanch tomatoes in boiling water a minute; remove and peel (it will strip off easily). Remove a slice (cap) from the top of each and remove pulp carefully to retain shape and prevent "breakthrough." Turn them upside down to drain. Sprinkle lightly with additional salt and chill. To serve, fill each with the Ratatouille, place on crisped romaine lettuce, garnish with lemon wedges and cucumber sandwiches. Serves 6.

If you have an overabundance of Ratatouille, use it for omelet filling, or heat it as a vegetable for your next dinner.

JELLIED GUACAMOLE

1 tablespoon unflavored
  gelatine
½ cup cold water
1 cup boiling water
1 tablespoon seasoned chicken
  stock or 1 chicken
  bouillon cube
2 tablespoons lemon juice

1 ripe avocado, peeled and seeded
2 teaspoons dried onion flakes
  with ½ cup water to dehy-
  drate or 1 tablespoon grated
  onion
2 dashes Tabasco
½ cup sliced ripe olives
pimiento strips

Garnish: curly endive, hard-cooked sliced eggs, tomato wedges
Crabmeat Dressing

Soften gelatine in cold water for 5 minutes; add hot water and stir until dissolved. Blend in seasoned stock or bouillon cube and dissolve. Place in refrigerator until of egg white consistency. Pour lemon juice into bowl; mash avocado in the juice or purée through a sieve into lemon juice. Soften onion flakes in water for 1 minute; drain, then add with Tabasco to avocado; blend well. Grease a 4-cup mold and add sufficient of the jellied mixture to cover bottom, about ¼ cup. Arrange a single layer of sliced olives as a border and alternate with pimiento strips. Add remaining olives and avocado mixture to remaining jellied mixture; pour over clear layer. Refrigerate until set. Turn out on platter, on curly endive, interspersed with egg slices and tomato wedges. Serve with Crabmeat Dressing. Serves 6 to 8.

Crabmeat Dressing

1 cup mayonnaise
½ cup half and half cream
2 teaspoons lemon juice
¼ teaspoon salt

¼ teaspoon paprika
½ teaspoon Worcestershire
1 6-ounce can or 1 cup fresh
  crabmeat, cartilage removed

1 tablespoon snipped parsley

Combine mayonnaise and cream; blend in lemon juice, salt, paprika, and Worcestershire; then toss in crabmeat. Serve dusted with parsley, in center of mold or separately.

I have served this mold bordered with 1 pound whole shrimp, or decorated on top by placing shrimp as a border in the jelly in place of the sliced olives. Either way it is very attractive. I might add that when you are pushed for time, the mold is delicious without any design, and all of the clear gelatine may be added to the avocado purée and poured into a greased mold, omitting decorations. An egg and tomato garnish tops this sophisticated dish.

LOBSTER SALAD PIQUANT IN ARTICHOKE CUPS

6 artichokes, cooked and chilled (see Index for preparation)	¾ cup French or Italian dressing Lobster Salad Piquant

Marinate each artichoke with 2 tablespoons of dressing. Chill a minimum of one hour. Drain and fill with Lobster Salad Piquant. Serves 6.

Lobster Salad Piquant

2 7-ounce cans lobster or 1 pound fresh lobster	1½ cups finely diced celery
4 tablespoons chili sauce	¼ teaspoon onion salt (optional)
2 teaspoons prepared horseradish	½ cup mayonnaise
dash Maggi sauce	¼ cup French Dressing

Separate lobster pieces; remove cartilage, but do not shred. Combine remaining ingredients and blend well; toss with lobster and refrigerate before serving.

For hot weather dining, just add

Buttered Rye Toast with Apricot Jam   Autumn Cucumbers
Apple Sauce Cake

Substitute shrimp or crabmeat for lobster. Double the recipe if used without artichokes. Substitute avocado halves for variety.

ARTICHOKE CUPS

6 artichokes   ¼ cup salad oil
boiling salted water   1½ tablespoons lemon juice
              1 clove garlic (optional)

To boil artichokes

Slice off 1 inch from top of artichokes, straight across with sharp knife; with scissors cut off discolored tips of petals and remove any brown from base. Cut off stem evenly and close to petals, leaving a level stub. Place in pan just large enough to hold them snugly upright. Pour in 1 inch of boiling salted water (½ teaspoon for each cup), oil, lemon juice, and garlic. Cover, bring to boil and reduce heat to gentle simmer; cook 25 to 45 minutes or until petal can be easily pulled from stalk. Add more water if needed; remove from pan, and drain upside down. Clear out the spiny "choke" within the artichoke, pulling it to clear the bottom, the gourmet morsel. Serve hot or cold as vegetable, salad or appetizer, as recipe directs. Serves 6, one for each; serves 12 when halved for first course.

For a first course, they may be split in half lengthwise and filled with seafood or a dip, such as Curry Dip; or a sauce, such as Hollandaise; Drawn or Brown Butter.
To open artichoke before removing choke, strike tips forcibly on flat surface and it will open flowerlike.

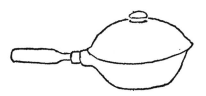

Gelatine as a cooking preparation was first introduced at the St. Louis World's Fair in 1904. In 1905, this classic American salad was presented in a cookery contest and won its originator third prize — a sewing machine — for her "receipt."

PERFECTION SALAD

2 3-ounce packages Mixed Vegetable gelatine
1 cup boiling water
½ cup sugar
1 teaspoon salt
1½ cups ice water
½ cup white vinegar

2 tablespoons lemon juice
1½ cups finely shredded cabbage
1 cup finely chopped celery
½ cup finely chopped green
pepper
1¾-ounce jar chopped pimiento,
drained

Garnish: curly endive, pimiento olives, hard-cooked eggs, quartered

Add gelatine to boiling water and stir until dissolved; blend in sugar and salt; stir until dissolved. Mix in ice water, vinegar, and lemon juice; place in refrigerator. Let stand until of jellylike consistency. Fold in cabbage, celery, green pepper and pimiento. Turn into well-greased 6-cup mold and chill in refrigerator until set. Unmold on platter; garnish with curly endive, quartered eggs, and olives. Serves 6 to 8.

To trim mold, pour in ½ cup of the jellied mixture before adding vegetables. Arrange a row of sliced pimiento olives through center; place in refrigerator until set but not too firm. Add vegetables to remaining chilled gelatin and pour over firm olive-trimmed layer. Chill until thoroughly set.

Grated carrots may be added.

PEPPERED MUSHROOM SALAD

½ pound button mushrooms
2 tablespoons salad or olive oil
2 tablespoons minced onion
1 medium green pepper, cut in
¼-inch strips
2 tablespoons lemon juice
½ teaspoon salt
⅛ teaspoon coarsely ground pepper

2 tablespoons brandy
3 heads Bibb lettuce
6 ½-inch slices tomato
1 6-ounce can pitted ripe
olives, drained
½ cup salami, cut in ¼-inch
strips

Cut stems of mushrooms even with caps; wash and drain well. Heat oil in skillet; add onion, green pepper, and sauté on medium heat until onion is lightly browned, stirring to prevent sticking. Add mushrooms and sauté additional 2 or 3 minutes. Stir in lemon juice, salt, and pepper; cover and simmer 5 minutes. Remove from heat; add brandy. Pour into a bowl; place in refrigerator and chill a minimum of 3 to 4 hours before serving. Arrange lettuce on platter and circle with tomato slices. Cover tomatoes with mushroom mixture and toss ripe olives over. Crisscross with salami strips. If additional marinade is desired, use any basic French Dressing

For more variety, add zucchini slices and/or celery hearts. A good living room appetizer-salad. Serves 6.

PINEAPPLE SHELLS MANOA

3 pineapples	1 6-inch watermelon wedge
¾ cups sugar	3 bananas, rolled in chopped
1 pint strawberries	nuts
1 melon, honeydew or cantaloupe	Fruit Dressing Manoa

Cut pineapples through crown into halves; hollow out the fruit to form shells — a grapefruit knife is fine. Remove core and cut the pineapple into ½-inch cubes. Sprinkle with ¼ cup of the sugar for each pineapple; return to shells. Wash and hull strawberries, reserving 12 unhulled berries for garnish. Cut honeydew into halves; remove seeds and scoop out balls with a melon cutter or small round measuring spoon. Prepare 1 cup watermelon balls in the same fashion. Just before serving, peel bananas; roll in coarsely chopped nuts and slice each into 6ths with French fluted cutter. Arrange strawberries, melon balls, and banana slices around each shell. Top with unhulled berries. Place on doilies or shiny green leaves on individual salad plates. Serve with Fruit Dressing Manoa, and use as a first course or luncheon entrée. Serves 6.

Fruit Dressing Manoa

1 tablespoon cornstarch	1 tablespoon Maraschino liquid
2 tablespoons water	1 cup sugar
⅓ cup lemon juice	2 eggs, well beaten
⅔ cup orange juice	1 cup heavy cream, whipped

Mix cornstarch and water; add fruit juices, sugar, and eggs. Cook in double boiler, stirring constantly until thick. Cool slightly and refrigerate. Just before serving, fold in whipped cream. Makes about 2 cups.

PRINCESS SALAD

1 small head iceberg lettuce	1 1-pound can green asparagus
4 ½-inch slices firm tomatoes	8 pimiento strips

½ cup Chiffonade Dressing

Cut lettuce into 4 equal slices and place each on salad plate. Layer each with tomato slice, then a pyramid of 3 asparagus stalks. Top the asparagus with 2 pimiento strips. Serve ice-cold with Chiffonade Dressing. Serves 4.

RASPBERRY CHEESE MOLD

1 10-ounce package frozen raspberries, thawed	1 cup (8-ounce package) cream-style cottage cheese
1 cup boiling water	
1 3-ounce package raspberry-flavored gelatine	⅓ cup mayonnaise
	2 tablespoons lemon juice

Garnish: curly endive, fresh berries

Drain raspberries, reserving juice. Pour boiling water over gelatine, stirring until dissolved. Add reserved juice. Chill until of jellylike consistency. Combine cottage cheese, mayonnaise, and lemon juice; blend in electric mixer or with rotary beater until smooth. Beat in the chilled gelatine mixture, then fold in raspberries. Pour into greased 1-quart mold or individual, greased 4-ounce molds. To unmold, run spatula around edge, and use hot towel on bottom of mold to release it. Reverse plate and mold; give it a sharp slap and it will drop out. Garnish with greens and fresh berries. Serves 4 to 6.

I served an enjoyable luncheon with small molds on individual plates, arranged with an open sandwich of tongue, chicken, and bacon strips, a garnish of sliced, hard-cooked eggs dusted with paprika, and a bright watercress bouquet to complete the appetizing picture.

Add Schnecken and coffee for dessert.

As I approached the dining room with my two guests, the doorbell rang unexpectedly, and my husband bravely inquired, "Is it time for lunch?" The salad had been duly apportioned on three plates, with less than a serving remaining.

In the refrigerator were the vegetable leftovers I had planned to use for dinner. Quickly I added them to the remnants of the prepared salad, poured in a little dressing, tasted it appraisingly, and found it comparable to the original. On it went to another lettuce-dressed dish, and we were four happy people, three pleased with the addition of the male company.

This is the chameleon-like salad I served; it has many faces.

RUSSIAN SALAD

1 cup cooked potatoes, diced	1 cup cooked, canned peas
1 cup cooked carrots, diced	2 cups cooked beef, diced small
1 cup beets, diced or julienne, freshly cooked or canned	½ cup Vinaigrette or ½ cup French Dressing
1 onion, thinly sliced (optional)	leaf lettuce
1 cup mayonnaise	

Garnish: capers

If you cook fresh vegetables, have them a little underdone so that they remain firm. Mix with the meat; toss with French Dressing. Marinate 1 to 2 hours. Serve on crisp leaf lettuce; pass mayonnaise separately. Serves 6.

The addition of Cherry Kümmel Soufflé Cake and coffee completes an ample luncheon.

This kind of recipe is fun, for it creates the opportunity to utilize a variety of "on-hand" preparations in refrigerator and on the pantry shelf. Vary to suit your mood and your ingredients.

Omit

> beef, and add ham or tongue, other meats or poultry
> meat, and add herring
> potatoes; add baby limas

Add

> 2 peeled, sliced apples for a change in texture
> 2 hard-cooked sliced eggs, for taste and additional quantity,
> or use as garnish

Substitute other vegetables

1 large Spanish or Italian red onion, thinly sliced

The vegetable ingredients may be 2 1-pound cans of mixed vegetables, or 2 10-ounce packages of the frozen variety. Stretch the amounts or reduce them and you have the salad for any number of occasions. I do urge you, though, to taste as you change. Cooking is fun.

SALAD BELLA

4 heads Bibb lettuce	1 pint large strawberries,
2 grapefruit, peeled and sectioned	not hulled

½ cup Bouquet Dressing or Great Salad Dressing

Wash and drain lettuce; wrap in a towel and refrigerate. To serve, arrange 1 head of lettuce on each salad plate and spread out leaves as for an open flower. Tuck grapefruit sections and washed strawberries among leaves. Pour about 2 tablespoons dressing over each salad. Serves 4.

Another salad arrangement for 4 persons: sprinkle each head of lettuce with 2 tablespoons bean sprouts; tuck slices of persimmon among the leaves for taste and color. Serve with Great Salad Dressing.

SALAD CAPRICE

6 navel oranges	French Dressing Caprice
2 red sweet onions	1 head iceberg lettuce

Peel oranges and cut in ¼-inch slices; remove loose outside leaves and slice onions thin. Combine in a bowl; toss lightly with French Dressing Caprice. Refrigerate 2 or 3 hours. To serve, drain oranges and onions and reserve marinade. Arrange a bed of shredded lettuce, "dress" with the reserved marinade, and top with oranges and onions. Serves 6 to 8.

French Dressing Caprice

½ cup olive or salad oil	½ teaspoon sugar
6 tablespoons lemon juice	1 teaspoon celery seed
1 teaspoon salt	¼ teaspoon paprika

Combine ingredients in a 2-cup jar and shake very well. Makes about ¾ cup.

This is an early in the day preparation, wonderful for a dinner party with poultry, especially with duck.

Cubed avocado is compatible as an additional ingredient.

Madrid is a modern city, with wide tree-lined boulevards, verdant parks and flourishing fountains of sculptured magnificance. Old Madrid is "just around the corner," where we ambled through narrow cobblestone streets to the huge square, and into an earlier era of sun-drenched yellowed buildings and rows of street vendors. A narrow, rugged byway led us to Casa Botin, for eons the restaurant rendezvous of bullfighters and their adoring following. Their food is hearty; their salads "things of beauty," pictures of rare composition. Such was

SALAD CASA BOTIN

1 cup diced celery	2 heads Boston lettuce
1 cucumber, thinly sliced	½ cup salad olives, or sliced
6 radishes, sliced	stuffed pimiento olives
2 large tomatoes (or 3 small)	1 tablespoon chopped chives, fresh
sliced	or frozen

Dressing Casa Botin
(Oil and Vinegar)

Wash and slice vegetables as indicated; refrigerate 1 to 2 hours.

Line a salad bowl with 2 rows of lettuce leaves to conform to bowl. Turn celery, cucumber slices, and radishes into center. Cover with overlapping tomato slices. Sprinkle with olives and chives. Just before serving, dress with Dressing Casa Botin. Toss so that all ingredients are coated, and serve individual portions, using the lettuce as cups for the remaining vegetables in the salad. Serves 6 to 8.

Dressing Casa Botin

½ teaspoon salt   6 tablespoons olive oil
⅛ teaspoon white pepper   3 tablespoons wine vinegar

Dust the salad with salt and pepper, then sprinkle with vinegar and oil and toss lightly until ingredients are coated. Do not allow it to stand longer than 15 minutes after "dressing" the contents of the salad bowl. This is the Spanish version.

A simple tossed salad with oil and vinegar dressing is a basis for many additional ingredients such as

⅛ teaspoon paprika   ⅛ teaspoon dry mustard   ⅛ teaspoon curry
¼ cup grated Parmesan cheese   ¼ cup crumbled Roquefort
2 slices Swiss cheese, cut in strips

Top with a mound of cottage cheese for a luncheon entrée.

SESAME SEED SPINACH

1 tablespoon peanut oil   4 tablespoons vinegar
4 tablespoons sesame seeds   1 tablespoon soy sauce
4 tablespoons sugar   1 pound spinach
3 slices sautéed bacon, crumbled

Heat oil in skillet; add sesame seeds and brown evenly. Caution! They burn quickly — use low heat. Remove from heat and add sugar, vinegar and soy sauce; stir. Wash spinach and wrap in towel; place in refrigerator to crisp. To serve, heat sauce quickly and toss with cold spinach. Arrange in individual salad bowls and sprinkle with bacon. Makes 4 generous servings.

SLAW DOWN UNDER

1 medium head cabbage, finely sliced	1 cup cooked string beans
3 medium onions, sliced paper-thin	6 radishes, sliced
1 cucumber, peeled and sliced	French Dressing Caprice

Layer cabbage and onions in bowl; cover with cold water and place in refrigerator for one hour. Drain and add cucumber, beans, and radishes. Pour French Dressing Caprice over; let stand 6 hours in refrigerator to chill thoroughly. To serve, toss lightly. This slaw keeps very well. Makes 8 servings.

Try adding ½ cup sliced black olives for a different flavor.

WAX BEAN RELISH
(salad)

1 10-ounce package frozen wax beans	1 large Bermuda onion, sliced very thin

1 large cucumber, unpeeled

Garnish: lettuce cups, paprika

Relish Dressing

⅔ cup Italian dressing, prepared or see Index	½ teaspoon snipped parsley
1 garlic clove, minced	¼ teaspoon oregano
	¼ cup finely chopped celery
¼ cup finely chopped onion	

Cook wax beans "al dente," one minute less than package directions. Drain and cool. Slice cucumber very thin (a metal slicer is excellent), there should be about 2 cups; then mix with beans and onion. Combine all ingredients in Relish Dressing; pour over bean mixture and toss lightly. Refrigerate until thoroughly chilled. To serve, toss and serve on lettuce cups, and sprinkle with paprika. Serves 6.

For an easy conversion to an excellent entrée or appetizer, add ½ pound cooked shrimp, cleaned, deveined and halved, and 1 cup canned kidney beans, drained. Add additional dressing if you wish.

Salad Dressings

French Dressing Assortment

Classic French Dressing is a ratio of three parts oil to one part vinegar or lemon juice. Olive oil is the connoisseur's choice, but salad oil makes a good dressing. The vinegar can be wine, tarragon, malt or cider.

To ½ cup vinegar add ¾ teaspoon salt and ¼ teaspoon freshly or coarsely ground white or black pepper. Blend well; add 1½ cups oil and beat until thick.

Choice of combinations is personal and certainly if your desire is for a more tart dressing you need feel no twinge of conscience in adding more vinegar or that spoonful of lemon juice.

½ teaspoon mustard gives tang.

1 teaspoon sugar gives balance.

½ teaspoon paprika adds color and flavor.

1 clove of garlic, halved, is delicious for those who enjoy it.

Herbs add interest but must be used with caution until you have experimented. Try a little at a time. Dill, chervil, chives, tarragon, or basil (so popular among many others), add a good accent.

Cheeses, chili sauce, anchovies, and capers are good additions. For fruit salads, the fruit juices, chutney or honey may be added.

When selecting ingredients, there is a wide choice of combinations, but in one area there is no deviation — fresh foods and greens must be fresh, and fruit the finest.

Never drown your salad. Use only sufficient dressing to make the leaves glisten.

BASIC FRENCH DRESSING

¼ cup olive oil   1 teaspoon salt
½ cup salad oil   ¼ teaspoon pepper
4 tablespoons vinegar   2 cloves garlic, cut in halves

Combine oils and vinegar in small jar. Add seasonings and garlic; cover and shake until well mixed. Garlic flavor is developed by allowing dressing to stand several hours in refrigerator. Remove garlic and shake well before using. Makes 1 cup.

ROQUEFORT DRESSING

To ⅓ cup Basic French Dressing add 2 tablespoons crumbled Roquefort cheese. Shake well. Chill.

CHIFFONADE DRESSING

⅓ cup French Dressing   1 tablespoon minced pimiento
⅛ teaspoon black pepper   ½ teaspoon minced onion
⅛ teaspoon paprika   ½ hard-cooked egg, finely
1 tablespoon minced parsley   chopped

To Basic French Dressing, add the pepper, paprika, parsley, pimiento, onion, and egg. Mix ingredients well and chill. Makes about ½ cup.

CHILI MAY DRESSING

½ cup sour cream   2 tablespoons chili sauce
½ cup mayonnaise   2 tablespoons pickle relish
        ½ teaspoon Worcestershire

Combine ingredients; blend well. Chill in refrigerator until served. Makes 1¼ cups.

CHIVE FRENCH DRESSING

2 tablespoons minced chives   1 teaspoon brown sugar
2 tablespoons finely chopped parsley   ⅓ cup French Dressing

Add chives, parsley, and brown sugar to Basic French Dressing.
Shake well. Chill. Makes about ½ cup.

DELTA DRESSING

3 green onions   ½ teaspoon coarsely ground pepper
1 stalk celery   ½ teaspoon oregano
1 clove garlic, minced   ½ teaspoon dried basil
¼ cup snipped parsley   ⅛ teaspoon crushed rosemary
1 teaspoon salt   1⅓ cups salad oil
          ½ cup tarragon wine vinegar

Chop onions, celery, garlic, and parsley together until finely
minced. Combine in a jar with remaining ingredients and shake
well. Let stand in refrigerator overnight so flavors may "marry."
Makes about 2 cups.

Princess Salad or any vegetable combination you may desire is
compatible with Dill Dressing; this is more tart than our classic
French.

DILL DRESSING

½ cup salad oil or   ½ teaspoon salt
    ½ cup olive oil   ¼ teaspoon coarsely ground pepper
¼ cup lemon juice   ½ teaspoon sugar
⅛ teaspoon garlic powder   ½ teaspoon dill weed

Blend all ingredients well; refrigerate. Pour over salad just
before serving. Makes 1¼ cups dressing.

DRESSING RICA

1 cup mayonnaise	1 teaspoon sugar
1 cup chili sauce	1 teaspoon lemon juice
¼ cup catsup	dash Tabasco
1 tablespoon horseradish	1 hard-cooked egg, diced fine

Combine all ingredients; blend well and chill. Makes 2½ cups dressing.

FRUIT DRESSING CELESTINA

2 egg yolks, beaten	1 cup orange juice
3 tablespoons sugar	¼ cup maraschino cherry liquid
½ teaspoon arrowroot or corn-starch	2 tablespoons lemon juice
	¼ teaspoon vanilla
1 teaspoon Angostura Bitters	

Combine yolks, sugar, and arrowroot in top of double boiler; blend in orange juice, cherry liquid, and lemon juice. Place over hot water and cook, stirring until mixture is clear and slightly thickened, about 5 minutes. Remove from heat; mix in vanilla and bitters; pour into bowl; cool, then chill. Makes about 1½ cups.

This dressing has a distinctive flavor which enhances and blends with the endless variety of fruit.

For another version, fold in ½ cup heavy cream, whipped. The flavor will be mellowed a little and the texture fluffier.

Both are so very good.

LORENZO DRESSING

½ cup salad or olive oil	½ cup chili sauce
½ cup white vinegar	¼ cup finely chopped watercress
1 teaspoon salt	

Combine all ingredients; mix until well blended. Chill thoroughly. Makes about 1½ cups.

BOUQUET DRESSING

7 tablespoons oil
6 tablespoons vinegar
6 tablespoons sugar
5 tablespoons catsup
2 tablespoons Worcestershire
½ teaspoon salt

1 tablespoon chopped watercress
   or parsley
1 tablespoon finely chopped
   green pepper
1 hard cooked egg, sieved
   (optional)

Combine all ingredients in a jar; shake well and refrigerate.
Shake well before serving. Makes 1¾ cups dressing.

GREAT SALAD DRESSING!

¾ cup chopped parsley
½ cup chopped shallots
3 teaspoons prepared mustard
1 tablespoon monosodium glutamate

1 teaspoon salt
¾ cup chopped chervil
1 cup tarragon vinegar
2 teaspoons Worcestershire

1½ cups mayonnaise

Combine ingredients, except mayonnaise, in blender and run
mixer at high speed for 3 to 8 minutes; add mayonnaise and run
mixer again for one minute. Refrigerate until thoroughly
chilled. Makes about 4½ cups.

This dressing is especially good with cold lobster; add a dash
of garlic salt.

HONEY DRESSING

1 cup sour cream   2 tablespoons honey
⅛ teaspoon grated nutmeg

Blend well; refrigerate. (Scarcely a recipe, but too good to
omit.)

ITALIAN DRESSING

½ cup prepared Italian dressing
3 tablespoons wine vinegar
½ teaspoon caraway seeds

⅛ teaspoon Italian
   seasoning or oregano
⅛ teaspoon salt

Combine all ingredients and blend well. Makes ¾ cup.

Prepared Italian dressing is a wonderful base for a selection of additional ingredients: add chopped watercress, parsley or pickles.

ITALIAN MAYONNAISE DRESSING

½ cup spicy Italian dressing
1 cup mayonnaise or salad
   dressing
1 tablespoon white vinegar

3 tablespoons sugar
1½ teaspoons celery seed
⅛ teaspoon salt
dash paprika

Blend all ingredients very well. May be stored in refrigerator. Makes 1½ cups dressing.

ROQUEFORT CREAM DRESSING

¼ teaspoon dry mustard
¼ teaspoon black pepper
¼ teaspoon monosodium glutamate
1 teaspoon horseradish

2 ounces crumbled Roquefort
   cheese
1 tablespoon white vinegar
salt

¼ cup sour cream

Combine all ingredients; mix well and refrigerate till serving time. About ½ cup; can be doubled except for pepper.

VINAIGRETTE DRESSING

½ cup wine vinegar
1½ cups olive or salad oil
1½ teaspoons salt
½ teaspoon paprika

2 tablespoons pickle relish
1 tablespoon chopped pimiento
1 hard cooked egg, finely chopped
   or sieved

Combine all ingredients in a jar; shake thoroughly to blend, and refrigerate. Makes about 1¾ cups.

It's Fun to Bake

• ♡ • ♡ • ♡ • ♡ • ♡ •

The Rising Bread

THE FUN of beating and kneading yeast dough and its responsive rise to gourmet heights has challenged the contemporary hostess cook. Home-baked bread is in fashion; its fragrance wafts the essence of hearth and hospitality.

BUBBLE COFFEE CAKE

1 package active dry yeast	½ cup dark brown sugar,
2 tablespoons warm water	firmly packed
2 tablespoons sugar	1 teaspoon cinnamon
½ teaspoon salt	½ cup walnuts or pecans,
¼ cup butter or margarine	coarsely chopped
½ cup hot milk	⅓ cup melted butter or
2 to 2½ cups sifted flour	margarine
1 egg	¼ cup seedless raisins

Add yeast to water; stir until blended. Combine sugar and salt in mixing bowl. Add ¼ cup butter to hot milk, stirring until melted, then add to combined sugar and salt. Cool to lukewarm; stir in 1 cup of the flour and beat until batter is smooth and elastic, about 100 strokes. Blend in yeast and egg. Stir in remaining 1½ cups flour (more flour may be added to make dough more firm, but if you have patience to work with the stickiness of 2½ cups of flour, the results are well worth the effort). Knead dough in the bowl until it becomes satiny. (It will not leave the fingers completely but is manageable.) Place dough in greased bowl, turning until it is oiled on all sides. Cover and let rise in warm place, away from drafts, until double in bulk, 1½ to 2 hours. Combine brown sugar, cinnamon and chopped nuts. Punch dough down and shape into balls the size of walnuts. Dip balls in melted butter or margarine; roll in brown sugar mixture, and arrange in a layer in a greased 9-inch tube pan. Sprinkle with seedless raisins. Top with remaining coated balls and pour over any remaining butter. Cover and let rise until double in bulk, about 40 to 50 minutes. Bake in a 375° oven 30 to 35 minutes or until browned.

CHRISTMAS COFFEE CAKE

2 packages active dry yeast or	1 teaspoon salt
2 cakes compressed yeast	3 eggs
½ cup warm water	½ cup milk, scalded, cooled
½ cup butter or margarine	5½ cups sifted flour
¾ cup sugar	(approximately)
grated rind of 1 lemon	1 cup chopped candied fruits
½ teaspoon nutmeg	½ cup slivered almonds

Soften dry yeast in warm water (compressed yeast in lukewarm water). Cream butter and sugar until light, then add lemon rind, nutmeg, salt and eggs; beat well. Add yeast and milk. Beat in flour gradually, using as much as needed to make a soft dough. Turn out on floured board; add fruit, and knead until smooth and elastic, about 10 minutes. Mound dough and place in a greased bowl, turning so it is completely oiled. Let rise until doubled in bulk in a warm place free from drafts. Butter a 2-quart form pan generously; sprinkle almonds in bottom and press into buttered sides. Spread dough evenly; cover, and set in warm place again to rise until doubled in bulk. Bake at 350° for 50 minutes to one hour. Turn out on a cake rack; let stand until slightly cool, then drizzle a thin Confectioners' Icing over cake and decorate with red and green candied cherries.

Confectioners' Icing

1 cup sifted confectioners' sugar
2 tablespoons warm milk or cream
½ teaspoon vanilla or other flavoring (orange extract with
grated peel; lemon extract with grated lemon rind)

Blend until smooth.

At luncheon with excitingly generous and bubbling Virginia Graham, the "Girl Talk" veered from sports to fashions to grandchildren and other engrossing subjects. Finally — over dessert — we discussed recipes.

Virginia, glamorous homemaker, gave me the formula for this superb coffee cake.

CHOCOLATE SWIRL COFFEE CAKE

1 6-ounce can evaporated milk	1 package active dry yeast
¾ cup sugar	½ cup warm water
½ teaspoon salt	1 6-ounce package (1 cup)
2 eggs	semisweet chocolate pieces
½ cup soft butter or margarine	½ teaspoon cinnamon
4½ cups sifted flour	Crumb Topping

Reserve ¼ cup evaporated milk; combine remaining milk with sugar, salt, and eggs in large bowl of electric mixer. Beat 5 minutes at medium speed; add butter and 2 cups flour, then beat until very smooth. Sprinkle yeast over warm water and stir until dissolved. Add yeast and 1 cup flour to first mixture, beat at medium speed 3 minutes; then blend in remaining 1½ cups flour, clearing sides of bowl by scraping to center. Cover; let rise in warm place until double in bulk, about 3 hours. Combine chocolate pieces, cinnamon, and reserved ¼ cup milk in saucepan and heat just to boiling; remove from heat and stir until mixture is smooth. Cool. Punch down dough, turn out on well floured board or pastry cloth; let rest a few minutes. Flour hands well; knead dough 20 times; roll on floured board into 10" x 15" rectangle. Spread with chocolate mixture, roll up from long side as for a jelly roll. Place seam side down in greased angel food pan (preferably with removable bottom). Press ends together to seal and carefully stretch roll to fit pan. Sprinkle with Crumb Topping. Cover and let rise in warm place until double in bulk — about 2 hours. Bake at 350° for 45 minutes or until cake tests done. Carefully remove from pan; cool on rack, crumb-topped side up, for one hour.

Crumb Topping

½ cup flour
⅓ cup sugar
¼ cup soft butter or margarine
½ cup chopped walnuts

1½ teaspoons cinnamon
½ cup grated German's
Sweet or chocolate bits

Mix flour, sugar, butter and cinnamon with fork until well blended and crumbly. Blend in chocolate and nuts.

CINNAMON TWISTS

1 package active dry yeast
¼ cup warm water
4 cups sifted flour
1 teaspoon salt
1 cup butter or ½ cup butter
    and ½ cup margarine

4 egg yolks
1 cup sour cream
1 teaspoon vanilla
1 teaspoon grated orange rind
1 cup sugar
1 egg white, slightly beaten

Topping: Cinnamon Sugar

Sprinkle yeast on warm water; set aside. Sift flour and salt into large mixing bowl and add butter; cut in as for pie with blender or knives until consistency of cornmeal. Beat yolks until thick, then add to flour mixture with sour cream, vanilla, orange rind, and yeast; mix very well. Cover and place in refrigerator to chill a minimum of 3 hours; dough may stand overnight. Sprinkle the pastry board with 2 tablespoons sugar, place dough on sugar and roll to a 12-inch square. Fold dough in thirds to a rectangle, 12″ x 4″, then fold in opposite direction to make a 4-inch square. There will be 9 layers of dough. Roll out to a 12-inch rectangle again, sprinkle with 2 tablespoons sugar and repeat 2 more times. Work quickly. Then, for this last rolling, make the rectangle 9″ x 16″, brush with egg white and sprinkle with remaining sugar. Cut dough from 9-inch side into three 3-inch strips, then cut each length into sixteen 1-inch strips; the dough will have layered look. Twist each strip 3 times and place on well-buttered cooky sheet about 1 inch apart. Bake in 375° oven, 20 minutes or until lightly browned. Remove at once, as sugar sticks, and dust while hot with Cinnamon Sugar. Makes 48 twists.

Though the recipe is lengthy, the procedure is simple. Do try these; they are delectable Danish type pastries.

They keep well in an airtight container and also freeze well. Before serving, heat, wrapped in foil, in 400° oven about 10 minutes. Allow an additional five minutes when frozen.

Cinnamon Sugar

Combine and blend well ⅓ cup sugar and 1 teaspoon cinnamon. To keep a quantity on hand, combine 1 cup sugar with 1 tablespoon cinnamon.

To paraphrase, "When in Denmark do as the Danes do," so in Copenhagen I hastened to order Danish pastry, my favorite coffee cake. Said the waiter, "Madam, you mean Wiener Brod." My protestations were to no avail, and when he arrived with my order, we were both correct. In Denmark, Danish Pastry is called Wiener Brod — translated, Vienna Bread. Why the reluctance of these nice people to make claim to title, I cannot imagine. Fortunately, I acquired this recipe while attending a class on Danish Cuisine.

DANISH PASTRY
("Wiener Brod")

⅓ cup warm water	¼ cup sugar
2 packages active dry yeast	¾ teaspoon salt
	2 ¾ cups flour
½ cup milk	¾ cup butter or margarine,
1 egg yolk, beaten	solidly cold

Glaze

| 1 egg yolk | Cream Cheese Filling or ½ cup |
| 1 teaspoon cream | preserves (approximately) |

Pour warm water in large mixing bowl (test the water as one tests the baby's bottle, by dropping it on the wrist). It should be comfortably, but definitely warm. Sprinkle yeast over water and stir until dissolved; mix in milk, egg yolk, sugar and salt. Stir in 2½ cups flour and beat vigorously until elastic and shiny for about 2 minutes or 250 strokes. Dust board or pastry cloth with 2 tablespoons of remaining flour; roll dough into ball; place on pastry board and dust with remaining 2 tablespoons flour. Pat with hands into rectangular shape, then roll to a 10" x 15" rectangle. Slice cold butter very thin and cover 10" x 10" part of dough. (I keep the butter in the freezer until ready to use. Slice as soon as possible.) Fold unbuttered 5 inches of dough over half of buttered side, then fold buttered side over the middle, making 3 layers. Fold in thirds in the opposite direction making 9 layers. Repeat rolling and folding 3 times more and place in refrigerator while making fillings. The dough is now ready for final rolling, shaping, filling, raising and baking. If, during rolling, dough becomes soft, place in the refrigerator for 30 minutes.

Pastry Shapes

COCKSCOMBS

Roll dough on floured board into a rectangle 12" x 15". Cut into twenty 3-inch squares. Spread a tablespoon of preserves or Cream Cheese Filling across each square; fold over into a rectangle and seal by pressing together. Cut 4 slits into dough, at right angles to edge. Place Cockscombs on greased cooky sheets, about 3 inches apart, curving slightly so that slits spread open. Cover, let stand in warm place, away from drafts for about one hour or until double in bulk. Place in 450° oven, reduce heat immediately to 375° and bake 15 minutes, or until golden brown. Serve warm. Makes 20.

To reheat, wrap in foil and place in 400° oven for 10 minutes.

POCKETBOOKS

Roll out dough on floured board to 12″ x 8″ rectangle and cut into 2-inch squares (lengthwise into 4 strips, crosswise into 6 strips). Place 1 tablespoon preserves or Cream Cheese Filling in center and draw 4 corners together sealing edges firmly. Place 3 inches apart on greased cooky sheets; brush tops with beaten egg yolk mixed with 2 tablespoons water. Bake as for Cockscombs. Makes 24.

Prepared prune and apricot fillings are excellent.

VANILLA BUNS

Roll dough to 12″ x 8″ rectangle; cut into 12 4-inch squares. Place 1 tablespoon Vanilla Cream or plum jam in center of each; fold corners to center, sealing open edges together and place on greased cooky sheet, seam side down 3 inches apart. Bake as for Cockscombs and Pocketbooks. Makes 12.

Cream Cheese Filling

1 8-ounce package cream cheese, softened, or 1 8-ounce package Neufchatel cheese	2 tablespoons sugar dash salt 1 tablespoon lemon juice

Combine ingredients and beat until blended and fluffy. For the diet-conscious, Neufchatel has fewer calories than cream cheese.

Chocolate Frosting

1 6-ounce package chocolate bits dash salt	1 tablespoon butter or 1 tablespoon margarine

Combine in top of double boiler; stir over heat until melted and smooth.

Vanilla Cream

3 tablespoons sugar 2 tablespoons cornstarch 2 egg yolks, beaten	¾ cup half and half cream or ¾ cup milk 1 teaspoon vanilla

Combine sugar and cornstarch in top of double boiler; blend in yolks, then cream. Cook over hot water, stirring until thickened, then cook an additional 5 minutes without stirring. Remove from heat, cool quickly, stir in vanilla.

For Chocolate Cream, add two 1-ounce squares of melted unsweetened chocolate after removing from heat.

ENSAIMADA
(Golden Muffins)

3½ cups sifted flour	¾ cup butter or margarine
¼ teaspoon salt	½ cup sugar
1 package active dry yeast	4 egg yolks
¼ cup warm water	⅓ cup evaporated milk

1 tablespoon sugar

Topping

2 egg whites, slightly beaten   1 teaspoon cinnamon
2 tablespoons sugar

Sift flour and salt together; dissolve yeast in warm water, then add 1 tablespoon sugar and ½ cup of flour mixture; beat very well. Cover; let rise in warm place 15 minutes. Cream butter and ½ cup sugar until very light and smooth (the electric mixer serves very well). Beat in egg yolks, one at a time, until blended; beat in evaporated milk alternately with remaining flour. Add yeast sponge and beat well until smooth. Turn into greased bowl; cover and let rise again, in a warm place free from drafts, for 2 to 2½ hours, or until doubled in bulk. Coat hands with flour and knead dough in bowl for 5 minutes (it will be quite oily). Turn onto lightly floured wax paper and cover with second sheet. Pat into a 1-inch thick square. Divide into 12 even sections; place each piece in a 3-inch muffin-pan cup; cover and let rise in warm place at least 1 hour. Brush tops with beaten egg whites and sprinkle with combined cinnamon and sugar. Bake in 375° oven 15 minutes; serve warm. Reheat if baked in advance. Makes 12 large muffins.

This is a very rich muffin, so for the calorie-conscious we suggest a smaller size. Cut the dough into 24 sections and place in 1½-inch muffin-pan cups.

The dough for these airy rolls may be refrigerated for 5 days — a luxury item.

FEATHERY ROLLS

¼ cup butter	¼ cup warm water
¼ cup vegetable shortening	1 egg, beaten
¼ cup sugar	½ teaspoon mace
¾ teaspoon salt	2½ cups sifted flour
½ cup boiling water	1 egg
1 cup rolled oats	1 teaspoon half and half cream or
1 package active dry yeast	water
	sesame seeds

Combine butter, shortening, sugar and salt with boiling water and stir until shortenings melt; add rolled oats and let stand until mixture is lukewarm. Dissolve yeast in warm water; add with egg and mace to oatmeal mixture. Add 1 cup flour and beat thoroughly, about 100 strokes. Add remaining flour gradually, blending well. Flour hands and knead dough in bowl to mix lightly and well; it will be satiny in a very few minutes. Cover with foil, then wrap bowl in tea towel, and let stand overnight in refrigerator. To bake, shape into rolls; place in greased pan, cover and let stand in warm place, free from drafts, 1½ to 2 hours until doubled in bulk. Combine egg and water; brush over rolls and sprinkle with sesame seeds. Bake in 450° oven 15 minutes or until browned. Makes about 30 small rolls.

To shape rolls

Parker House: Flatten into 1-inch circle ¼ inch thick; press a line with back of knife just off center. Fold larger side over smaller one. Place on greased cooky sheet.
Clover Leaf: Makes balls the size of marbles; put three together in small muffin tins.
  Serve warm; they reheat very well.

HERB BREAD

1 loaf French bread   Herb Butter

Slice the bread in half lengthwise; spread cut side of bread generously with Herb Butter. Replace the two halves and wrap in aluminum foil, sealing well. Place in 350° oven and heat 20 minutes or until bread is crisp and piping hot. Serve from opened foil; cut in 1½-inch slices.

Herb Butter

½ cup butter, softened   ¼ cup chopped chives or green
½ cup chopped parsley   onions

Cream the ingredients together until well blended.

LIGHT-AS-A-FEATHER BREAD

1 package active dry yeast   ¼ cup evaporated milk
¼ cup warm water   1 teaspoon salt
½ cup butter or margarine   ½ cup sugar
½ cup scalded milk   4½ cups flour, sifted
3 medium-size potatoes, boiled and 1 egg, well beaten
  mashed (about 1 cup)

Sprinkle yeast on warm water, 105° to 110°, and dissolve. Add butter to scalded milk and stir until melted. Add milk to hot mashed potatoes and beat well; add evaporated milk and salt; cool. Combine sugar and dissolved yeast and add to cooled potato mixture. Beat well, then blend in 1 cup of flour. Cover and let stand in warm place until light and foamy. Sponge will bubble actively in about one hour. Add egg, then sift in flour gradually. Knead with floured hands in bowl as it is added (dough will be sticky) for about 10 minutes or until dough leaves sides of bowl. Place in greased bowl, turning so that it is completely oiled. Cover and set in warm place, about 85°, until doubled in bulk, for approximately 2 hours. Shape ⅓ of dough into a loaf in 5" x 8" greased pan and bake in 375° oven 25 to 30 minutes. Test by tapping; loaf will sound hollow. For 1 loaf. See next page for rolls.

Shape the balance of the dough into 30 small balls. Place in small greased muffin tins, or on greased cooky sheet. Cover and let stand until double in bulk. Bake in 375° oven 15 to 20 minutes. For 30 small rolls.

These keep well and are delicious when reheated.

To freeze, bake rolls for only 10 minutes. Cool and wrap in freezer bags or foil.

To serve, do not thaw. Remove from foil and place in 450° oven for approximately 15 minutes until heated and browned.

MONKEY BREAD

1 package active dry yeast or	½ cup butter or margarine
1 cake compressed yeast	1 cup milk, scalded
2 tablespoons warm water	3½ cups sifted flour
4 tablespoons sugar	(approximately)
1 teaspoon salt	¼ cup melted butter

Add yeast to warm water (use lukewarm water for compressed yeast) and stir until dissolved. Combine sugar and salt in mixing bowl. Add ½ cup butter or margarine to milk, stirring until melted, then add to combined sugar and salt. Cool to lukewarm; add yeast mixture. Add flour gradually, beating well. Additional kneading with the hands improves the texture of the dough. Place in a greased bowl, turning so that dough is oiled completely. Cover with a towel and let rise in a warm place until double in bulk; about one hour. Punch down and roll out on a lightly floured board to ¼-inch thickness. Cut into 2½-inch diamond pieces. Dip each piece in melted butter and layer in a 9-inch ring mold to ½ the depth of mold. Let rise again until doubled in bulk; about 45 minutes. Bake at 400° for 30 minutes or until golden brown.

This recipe may be a coffee cake as well. Dip diamonds in butter, then dredge with a mixture of 1 cup brown sugar, 1 teaspoon cinnamon, 2 teaspoons rum flavoring. Proceed as for the bread.

PECAN SCHNECKEN

1 cup sour cream	1 teaspoon salt
1 ¾ ounce compressed yeast or	3 eggs, well beaten
1 package active dry yeast	3½ cups flour
¼ cup lukewarm water or	¼ cup melted butter
warm water	Raisin Filling
1 cup butter	48 pecan halves
⅓ cup sugar	Brown Sugar Syrup

Allow sour cream to stand at room temperature 1 hour. Dissolve compressed yeast in lukewarm water (dry yeast in warm water). Cream butter and sugar until fluffy, then stir in sour cream, salt, dissolved yeast, and eggs. Beat in 1 cup of flour at a time, beating well after each addition. Cover tightly with foil and a towel and place in refrigerator overnight. Remove and let stand in warm place free from drafts for 2 hours. Divide dough in half; place on lightly floured board and roll each into a rectangle, ¼-inch thick, about 18 inches long. Spread each with half the melted butter and half the Raisin Filling. Roll from long end as for a jelly roll; then slice each roll into 12 pieces, 1½ inches wide. Butter 24 muffin tins and place 2 pecan halves in each, rounded side down. Pour 1 tablespoon Brown Sugar Syrup over nuts and place a slice of rolled dough, cut side down on top of nuts and syrup. Cover and set in warm place to rise until double in bulk. Bake in 375° oven 12 to 18 minutes or until evenly browned. Makes 2 dozen.

Raisin Filling

½ cup raisins	½ cup coarsely chopped
½ cup sugar	pecans
1½ teaspoons cinnamon	

Soak raisins in hot water 15 minutes, then drain thoroughly. Combine with sugar, cinnamon, and pecans; mix well.

Brown Sugar Syrup

½ cup butter	1 cup brown sugar
3 tablespoons water	

Place butter, brown sugar, and water in saucepan and let it come to a boil; cook 3 minutes until blended.

RAISED FRUIT COOKIES

1 cake compressed yeast or
   1 package active dry yeast
4 tablespoons sour cream
2 cups flour

1 egg yolk, slightly beaten
1 cup salted butter or
   margarine, softened
½ cup prepared prune filling

confectioners' sugar

For compressed yeast, heat sour cream to lukewarm; if using dry yeast, heat sour cream to warm. Soften yeast in cream and stir until dissolved; add flour gradually, then mix in egg yolk and butter; blend well. Let dough rest for 15 minutes; divide in half, then roll each out on lightly floured board to ⅛-inch thickness. Cut into 2-inch rounds with cooky cutter; make a depression in center of each cooky with rounded bottom of thimble or with the ¼ teaspoon measuring spoon. Fill each with ½ teaspoon prune filling or Lekvar; place on ungreased cooky sheet and bake in 425° oven 10 minutes or until lightly browned. Cool and sprinkle with confectioners' sugar. Makes about 4 dozen.

The prepared fillings come in 12-ounce cans in a variety of flavors, and are excellent. Substitute any of your choice; a combination of toppings make an interesting assortment.

The following is a well-known Hungarian specialty, a prune filling called Lekvar, which you may want to try.

LEKVAR

2 pounds prunes
½ teaspoon ground cinnamon

grated rind of 1 lemon
⅛ teaspoon ground cloves

Wash prunes and place in saucepan; cover with water and let stand 2 hours. Drain, reserving 1 cup of the water in which they were soaked. Pour this liquid over prunes in saucepan and bring to boil; reduce heat and simmer ½ hour. Remove prunes, reserving all liquid; remove pits and chop prunes coarsely, then return to liquid. Add cinnamon, lemon rind, and cloves; simmer very slowly, stirring constantly until thick and glossy.

Hungarian cooks say it is done when the wooden stirring spoon stands erect without assistance.

ROYAL CREAM CHEESE COFFEE CAKE

1 teaspoon salt	¾ cup sugar
½ teaspoon ground cardamom	2 packages active dry yeast
¼ teaspoon ground nutmeg	¼ cup warm water
4½ cups flour	1 whole egg plus
¾ cup milk	3 yolks, slightly beaten
1 cup butter	additional flour as needed

Nut Filling   Raisin Filling   Cheese Filling
Topping

Sift salt, cardamom, nutmeg, and 4 cups flour together into large bowl. Scald milk; remove from heat; add butter and sugar; stir until dissolved. Cool mixture to lukewarm. Dissolve yeast in warm water (185°). Make a well in flour mixture; pour in dissolved yeast, milk mixture, and eggs. Beat until very smooth (150 strokes if by hand); add remaining ½ cup flour if dough is too sticky to handle (the less flour used, the lighter the dough). Cover and let stand at room temperature for one hour; refrigerate, well covered, overnight.

Remove from refrigerator; let stand 1 hour, then place on floured board and knead until dough is smooth and elastic, about 5 minutes. If necessary, add sufficient flour to manipulate dough easily, using as little as possible. Place in greased bowl; cover and let stand in warm spot away from drafts for one hour.

Divide dough in half for 2 cakes. Place half of dough on floured board; dust lightly with flour and roll into a rectangle 10″ x 15″. Use half of each filling for a single cake. Brush dough with melted butter; sprinkle with Nut Filling and Raisin Filling, leaving a border of 1 inch on the dough. Dot with Cheese Filling until well covered, using 1 teaspoon at a time, about ½-inch apart. Roll as for jelly roll from 10-inch side, sealing ends well. Place in greased and floured 9½″ x 5½″ loaf pan; brush top with melted butter and sprinkle with 2 tablespoons reserved Nut Filling. Cut diagonal gashes 1 inch apart and ½-inch deep across top of loaf. Cover and let stand in warm place away from drafts for 2½ hours or until tripled in size. Brush tops with half and half cream; place in 350° oven and bake 40 minutes. Place on rack and remove from pan when cool.

FILLING FOR TWO
ROYAL CHEESE COFFEE CAKES

Use half of each of the following for 1 cake.

½ cup melted butter

Nut Filling

1 cup walnuts or pecans, finely ground	½ teaspoon cinnamon
	1 cup white sugar

Combine ingredients and blend well. *Reserve 4 tablespoons for Topping.*

Raisin Filling

1 cup seedless yellow raisins   ½ cup light brown sugar
scalded and drained

Combine lightly.

Cheese Filling

1 8-ounce package cream cheese	¼ teaspoon vanilla or
1 3-ounce package cream cheese	¼ teaspoon lemon juice
½ cup sour cream	1 teaspoon sugar

Cream ingredients together until smooth and fluffy.

Topping

4 tablespoons reserved Nut Filling (see above)
2 tablespoons half and half cream

This dough may be kept in the refrigerator for a week. Place in greased bowl and cover. Use it for small filled cakes or other Pastry shapes.

For filled cakes, cut dough in 4-inch squares and fill with jam or nut filling. Fold into triangles; let rise until doubled in bulk. Brush with milk and bake in 350° oven 20 minutes or until lightly browned.

Use this dough for Cinnamon Bread. Roll to ½-inch thickness; sprinkle well with Cinnamon Sugar and dot with butter.

Roll to fit 9″ x 5″ bread pan. Proceed with raising and baking as for Royal Cream Cheese Coffee Cake.

Cinnamon Sugar

> 1 cup sugar blended with 1 tablespoon cinnamon

SALLY LUNN

1½ tablespoons active dry yeast	2 egg yolks, well beaten
¼ cup warm water	2 egg whites, stiffly beaten
2½ cups flour	½ cup butter, melted
¼ cup sugar	½ cup vegetable shortening
2 teaspoons salt	1 cup warm milk

Sprinkle yeast over warm water; dissolve. Combine flour, sugar, and salt. Beat egg yolks in the large bowl of the electric mixer (beat the whites first, set aside, to save beater washing); stir butter and shortening into yolks, then beat in milk, flour mixture, and egg whites; beat thoroughly. Cover and place in a warm place, free from drafts, until doubled in bulk, for about 2 hours. Punch down the dough and beat thoroughly, about 100 strokes. Pour into buttered 10-inch fluted pan and cover again; set aside in warm place about 1½ hours until doubled. Bake in 325° oven 20 minutes, then raise temperature to 375° and bake an additional 30 minutes. Turn out on platter and serve piping hot with butter aplenty. Serves 6.

Reheats well.

SIMPLE SIMON COFFEE CAKE

½ cup half and half cream	¼ cup sour cream
2 cakes compressed yeast or	3 eggs, well beaten
2 packages active dry	4 cups flour
yeast	1 teaspoon salt
1 cup butter or margarine	Apricot, Prune, or Cheese Filling
½ cup sugar	egg yolk, slightly beaten

Heat cream (lukewarm for compressed yeast, warm for dry yeast) and sprinkle yeast over; dissolve. Cream butter and sugar together until fluffy; add sour cream, eggs, and yeast. Beat very

well. Sift flour and salt together and add 1 cup to yeast mixture;
beat well. Add remaining flour gradually, mixing thoroughly.
Place in greased bowl, turning so that dough is completely oiled,
then cover with wax paper and towel; refrigerate overnight.
Cut dough in half and place on floured wax paper; sprinkle
lightly with flour and cover with second sheet of wax paper,
then roll to ½-inch thickness between the sheets to a 9″ x 15″
rectangle. Lift paper occasionally to prevent sticking. Remove
paper, then place dough carefully in 9″ x 5″ loaf pan, allowing
it to drape over sides. Pour filling over bottom and bring dough
to center, pinching to seal securely. Brush with egg yolk;
place in 350° oven at once; do not allow to rise. Bake 1 hour.
The remaining dough will keep up to 5 days in the refrigerator.
Use it for another loaf or small rolls, using the fillings suggested,
or sprinkling with cinnamon, sugar, nuts, and/or raisins.
Makes 2 cakes.

Cheese Filling

1½ cups dry cottage cheese	½ teaspoon vanilla
2 tablespoons flour	¼ cup currants or raisins
2 tablespoons half and half cream	2 egg whites, beaten stiff with ⅛ teaspoon salt
3 egg yolks, beaten slightly	1 egg white, slightly beaten
¼ cup sugar	¼ cup slivered almonds
1 tablespoon melted butter	(optional)

Press cheese through sieve; add flour, cream, and mix well. Mix
eggs, sugar and butter together and add to cheese, then add
vanilla, currants, and fold in beaten egg whites. After sealing
dough, brush top with remaining egg white and sprinkle with
almonds.

Apricot or Prune Filling

1 cup puréed cooked prunes or prepared canned prune or apricot filling	1 teaspoon grated lemon peel dash nutmeg

Blend all ingredients to spread smoothly over dough. You may
spread filling on rectangle of dough and roll as for jelly roll.
Seal ends tightly and bake in greased pan.

BEE HIVES

1 cake compressed yeast
2 tablespoons lukewarm water
2 tablespoons flour
1 tablespoon sugar
2 tablespoons butter
1 egg yolk
¼ cup sugar
¼ teaspoon salt
1 tablespoon grated lemon rind

¾ cup lukewarm milk
2¼ cups flour
¾ cup almonds, blanched
  and slivered
2 tablespoons citron, chopped
2 tablespoons raisins
¼ teaspoon cinnamon
3 tablespoons chocolate bits
3 tablespoons butter, melted

Dissolve yeast in lukewarm water. Add 2 tablespoons flour, 1 tablespoon sugar, and stir. Cover and set in a warm place to rise until doubled in bulk. Cream butter, add egg yolk, sugar, salt, lemon rind, yeast mixture, milk, and flour. Beat until dough loosens from beater. Cover and let rise in warm place, free from drafts, until double in bulk — about 1 to 1½ hours. Roll out on floured board to ¼-inch thickness; cut in half and roll each until about a 12-inch square. Sprinkle with almonds, citron, raisins, cinnamon, and chocolate bits. Roll up like jelly roll, then cut into 1-inch slices. Dip in melted butter and place in shallow buttered pan cut side down, close together. Cover again and let rise in warm place 30 minutes. Bake at 350° for 25 to 30 minutes. Makes 24 hives.

NOTE: In the foregoing recipes, the package of active dry yeast weighs 1¾ ounces; the cake of compressed yeast weighs ¾ ounce.

Cake Walk

APPLE STRIPS

Crust
1 cup butter
½ cup sugar
2 egg yolks
½ teaspoon vanilla
⅛ teaspoon salt
2¾ cups sifted flour

Apple Filling
4 to 5 medium apples
(about 2 pounds)
½ teaspoon lemon juice
½ cup sugar
½ cup dry bread crumbs
½ teaspoon cinnamon
½ teaspoon grated orange or lemon rind
⅛ teaspoon salt
egg whites or milk

Cream butter and sugar until light and fluffy; add yolks, vanilla and beat thoroughly. If possible use an electric mixer. Add salt and flour gradually and blend well. Use half the dough to line a 9″ x 9″ x 2″ cake pan, pressing firmly with fingers or back of spoon. Press remaining dough into flat round, and refrigerate. Refrigerate lined pan. Peel apples; core and grate or chop coarsely; sprinkle with lemon juice. Combine sugar, bread crumbs, cinnamon, orange rind, salt and toss with apples; turn into lined pan. Remove unused dough and roll between sheets of floured wax paper to 9½-inches square. Remove top sheet and invert dough over filled pan. Peel off wax paper carefully and seal edges of dough firmly. Brush with unbeaten egg whites or milk. Bake in 350° oven 30 to 40 minutes or until browned. Cool on rack, then cut into 3″ x 1½″ slices. Makes 18.

One-half the recipe will fill an 8-inch pie pan. Make two; use one and freeze the other.

Delicious à la mode.

For a pastry tray, cut them into 1½-inch squares.

Do you like raisins? Add ¼ cup of the seedless kind.

Drizzle with Confectioners' Icing, lemon flavored.

There are approximately 4 small apples per pound.

APPLESAUCE CAKE

½ cup butter or margarine
1 cup sugar
1 egg, well beaten
1 teaspoon vanilla
1 cup dates, chopped fine
1 cup nuts, coarsely chopped
1 cup raisins, chopped

2 cups sifted cake flour
¼ teaspoon salt
1 teaspoon cinnamon
¼ teaspoon ground cloves
2 teaspoons baking soda
1½ cups applesauce
    (room temperature)

Cream butter and sugar until well blended and light; beat in egg and vanilla. Combine dates, nuts and raisins and sprinkle with a tablespoon or two of the sifted flour to coat. Resift balance of flour with salt, cinnamon, cloves and soda. Mix with butter mixture until smooth, add flour-dusted fruit and nuts, then stir in applesauce. Pour into well greased 9-inch tube pan or loaf pan. Bake in 350° oven 45 minutes to one hour, or until done when tested. Sprinkle with confectioners' sugar, or spread with your favorite icing.

BLACK WALNUT FLUFF CAKE

½ teaspoon rum flavoring
6 egg yolks, well beaten
2 cups sugar
2 cups sifted cake flour
3 teaspoons baking powder
½ teaspoon salt
½ teaspoon cream of tartar

1 teaspoon instant coffee
¾ cup finely chopped black
    walnuts
¼ cup finely chopped pecans
1 cup water
6 egg whites

Add rum flavoring to egg yolks, beat again until thick, then beat in 1 cup sugar gradually. Combine flour, baking powder, salt, coffee, and ½ cup sugar; sift together. Add dry ingredients to yolk mixture in 4 parts, alternating with water, starting and ending with flour mixture. Use electric mixer if possible. Beat egg whites until frothy, add cream of tartar, beat until soft peaks form. Add remaining ½ cup sugar gradually; beat until stiff and glossy. Fold yolk mixture into egg white meringue, using rubber scraper or wire whisk. Cut through batter carefully until blended. Turn into ungreased 10-inch tube pan;

place in 350° oven and bake one hour and 10 minutes. Invert pan on neck of soft drink bottle and cool thoroughly. Remove cake by cutting carefully against sides of pan and around tube in center. Dust with confectioners' sugar, or ice with Rum Icing. Makes 25 slices.

Traditionally Southern, this Jam Cake is claimed from Mississippi to all radiating points. Also known as Woodford Pudding, it is said to belong to Woodford County, Kentucky. A more complicated recipe locates its origin in Tennessee, and the following came from Atlanta with a bride's trousseau.

BLACKBERRY JAM CAKE
(Woodford Pudding)

¾ cup butter or margarine
1 cup brown sugar
1½ cups sifted cake flour
1 teaspoon baking soda
2 teaspoons cinnamon
¼ teaspoon allspice
dash salt

½ teaspoon nutmeg
2 eggs, well beaten
3 tablespoons sour cream
1 cup blackberry jam
½ cup pecans, coarsely chopped
    (optional but good)

Cream butter and sugar together until frothy and light. Sift flour, soda, cinnamon, allspice, salt and nutmeg together. Combine eggs and sour cream; add to butter mixture alternately with dry ingredients. Blend or beat gently only until mixture is thoroughly combined. Fold in jam and blend lightly again; add nuts carefully and pour into greased and floured tube pan or two 8-inch layer cake pans. Bake in 350° oven 30 minutes or until cake springs back when depressed with finger. Remove from oven and place on rack to cool. Frost with a white butter cream icing or with Caramel Icing.

Black Raspberry Jam or preserves can be substituted in batter.

Caramel Icing

1 cup brown sugar; heated until melted and syrupy; blend in 2 teaspoons butter and spread while hot.

Woodford County suggests omitting icing and serving with Whiskey Sauce.

Whiskey Sauce

> 1 cup sugar   2 eggs, beaten
> ½ cup butter   1 cup half and half cream
> 1 tablespoon bourbon (or to taste)

Combine sugar, butter, eggs and cream in top of double boiler; stir over hot water until thickened. Add bourbon.

BLUEBERRY CHEESE CAKE

1 cup quick oats, uncooked
⅓ cup sifted flour
⅓ cup firmly packed brown sugar
½ teaspoon salt
¼ cup melted butter or margarine

½ cup sugar
3 eggs, well beaten
1 8-ounce package cream cheese, softened
1 cup blueberries (fresh or frozen)
confectioners' sugar

Combine oatmeal, flour, brown sugar, and salt in 8-inch square pan. Add melted butter and mix thoroughly. Toast mixture in pan in 350° oven about 10 minutes, then spread evenly in pan. Add sugar gradually to eggs, beating constantly; add cream cheese and mix well. Stir in berries lightly and pour mixture over oatmeal crust. Bake in 350° oven 30 minutes or until topping is set. Cool, place in refrigerator, and chill for several hours. Just before serving, sprinkle with confectioners' sugar and cut into 9 squares. Serves 9.

CHOCOLATE WHIPPED CREAM CAKE

3 squares unsweetened chocolate
1 cup boiling water
2 eggs
1 cup light brown sugar
1 cup granulated sugar

2 cups sifted flour
2 teaspoons baking soda
1 teaspoon salt
1 cup sour cream
1 teaspoon vanilla

Whipped Cream Filling

1 pint heavy cream, whipped	1 tablespoon confectioners'
2 tablespoons instant coffee	sugar, sifted

Add chocolate to boiling water in saucepan. Bring to boil while stirring; reduce heat, then cook gently until slightly thickened. Cool. Beat eggs, add brown and white sugars, continuing to beat until thick and creamy. Sift flour, soda, and salt together; combine sour cream and vanilla. Add flour mixture to egg mixture alternately with sour cream mixture, beginning and ending with flour. Blend in cooled chocolate. Grease two 8-inch cake pans and line with wax paper; grease again and flour lightly. Pour in batter and bake in 350° oven until done when tested, about 30 to 35 minutes. Cool 10 minutes, then remove from pan, place on racks and cool completely. Split each layer in half, making 4 layers.

Prepare Whipped Cream Filling: beat confectioner's sugar and instant coffee into cream until smooth and blended. Spread between layers of cake. Place paper doily over top layer and sprinkle evenly with 1 tablespoon confectioners' sugar. Remove doily carefully to leave design. Place cake on wax-covered doily on cake plate. Store in refrigerator until serving time.

CONNECTICUT BREAKFAST CAKE

This recipe, sometimes titled plain Breakfast Farmer Cake, is seventy-five years old.

1 cup sugar	½ teaspoon soda
¼ cup butter	1 cup sour milk or buttermilk
¼ cup margarine	1 cup nuts, raisins, prunes,
2 whole eggs	dates, figs or chopped fruit
2 cups flour	of your choice
1 teaspoon baking powder	

Cream sugar and shortening together until light and fluffy. Add eggs and blend well. Sift flour, baking powder and soda together. Add to egg mixture alternately with milk, ending with flour and then fold in chopped nuts and fruit. Pour into an

8" x 8" x 2" greased and floured pan and bake at 375° for 35 to 40 minutes or until done. Dust top with confectioners' sugar.

Leftover compote, drained and chopped, makes a fruity tea cake. Substitute for 1 cup *fruit of your choice* listed in ingredients.

CREAM PUFFS

1 cup water	$\frac{1}{4}$ teaspoon salt
$\frac{1}{2}$ cup butter or margarine	1 cup sifted flour
4 medium eggs	

Combine water, butter, and salt in saucepan and bring to boiling; lower heat. Add flour all at once, beating thoroughly and rapidly. (I like a wooden spoon.) Beat until mixture forms ball and leaves the side of pan. Remove from heat and add eggs, one at a time; beat mixture thoroughly about one minute for each egg. Continue beating until dough is shiny and satiny and breaks away when spoon is raised.

For Large Cream Puffs

Drop 12 rounded tablespoonfuls, about 2 inches apart, on ungreased cooky sheet. Place in 450° oven and bake 15 minutes; reduce oven to 350°, then bake 30 minutes or until brown. Puffs should sound hollow when lightly tapped with fingertip. Turn out on wire rack to cool, avoiding drafts.

Cut off tops crosswise, using a sharp knife. Remove any bits of soft dough. Fill with ice cream, Whipped Cream Filling or Custard Filling. Replace tops and sprinkle with confectioners' sugar; or frost with Chocolate, Caramel, or Apricot Glaze; or serve with favorite sauce. Makes 12.

For Chocolate Puffs

Add $\frac{3}{4}$ cup Dutch type cocoa to flour.

For Tiny Puffs

Drop by rounded teaspoonful, 2 inches apart on ungreased cooky sheet. Bake in 400° oven for 15 minutes; reduce heat, and bake 10 minutes. Makes about 50 puffs.

Recipe may be halved. Use for hors d'oeuvres, or fill as for Large Cream Puffs.

Whipped Cream Filling

1 cup heavy cream	1 teaspoon vanilla
½ cup sifted confectioners' sugar	¼ teaspoon almond extract

In medium bowl, combine cream, sugar, and extracts. Refrigerate, covered, at least one hour — until very well chilled. Refrigerate rotary beater also, and beat mixture just until stiff. Makes 2 cups.

For Coffee Cream Filling, omit almond extract and add 2 teaspoons instant coffee.

Custard Filling

1½ cups milk	¼ teaspoon salt
¼ cup sugar	2 egg yolks
1½ tablespoons cornstarch	1 teaspoon vanilla

Pour milk into saucepan; heat until scalded (when bubbles form around edge of pan). Combine sugar, cornstarch, and salt; blend well and stir quickly into hot milk. Cook, continuing to stir, over medium heat, until mixture boils. Reduce heat, and simmer one minute. Beat a small amount of hot mixture into egg yolks, then return to saucepan; cook, stirring, over medium heat, until mixture boils and thickens. Stir in vanilla. Place a sheet of wax paper directly on the surface to prevent film forming. Refrigerate filling and refrigerate again when puffs are filled as a temperature safeguard. Makes approximately 1⅓ cups.

Chocolate Glaze

1 6-ounce package semisweet chocolate bits	2 tablespoons shortening
	2 tablespoons light corn syrup
3 tablespoons milk	

In top of double boiler, over hot, not boiling water, melt chocolate pieces with shortening. Add corn syrup and milk, stirring until smooth and well-blended. Let cool slightly, and pour warm glaze over cooled, filled cream puffs placed on wire rack, with pan underneath. Makes 1 cup.

Caramel Glaze

½ pound caramels   ¼ cup water

Remove paper wrapping from caramels. Place caramels in top of double boiler with water. Melt over hot, not boiling water. Stir to mix well. Pour warm glaze over cooked, filled cream puffs placed on a wire rack, with pan underneath. Makes ¾ cup.

Apricot Glaze

½ cup apricot preserves   1 tablespoon cognac

Heat preserves in saucepan just until melted; stir in cognac. Pour over puffs as for Caramel Glaze.

DATE AND NUT TORTE

½ pound butter
1 cup sugar
2 egg yolks, well beaten
1 cup sour cream
1 teaspoon baking soda
1 teaspoon vanilla

1 cup chopped walnuts
1 cup dates, pitted and finely cut
grated rind of 2 oranges
2½ cups cake flour
1 teaspoon baking powder
2 egg whites, beaten stiff

Topping: juice of 2 oranges

Cream butter and sugar together; beat in egg yolks. Combine sour cream with baking soda and mix with butter mixture. Blend in vanilla, walnuts, dates, and orange rind. Sift flour and baking powder together; add to other ingredients and beat well. Fold in beaten egg whites; pour into 9-inch greased spring tube pan. Place in 350° oven and bake one hour. Remove from oven and pour juice of oranges over the cake. Let cool and remove rim of pan.

DOUBLE CHOCOLATE CAKE

½ cup cocoa   pinch of salt
¾ cup boiling water   ½ teaspoon baking powder
¼ cup butter   ½ teaspoon soda
2 cups sugar   ½ cup sour cream
2 cups sifted cake flour   1 teaspoon vanilla
3 egg whites, stiffly beaten

Combine cocoa and boiling water to make a paste. Cool; cream
butter and sugar until fluffy; add cool cocoa paste and blend
well. Sift remaining dry ingredients together, then add alternately to sugar mixture with sour cream, mixing well. Add
vanilla, then fold in egg whites. Pour into 2 8-inch greased and
floured layer cake pans and bake in 350° oven 30 minutes.
Remove from pans; turn out on cake racks and when cool split
each layer in half. Spread layers and frost cake with Ice Cream
Frosting.

Ice Cream Frosting

2 cups confectioners' sugar   ½ teaspoon vanilla
½ cup milk   4 squares (4 ounces)
2 eggs   unsweetened
pinch of salt   chocolate
6 tablespoons butter

Combine sugar, milk, eggs, salt and vanilla in a mixing bowl.
Place in another bowl filled with ice and water. Melt chocolate
and butter in double boiler and while warm add to first mixture.
Beat with electric or rotary beater until thick enough to hold
its shape. Frost cake at once.

After introducing Fallen Torte on the Jim Conway television show from Chicago, I was deluged, delighted too, with requests for the recipe. Here is a re-run for those who weren't tuned in.

FALLEN TORTE

8 egg whites	1 teaspoon vanilla
dash salt	8 egg yolks
1¼ cups confectioners' sugar	Coffee Cream
½ cup cocoa	¼ cup shaved Chocolate Curls

Separate eggs and allow whites to stand about one hour at room temperature; add salt and beat until stiff and glossy, but not dry. Sift sugar and cocoa together and set aside. Add vanilla to yolks and beat until thick and lemon colored; blend in combined sugar and cocoa, then beat again until very thick. Fold in egg whites blending well and carefully; push the batter into ungreased 9-inch spring form and bake in 325° oven 40 to 45 minutes until set. Do not open the oven door while baking. Remove from oven and place on rack to cool. The *center will fall.* Fill with Coffee Cream and border with a sprinkling of shaved Chocolate Curls. Remove rim of spring form pan and place cake on doily-covered serving plate. Serves 8 to 10.

The cake may be assembled an hour in advance and refrigerated. It is delectable.

Coffee Cream

1 cup heavy cream, whipped	2 tablespoons confectioners' sugar
	1 tablespoon instant powdered coffee

Fold all ingredients together and blend well.

The whipped cream may be flavored with a substitute for the coffee, such as mint, liqueurs, rum or Dutch cocoa.

Chocolate Curls

With a vegetable peeler, shave thin strips from a bar of semi-sweet baking chocolate.

GOLD COAST CHEESE CAKE

Crust

26 graham crackers, finely crushed   ¾ cup melted butter

Combine crumbs and melted butter; line a 10-inch greased spring form with mixture, pressing against sides and bottom with back of spoon; set aside.

Cake Filling

2 8-ounce packages cream cheese,   1 cup sugar
      softened   1 teaspoon vanilla
5 whole eggs   1 teaspoon almond extract
                  2 tablespoons lemon juice

Cream the cheese until smooth and add remaining ingredients; mix and blend well. Pour into prepared spring form and place in 300° oven; bake 30 minutes. Remove from oven and place on cake rack until cooled.

Topping

1 quart sour cream   1 teaspoon almond extract
1 teaspoon vanilla   1 cup sugar

Combine topping ingredients and mix well. Spread over top of cake. Return to oven and bake 8 minutes in 475° oven. Place on rack, let cool thoroughly, then refrigerate overnight. Remove rim but not bottom, and place cake on doily-lined plate.

GOSSAMER ANGEL FOOD CAKE

1¾ cups egg whites (12 to 14)   1½ teaspoons cream of tartar
   ½ teaspoon salt   1 teaspoon vanilla extract
1¼ cups sifted cake flour   ½ teaspoon almond extract
1¾ cups sugar   powdered sugar

Be cautious and separate eggs one at a time in sauce dish before dropping into measuring cup. If a yolk breaks, only one egg is lost. Pour egg whites into large bowl of electric mixer, add salt and let stand until warmed to room temperature, about one hour.

Sift flour with ¾ cup sugar, then resift 3 more times; set aside. Beat egg whites at high speed until foamy, add cream of tartar; continue beating until soft peaks form when beaters are raised. Beat in remaining sugar, 2 tablespoons at a time, at moderate speed; beat well after each addition, and until *very stiff peaks* form; fold in extracts gently with wire whisk or rubber spatula. Sift flour mixture into egg white mixture, ¼ at a time, using 15 strokes of whisk while turning bowl. Caress the batter lovingly and gently; bring the whisk from underneath, up through the batter then over so that the mixture is aerated and well blended. Give it a final 15 strokes for good measure. Carefully push batter into ungreased 10-inch angel tube pan, pass a knife through batter, circling pan twice to break up air bubbles. Smooth top evenly and spread to edge of pan; bake on low rack in a 375° oven, 35 to 40 minutes or until done when tested. Remove and invert pan to cool about 2 hours; rest tube opening on mouth of soft drink bottle so cake cannot touch surface. Loosen sides and bottom with knife; around tube, the fineness of an ice pick is helpful. Turn out on cake plate; dust with powdered sugar, frost, fill or use in many suggested ways in desserts. Serves 12.

MACAROON TORTE

2 cups sugar	1 tablespoon almond extract
6 egg whites, beaten stiff	2 teaspoons baking powder
1½ cups finely crushed	1 quart fresh strawberries or
unsalted soda crackers	2 10-ounce packages
2 cups finely chopped pecans	frozen raspberries, defrosted
1 cup heavy cream, whipped	

Beat sugar gradually into shiny beaten egg whites; combine cracker crumbs, nuts, baking powder, and fold into egg whites; then fold in almond extract. Spread out in 2 well greased and floured 9-inch cake pans (the loose-bottomed type is recommended for this torte). Bake in 325° oven 40 minutes. Remove from pans while warm and turn on to racks to cool. To serve, place each layer on a cake plate; cover with 1 pint of berries, topped with whipped cream. Each cake serves 6.

You may layer the two cakes, using 1 package berries and 1 cup whipped cream between layers, with the other berries and cream over the top. Circle cream topping with ¼ cup frozen berries, drained, or fresh berries.

PEACHES AND CREAM CAKE

6 3-inch slices sponge cake	Custard Royale
4 cups sliced fresh peaches or	⅓ cup apricot jam
2 1-pound cans, drained	2 tablespoons water
1 tablespoon brandy	

Place cake on individual shallow dessert plates; cover with sliced peaches. Spoon Custard Royale over each and refrigerate until well chilled. Combine jam and water in a saucepan, heat until blended; add brandy and cool. To serve, pour cooled jam mixture over custard topped peaches. Serves 6.

Custard Royale
(Natilla Realeza)

This is a soft custard topping.

1½ cups milk	3 eggs, slightly beaten
½ cup sugar	1 tablespoon sherry
¼ teaspoon salt	2 teaspoons vanilla

Scald milk in upper part of double boiler and remove from heat. Mix sugar, salt, and eggs together and into it pour a small amount of scalded milk, stirring constantly, then return to remaining scalded milk in top of double boiler, continuing to stir. Cook over boiling water until mixture thickens and coats the mixing spoon with a thin film. Remove from heat, stir in sherry and vanilla. Cover, cool and refrigerate. Makes about 2 cups.

This sauce is a delicious topping for shortcake made with biscuit dough, or for a sponge cake base. I have used it with a base of butter crackers, heated, covered with fruit, then topped with the sauce. They are called Golden Puffs and are delectable.

RUM TORTE

1 6-egg sponge or Sunshine Cake, sliced into 4 layers

Filling

½ cup butter	6 tablespoons light rum
1 cup confectioners' sugar	1 tablespoon unflavored gelatine
4 egg yolks, beaten	2 tablespoons cold water

4 egg whites, stiffly beaten

Topping

1 cup heavy cream, whipped	1 teaspoon vanilla
1 tablespoon confectioners' sugar	¼ cup toasted almonds, slivered

Cream the butter with confectioners' sugar until fluffy. Beat in egg yolks and add ¼ cup rum (4 tablespoons). Sprinkle gelatine on water, then dissolve over heat while stirring. Blend into butter mixture; fold in egg whites and let stand in refrigerator 10 minutes, until just thick enough to spread. Sprinkle layers with remaining 2 tablespoons of rum and spread each with filling. If filling runs, scoop it up over cake. Place in refrigerator 2 to 6 hours until firm. Cut into 14 portions; do not separate; combine cream, sugar and vanilla; frost entire cake. Toss almonds over top and tuck a few lemon leaves around the base on the platter. Serves 14.

An angel cake serves very well.

SUNSHINE CAKE

6 eggs	1 cup sifted flour
1 cup sugar	1 teaspoon cream of tartar
1 teaspoon lemon extract	¼ teaspoon salt

Separate eggs; beat yolks until thick and lemon colored. Add ½ cup sugar and lemon extract, continuing to beat until well blended. Sift flour three times; combine with remaining ½ cup sugar and sift together. Place egg whites in large bowl; beat until frothy, then add cream of tartar and salt. Continue beating until stiff and shiny and soft peaks hold when beaters are raised. Fold flour mixture into egg yolk mixture carefully until well blended, then fold into egg whites, cutting through and over batter with a rubber spatula or wire beater to aerate as thoroughly as possible. Push the batter carefully into a 9-inch ungreased angel food pan and bake 20 minutes in 325° oven; raise temperature to 350° and bake an additional 20 to 25 minutes, or until cake springs back when dented with a finger. Invert on prongs of cake pan, or over mouth of soft drink bottle. Cool thoroughly. To remove, cut around pan with sharp knife. Serves 6.

To make a larger cake, increase recipe by adding ½ to original.

STRAWBERRY CLOUD CAKE

1 package frozen strawberries, defrosted and drained
¾ cup strawberry juice and   1 3-ounce package strawberry gelatine
    water   4 eggs
1 package white cake mix   ½ cup salad oil
Fluffy Frosting

Drain berries, measure juice and add sufficient water to make ¾ cup. Combine cake mix, gelatine, eggs, and beat with rotary beater or in electric mixer on low speed for 2 minutes. Add oil and liquid (juice and water) and beat for an additional 2 minutes. The batter will be thin. Fold in drained strawberries. Pour into greased and floured 9" x 13" pan or two 8-inch cake pans; place in a 350° oven and bake 35 minutes or until done when pierced with tester, or cake should spring back from touch of finger. Cool and frost with Fluffy Frosting, tinted pink, or with sweetened whipped cream; garnish with whole strawberries.

The flavor mellows as it stands. To bake this the previous day is a must. It makes a beautiful birthday cake, and with a drop or two of red coloring added to the frosting may well be the basis for complete pink party decor. Frost just before serving.

Fluffy Frosting
(7-minute)

2 egg whites	¼ teaspoon cream of tartar
1½ cups sugar	⅓ cup water
dash salt	1 teaspoon vanilla

Combine all ingredients except vanilla in top of double boiler and place over boiling water. Beat with rotary beater, preferably electric hand beater, about 7 minutes or until mixture puffs into fluffy thick consistency. Fold in vanilla and spread at once. Covers 1 large cake, or will fill and frost 2 8-inch layers.

For a smaller cake use

1 egg white	⅛ teaspoon cream of tartar
1½ cups sugar	¼ cup water
dash salt	1 teaspoon vanilla

Proceed as above.

For a mocha flavor

Beat in 1 teaspoon instant coffee just before removing from heat. Add it to taste, and increase the amount to 1½ teaspoons if you wish. Tint with a drop or two of vegetable coloring, as desired.

This standby is so old-fashioned that our specialty books tend to omit it. Added are themes for your choice: Here a shortcake ring.

STRAWBERRY SHORTCAKE DÉLICE

Standard Rich Biscuit Batter

2 cups sifted all-purpose flour	½ cup shortening, butter
2 tablespoons sugar	or half butter, half
½ teaspoon salt	vegetable shortening
4 teaspoons baking powder	1 egg beaten
⅔ cup half and half cream	

Short cake topping

soft butter	flat green leaves
2 pints strawberries, sliced,	6 large reserved berries
sugared to taste	Cream Délice

Sift flour, sugar, salt and baking powder together into a large bowl. Cut in shortening with knives or a pastry blender, as for pie. It should resemble coarse meal. Combine egg and cream; pour into flour mixture using just sufficient to bind. Turn onto a floured board; knead gently about 15 times. Roll or pat to ¼-inch thickness and spread in greased 9-inch ring mold. Place in 450° oven and bake 15 to 18 minutes until golden brown. Remove to cake rack; cool about 3 minutes, then turn out and split into 2 layers. Spread bottom layer with soft butter; carefully arrange on serving platter and cover bottom layer with half the berries; add top layer and cover with remaining berries. Arrange leaves and clusters of whole berries as a border. Fill center with Cream Délice and sprinkle with additional brown sugar. Serves 6 to 8.

To form dough into proper size

Roll it, then cut with edge of floured 9-inch ring mold turned upside down.

Cream Délice

2 cups sour cream	4 tablespoons light brown sugar sifted
	1 tablespoon kirsch (optional)

Combine sour cream, brown sugar and kirsch; blend well.

Make individual servings by rolling dough and cutting into 2½-inch circles. Bake about 10 minutes.

For topping use 1 cup heavy cream, whipped, ⅛ teaspoon nutmeg, and ½ teaspoon grated orange peel.

Omit kirsch and add 1 teaspoon grated orange peel to sour cream.

Line an 8-inch shallow square pan with dough, split the layers, spread with half the berries and half whipped cream, cover with second layer and repeat. Use 1 cup heavy cream, whipped and sweetened, if desired.

TOASTED MERINGUE SPICE CAKE

¾ cup butter
2 cups brown sugar
2 egg yolks, well beaten
2⅓ cups flour
1 teaspoon baking powder
1 teaspoon ground cloves

1 teaspoon ground cinnamon
¾ teaspoon salt
1 teaspoon soda
1¼ cups sour milk or buttermilk
1 teaspoon vanilla
Meringue

Cream butter and sugar until light and fluffy; add beaten egg yolks. Sift together flour, baking powder, cloves, cinnamon, salt. Dissolve soda in milk; beat into butter mixture alternately with dry ingredients. Add vanilla and blend well. Pour into greased 9" x 13" pan. Spread with Meringue and bake at 325° for 50 minutes or until done when tested. Cool in pan on rack, then cut into 3-inch pieces. Makes 12 squares.

Meringue

1 cup firmly packed brown sugar   3 egg whites, beaten stiff
¼ cup coarsely chopped pecans

Sift sugar into beaten egg whites, beating until smooth, thick and glossy. Spread over cake; sprinkle with chopped nuts and bake as directed.

TOFFEE BAR CAKE

2 cups sifted flour
2 cups brown sugar, firmly packed
¼ pound butter or margarine
1 teaspoon baking soda
½ teaspoon salt
1 teaspoon vanilla

1 egg, slightly beaten
1 cup milk
4 1½-ounce almond toffee bars (candy), coarsely crushed
½ cup chopped nuts

Mix flour and brown sugar together; cut in butter as for pie crust until consistency of coarse meal. Reserve ¾ cup of this crumb mixture for topping. Add baking soda, salt, vanilla, egg and milk to remainder and beat well. Pour into 9" x 13" greased baking pan. Mix reserved crumbs with crushed toffee bars and nuts; sprinkle evenly over top of batter. Bake in 350°

oven 30 to 35 minutes. To serve, cut in 3-inch squares. Makes 12 portions.

A good old-timer!

UPSIDE DOWN CAKE

Brown Sugar Fruit Glaze

1 1-pound can sliced pineapple, drained or 1 1-pound can peaches or apricots, drained

½ cup brown sugar
¼ cup butter, melted
12 maraschino cherries or walnut halves

Melt butter and brown sugar in an 8-inch round baking pan 3″ deep or in an 8″ iron skillet. Place fruit cut side down with cherry or walnut underneath in center, to form a pattern when turned out.

Cake Batter

¼ cup butter
½ cup sugar
1 cup cake flour
½ teaspoon salt

1½ teaspoons baking powder
1 egg
½ cup milk
½ teaspoon vanilla

½ teaspoon almond extract

Cream butter and sugar together. Sift flour, salt and baking powder together, then add to butter mixture. Add egg, milk, and flavorings; beat well. Pour over fruit and brown sugar glaze in pan. Bake in 350° oven 45 minutes. Remove from oven and let cool 5 minutes, then invert over cake plate. Serve warm with whipped cream if desired. Serves 6 to 8.

WONDERFUL CHOCOLATE CAKE

2 1-ounce squares unsweetened chocolate	1½ cups sugar
	2 eggs, well beaten
½ cup water	2 cups sifted cake flour
6 tablespoons butter or margarine	1 teaspoon baking soda
	1 cup sour cream

1 teaspoon vanilla

Place chocolate and water in top of double boiler and heat until chocolate is melted. Cream butter and sugar together. If using electric mixer, beat only at low speed, just enough to blend thoroughly; stir in eggs only until mixed. Sift flour again with baking soda, then add to butter mixture, alternately with sour cream; mix lightly, starting and ending with flour. Blend in chocolate mixture and vanilla. Bake in a 9″ x 13″ x 2″ pan, well greased, at 350° for 40 to 45 minutes or until cake pulls away from sides of pan. Dust with confectioners' sugar or frost with Glossy Chocolate Frosting. Cut into 3-inch squares.

Glossy Chocolate Frosting

3 1-ounce squares unsweetened chocolate	¼ cup water
	1 cup sugar
¾ cup evaporated milk	dash salt

1 teaspoon vanilla

Melt chocolate in top of double boiler; combine milk, water, sugar, salt, and stir into chocolate. Cook over hot water 20 minutes, then beat with rotary beater 1 minute or until smooth. Stir in vanilla; cool.

This icing may be made in advance. It will store well in refrigerator, tightly sealed.

Morsels and Muffins

ALMOND ZWIEBACK

6 egg whites, stiffly beaten
¾ cup sugar
1 cup flour, sifted
1 teaspoon baking powder
⅓ cup melted butter

1 teaspoon vanilla
¼ cup finely slivered almonds, toasted
⅓ cup confectioners' sugar, sifted

Beat egg whites until glossy but not dry, then beat in sugar gradually, 2 tablespoons at a time, until well blended. Sift flour with baking powder and fold into egg whites alternately with melted butter; blend in vanilla. Push gently into greased 9″ x 5″ loaf pan and sprinkle with almonds. Bake in 350° oven 40 minutes or until golden brown. Cool and remove from pan; wrap in foil or plastic wrap and let stand overnight. Cut in ½-inch slices across width, as for bread, and coat with confectioners' sugar on both sides. Place slices on cooky sheet and toast in 350° oven about 15 minutes or until lightly browned. Remove from pan and cool until crisp and crunchy. Makes about 18.

To toast almonds

Melt 1 tablespoon butter in small skillet and add ¼ cup slivered almonds. Stir over medium heat until browned; watch carefully as the nuts burn quickly.

BLACK CHERRY MUFFINS

1½ cups flour
¼ cup sugar
2½ teaspoons baking powder
½ teaspoon salt
¾ cup milk

3 tablespoons melted butter or margarine
1 egg, well beaten
¾ cup pitted sweet cherries or drained canned cherries

Sift flour, sugar, baking powder and salt into mixing bowl.

Beat milk, butter and egg together; add to dry ingredients and stir just sufficiently to blend in flour; batter should be lumpy. Fold in cherries lightly and spoon into well-greased muffin tins, filling ⅔ full. Bake in 400° oven 25 to 30 minutes for 3-inch muffins, 15 to 18 minutes for 2-inch muffins, or until golden brown. Makes 8 3-inch muffins; 14 2-inch muffins.

Though fresh sweet cherries have their particular delicacy, canned drained cherries may be substituted.

CINNAMON STRIPS

⅓ cup brown sugar   1 1-pound loaf unsliced bread
⅓ cup granulated sugar   ½ cup butter or margarine,
1 tablespoon cinnamon   melted

Combine brown sugar, granulated sugar, and cinnamon. Remove crust from bread and cut into 1-inch slices. Cut each into 3 strips. Roll lightly in butter, then in sugar mixture, coating well. Place on a cooky sheet and bake in 350° oven for 15 minutes. Makes 15 strips.

LOCKSMITH'S APPRENTICES

12 large prunes   Cream Cheese Pastry
12 blanched almonds   confectioners' sugar

Wash prunes and soak overnight in water to cover. Cook for about 15 minutes in water in which they were soaked; do not permit prunes to become too soft. If a sweeter taste is desired, add sufficient sugar the last 5 minutes of cooking. Cool; remove pits and replace with an almond. Place each on a 2½-inch round of pastry; cover with a second round; seal firmly with tines of a fork. Bake in 450° oven 15 minutes; remove from oven and dust with confectioners' sugar. Makes 12 "Apprentices."

Use halved walnuts instead of almonds. Good, too.

This recipe may be doubled. Use dried apricots instead of nuts for another variety.

Do not worry if the prune mashes in removing the pit. Nonchalantly shape it around the nut and proceed; it tastes just as great.

Kitchen Sorcery

The word Apprentice reminds me of a favorite tale. In a fervid burst of cleaning energy, a young housewife poured detergent into her dishwasher, and found herself overrun with billows of bubbles. Like a modern Sorcerer's Apprentice, the more she tried to stop them, the thicker and faster they multiplied, seeping through the closed cover of the machine in glistening globules, trailing onto the floor. Frantic attempts to dissolve the accumulation only caused it to multiply. In desperation she called her knowing contemporaries, one of whom finally gave her the magic formula — a cup of vinegar. Quickly she poured it down the drain, and the towering foam submissively collapsed and followed.

The delightful old story of the Sorcerer's Apprentice has been set to exciting, descriptive music by the composer Dukas. The Apprentice had been warned not to tamper with secret devices during the Sorcerer's absence, but temptation was too great. Carrying the water from the well proved a burdensome task, and with sly decision he transformed the broom into an animate object, as a helpmate. The broom went to work with speed and vigor; filled the receptacle to overflowing, continuing the appointed task until all was deluged, while the Apprentice dashed about in frantic, fruitless effort to stop the catastrophe. He did not know the magic stop order. Eventually the Sorcerer returned and performed the proper hocus-pocus, which, like the cup of vinegar our housewife used, curtailed the flow. He vented his ire upon his apprentice to increased tempo in the climax of the composition.

PECAN BANANA BREAD

⅓ cup butter or margarine	½ teaspoon salt
1 cup sugar	2 teaspoons baking powder
2 eggs	½ teaspoon soda
1 cup mashed bananas	1 cup chopped pecans
(2 bananas)	1½ tablespoons milk or
2 cups flour	buttermilk

Cream together the butter and sugar; beat in eggs thoroughly;

add bananas, blending well. Sift together flour, salt, baking powder, and soda, then add nuts. Stir dry ingredients into creamed butter and sugar alternately with milk. Stir until well blended, then spoon into well greased 9" x 5" loaf pan. Bake at 350° for one hour.

SPEEDY MONKEY BREAD

3 packages prepared refrigerated buttermilk biscuits

½ cup melted butter or margarine

Remove biscuits from package; cut each in half. Dip the pieces in melted butter and place in 9" x 5" loaf pan. Layer until all are used. Bake according to package directions. Makes 1 loaf. Each guest pulls his portion.

WHOLE WHEAT MUFFINS

1 cup 100% whole wheat flour
½ cup all-purpose flour
2 teaspoons baking powder
2 teaspoons sugar
½ teaspoon salt
¼ teaspoon pumpkin pie spice or cinnamon

⅓ cup non-fat milk powder
¾ cup water
1 egg white, slightly beaten
2 tablespoons melted butter
2 tablespoons melted vegetable shortening

Pour whole wheat flour into bowl; combine all-purpose flour, baking powder, sugar, salt, spice, and sift into whole wheat flour, blending well. In another bowl, dissolve milk powder in water, then add egg white, butter, and vegetable shortening; mix well. Pour liquid mixture into dry ingredients, mixing quickly and only sufficiently to dampen flour evenly. The mixture will be slightly lumpy; do *not* stir until smooth. Pour into 6 3-inch greased muffin tins and place in 425° oven; bake 15 to 20 minutes until lightly browned or done when tested. Makes 6 large muffins or 8 medium.

To test cakes

The old-fashioned straws plucked from our kitchen brooms

have been replaced by slim metal spears available at the variety stores. Pierce your cakes (or muffins) gently and if clear when removed, your recipe is done.

For a diet need

Use wheat germ instead of all-purpose flour, and substitute vegetable shortening for the butter, using 4 tablespoons vegetable shortening in all. Delicious both ways.

WONDROUS POPOVERS

2 eggs, slightly beaten	1 cup instantized flour
1 cup milk	½ teaspoon salt

Grease 6 deep custard cups or muffin cups heavily. Combine eggs, milk, flour and salt. Stir just until smooth; do not beat. Fill custard cups ½ full, or muffin tins ¾ full. Bake in 425° oven 40 to 45 minutes or until deep golden brown. Remove from cups immediately and serve at once, with preserves, and lots of butter.

Ovenware glass cups make higher popovers, easier to remove. These popovers make excellent cases for creamed dishes.

The Pie Cycle

PASTRY LEAVES AND FANCIES

When making pie crust, form a ball of remaining scraps; roll as thin as possible, then cut into ornate shapes:

Leaves to top a top-crusted pie   Christmas trees
Hatchets for Washington's birthday   Bells

or what pleases you.

For the decoration on top of a crust, place it on crust before baking; moisten your "cut-outs" and place in design. For an open pie, place the cut-outs on a cooky sheet and bake 10 to 15 minutes or until golden. To serve, place them over the filling after pie is baked.

For lattice tops, cut ½-inch strips of pastry, attach parallel strips to one side, weaving in opposite strands. The entire top may be woven on wax paper and chilled, then flipped over the pie. Seal ends to the rim.

Brushing with the slightly beaten yolk of egg produces a brown glow. The white of egg gives gloss but does not offer the depth of brown.

CREAM CHEESE PASTRY

1 cup butter, softened	¼ cup sour cream
1 cup (1 8-ounce package) cream cheese, softened	2½ cups flour
	1 teaspoon salt

The butter and cream cheese should be at room temperature. Cream together and beat in the sour cream. Add flour and salt gradually; continue beating by hand. Pat dough into a flat disk; wrap in wax paper, and chill several hours. Bake as directed for individual recipes.

This dough is good for filled cookies, pies, filled hors d'oeuvres and filled tarts. It freezes well for several weeks; before freezing, shape and/or fill and do not thaw before baking. The general rule for small tarts is 400° for 20 to 25 minutes.

MARVELOUS PIE CRUST
(single crust)

¼ cup cold water	1¼ cups instantized flour
½ cup shortening	½ teaspoon salt

Measure ingredients into small bowl of electric mixer and turn on speed to lowest point until dough forms, 15 to 30 seconds. Shape into firm ball, flatten on wax paper and roll between 2 floured sheets to ⅛-inch thickness. For pie shell, fit into pan, trim edges allowing 1 inch overdrop, then tuck it under, even with rim; flute with fork or fingers. Prick well, bake in 450° oven 10 to 12 minutes.

For double crust

2 cups instantized flour	⅓ cup plus 1 tablespoon water
¾ cups shortening	1 teaspoon salt

This method works only with instantantized flour.

COGNAC ANGEL PIE

Meringue Shell

2 egg whites	¼ teaspoon cream of tartar
⅛ teaspoon salt	½ cup sugar
	½ teaspoon vanilla

Cognac Custard

Place egg whites in large bowl (the electric mixer is fine) and beat until frothy. Add salt and cream of tartar; beat until soft peaks form. Add sugar, 2 tablespoons at a time, beating after each addition until sugar is blended. Continue beating until mixture stands in very stiff peaks, then fold in vanilla. Spoon into lightly greased 8-inch pie pan; make a nestlike shell, building sides up ½-inch above edge of pan. Bake at 300° for 50 to 55 minutes. Remove from oven and cool to room temperature; fill with Cognac Custard or Chocolate Filling, if preferred. 6 to 8 servings.

Cognac Custard

1½ cups milk	dash salt
1 3-ounce package vanilla pudding and pie filling mix	2 tablespoons cognac
	1 teaspoon rum flavoring
2 egg yolks, well beaten	½ cup sour cream
Garnish: Chocolate Curls	

Combine milk and vanilla pudding mix in saucepan. Place over medium heat and stir until a rolling boil is reached. Stir small amount of custard gradually into the yolks, then return to pudding mixture. Cook, stirring for 5 minutes; add salt, cognac, rum flavoring, then gently fold in sour cream. Pour into cooled Meringue Shell.

For a soufflé-like crust place in refrigerator 4 to 5 hours or overnight. To serve, decorate with border of Chocolate Curls.

If a crisp meringue crust is preferred, prepare pie the same day. Do not refrigerate; instead, assemble pie 1 hour before serving. The custard may be made in advance and refrigerated, but do not place shell in refrigerator, as chilling softens meringue.

For an alternate, use Chocolate Filling recipe.

Chocolate Filling

1 package (1/4 pound) sweet chocolate	3 tablespoons water
	1 teaspoon vanilla
1 cup heavy cream, whipped	

Place chocolate and water in saucepan over low heat. Stir until chocolate is melted; cool until thickened; add vanilla. Fold chocolate mixture into whipped cream; pile lightly into meringue shell. Chill 2 hours before serving. Makes 6 to 8 servings.

Either filling is a delicious custard dessert. Serve in sherbet glasses, and add a cooky.

CONCORD GRAPE PIE

4 cups Concord grapes	dash powdered cloves
1 cup sugar	2 egg yolks, beaten
1/8 teaspoon salt	2 egg whites, beaten stiff
2 tablespoons flour	1 tablespoon butter or margarine
1 unbaked 2-crust pie shell with lattice strips	

Remove grape stems. Pop each grape out of its skin; reserve the skins. Pour pulp into a saucepan, heat to boiling. Press through a sieve to remove seeds, and add pulp to reserved grape skins. Mix together sugar, salt, flour, and cloves; sprinkle 2 tablespoons of this mixture on the bottom of pastry-lined pie pan; mix remainder with the grapes. Add egg yolks, then fold in egg whites carefully. Fill the pie shell, dot with butter and adjust top crust or lattice strips across pie. Bake 45 minutes in 425° oven. Serves 6.

See Index for pie crust.

LEMON CHEESE PIE

20 vanilla wafers	1 8-ounce package cream cheese
⅓ cup melted butter	2 cups milk
⅛ teaspoon cinnamon	½ lemon, juice and grated rind
1 package instant lemon pudding	

Roll vanilla wafers between sheets of wax paper until finely crumbled. Add butter and cinnamon, mix thoroughly; reserve ⅓ cup for topping. Press remaining crumb mixture in 8-inch pie pan to make an even crust. Bake in 350° oven 5 minutes, cool. Soften cream cheese and mix well with one cup of milk; add juice and rind of lemon, then second cup of milk and instant pudding. Stir only until well mixed, pour into cooled shell and spread remaining crumbs over the top of filling. Chill a minimum of 2 hours or until cold and set. Serves 6.

This is a timesaving delicious dessert, as it may be made either early in the day or the previous day.

Hazel, who has been with us lo, these many years, is a great pie and potato maker, best among her many preparations. To glean this pie recipe was a major achievement, for she "just does this" or "puts in that" and somehow I couldn't often divide the sum into component parts. The following is a "high and mighty" facsimile.

LEMON MERINGUE PIE

Flaky Pie Crust

> 1¼ cups flour   ¼ teaspoon baking powder
> ¼ teaspoon salt   ½ cup vegetable shortening or lard
>   2 tablespoons ice water (approximately)

Have ingredients cold. Sift flour, salt, and baking powder together. Cut the shortening into flour mixture with 2 knives or pastry blender until consistency of small peas. Add water very slowly, tossing dough until just sufficient to hold it together. Turn out on lightly floured wax paper; cover with second sheet of paper. Roll ¼-inch thick until 1-inch larger than diameter of 9-inch pan. Fit loosely into pan; trim edges evenly, then turn back to make a rim and flute with fingers or edging cutter. Refrigerate ½ hour before baking. Bake in 425° oven 12 minutes or until lightly browned. Cool, pour in Lemon Filling, spread with Meringue, sealing well at crust to prevent shrinking. Bake in preheated 350° oven 12 minutes. Serves 6 to 8.

Lemon Filling

> 1 cup sugar   1 tablespoon butter or margarine
> ¼ cup cornstarch   grated rind of 1 lemon
> 1½ cups boiling water   juice of 2 lemons (about ⅓ cup)
> 4 egg yolks, beaten well   2 tablespoons meringue (from topping)

Combine sugar and cornstarch in top of double boiler; add boiling water slowly and simmer until clear, stirring constantly. Add yolks gradually, stirring constantly, then add butter. Cook over boiling water until thickened sufficiently to hold its shape when dropped from a spoon. Place pan of filling in pan of cold water to cool quickly. While cooling, fold in 2 tablespoons of meringue.

Meringue Topping

> ⅛ teaspoon salt   ¼ teaspoon cream of tartar
> 4 egg whites   ½ cup sugar
>   ¼ teaspoon lemon juice

Add salt to egg whites and beat until foamy. Add cream of

tartar and beat until soft peaks hold when beaters are raised. Add sugar, 1 tablespoon at a time, beating well, until thick and glossy; fold in lemon juice.

MILE HIGH STRAWBERRY PIE

Make the crust first — to prepare pie shell

Half Mile High Crust

1½ cups flour	1 teaspoon salt
½ teaspoon sugar	½ cup salad oil
2 tablespoons milk	

Sift flour, sugar, and salt into 10″ spring form pan. Combine oil and milk in measuring cup and pour over flour mixture in pan; blend all ingredients well. Press firmly into bottom and about 1 inch up the sides of pan. Place in 425° oven and bake 12 to 15 minutes or until lightly browned. Set aside to cool while Mile High Filling is being prepared.

Mile High Filling

2 egg whites	⅔ cup sugar
1 16-ounce package frozen	1 tablespoon lemon juice
strawberries, defrosted	1 teaspoon vanilla
and drained	1 cup heavy cream, whipped
Garnish: fresh strawberries, lemon leaves	

Break egg whites into large bowl of electric mixer and beat slightly; add strawberries, sugar, and lemon juice. Beat 15 minutes at high speed until mixture holds firm peaks. Fold vanilla into whipped cream, then fold into strawberry mixture. Pile lightly into prepared spring form pan; place in freezer a minimum of 12 hours (overnight). Remove 15 minutes before serving and garnish with fresh berries. Loosen crust from rim with a sharp knife, then place pie with pan bottom on serving platter. For a special look, border with leaves and beautiful berries. Serves 8 to 10.

This dessert freezes very well and may be made several days in advance.

PUMPKIN CHIFFON PIE

¾ cup milk	2 tablespoons (2 envelopes)
2¼ cups canned pumpkin	unflavored gelatine
1½ cups brown sugar	⅓ cup cold water
⅛ teaspoon salt	1½ cups heavy cream, whipped
¾ teaspoon ginger	¾ teaspoon grated orange rind
¾ teaspoon cinnamon	⅓ cup sugar
⅓ teaspoon nutmeg	Caramelized Almonds
5 large eggs, separated	1 10-inch pie shell, baked

Combine milk, drained pumpkin, sugar, salt, ginger, cinnamon, nutmeg in top of double boiler; heat to boiling; place over hot water in double boiler. Beat egg yolks slightly and stir in a small amount of milk mixture, then pour back into top of boiler. Cook, stirring until thickened. Add gelatine to cold water and soak for 5 minutes; add to milk and pumpkin mixture, stirring until dissolved and until mixture thickens and coats a silver spoon. Cool slightly. Beat egg whites until stiff and glossy but not dry, and fold in. Place in refrigerator and chill, but do not allow it to set. Combine whipped cream, orange rind, and ⅓ cup sugar, then fold into pumpkin mixture; chill again until thick but not set, and pour into pie shell. Refrigerate until set. To serve, sprinkle with Caramelized Almonds. Serves 8.

To Caramelize Almonds

Combine ¼ cup sugar and 1 cup slivered almonds in skillet and place over low heat. Stir constantly and briskly until sugar melts to a light brown. Watch carefully that it does not burn. Pour into 9-inch buttered shallow pan and let set. Crumble into small pieces.

This is really candy Almond Brittle; Peanut Brittle may be made the same way. Break into convenient-sized pieces.

Spanish Acquisition

Though we think of Sweet Potato Pie as our very own Southern claim, it was Henry VIII of England who, because of his fondness for sweet potatoes, first had them turned into a pie filling. The potatoes had come to him by way of Spain, brought back by Cortez from the New World.

SWEET POTATO PIE

1 16-ounce can sweet potatoes	2 eggs, slightly beaten
¼ teaspoon nutmeg	¼ cup butter or margarine
¼ teaspoon allspice	1 cup evaporated milk
½ teaspoon cinnamon	¼ cup coarsely chopped nuts
½ teaspoon salt	2 tablespoons cognac (optional)
½ cup sugar	1 unbaked 9-inch pastry shell

Drain potatoes, saving liquid. Add water sufficient to make ½ cup. Mash potatoes in a medium-size saucepan; add liquid and cook over medium heat until mixture reaches simmering point. Remove from heat and stir in spices, salt, sugar, eggs, butter, and evaporated milk. Return to low heat and cook for 5 minutes, stirring constantly until butter is melted. Stir in nuts and, if desired, 2 tablespoons cognac. Pour into pastry shell. Bake in 425° oven 20 to 25 minutes. Cool on rack. Decorate with Pastry Leaves. Serves 6 to 8.

Cooky Jar

BUTTER CRISPS

1 cup butter	1 teaspoon baking soda
1¼ cups sugar	1 teaspoon cream of tartar
4 egg yolks, beaten	2 cups flour
1 teaspoon vanilla or almond extract	

Cream butter and sugar together; add egg yolks and mix well. Combine baking soda, cream of tartar, flour and add to cooky mixture; add vanilla and blend thoroughly. Roll into a ball; wrap in wax paper; place in refrigerator overnight. Break off pieces the size of large marbles; flour hands well and roll balls

between palms. Place on cooky sheet 1 inch apart; bake in 375°
oven about 10 minutes or until lightly brown. Makes about
4 dozen.

CHOCOLATE MINT STRIPS

2 1-ounce squares unsweetened chocolate
½ cup butter or margarine
2 eggs
1 cup sugar
½ teaspoon peppermint extract
½ cup sifted flour
dash salt
½ cup chopped unblanched almonds
Peppermint Icing
Chocolate Glaze

Melt chocolate with butter in top of double boiler over hot
water. Beat eggs until frothy; stir in sugar, chocolate mixture
and peppermint extract. Add flour, salt, almonds; mix thoroughly. Pour and spread in well-greased 9-inch square pan.
Place in 350° oven and bake 20 to 25 minutes. Remove and cool
on racks. Spread top with thin coating of Peppermint Icing and
place in refrigerator. When cold, drizzle Chocolate Glaze over
icing. Tilt cake back and forth until glaze covers surface.
Cut into 1″ x 3″ strips. Makes 27 strips.

Peppermint Icing

2 tablespoons soft butter or margarine
1 cup sifted confectioners' sugar
1 tablespoon cream
¾ teaspoon peppermint extract

Cream butter and sugar; add cream and extract. Stir until
smooth.

Chocolate Glaze

½ 1-ounce square unsweetened chocolate
1 tablespoon butter or margarine

Melt chocolate and butter in double boiler over hot water. Mix
thoroughly.

These professional-looking pastries deserve a proper salute from their musical namesake.

CORNETS DOLCE

The recipe stated "2 eggs; weigh them with their shells and add the same weight of sugar, butter and flour." The eggs I used were medium large, and the measurements went this way when weighed on my slim little recipe scale. I used the electric mixer.

Cornets

2 eggs
1 cup confectioners' sugar
6 tablespoons butter or margarine, melted

1⅓ cups flour
½ teaspoon almond extract
dash salt

Break eggs into bowl of electric mixer; beat until creamy; add sugar and beat again until light and fluffy. Pour in butter gradually while continuing to beat, then blend in flour, almond extract and salt; beat at medium speed for 5 minutes. Butter a cooky sheet well, and drop 1 tablespoon of batter for each cornet. Spread in a thin oval with a rubber spatula; allow space as cooky will spread to about 5 inches in length. Bake in 375° oven 8 to 10 minutes or until edges are golden. Turn off oven; open oven door but do not remove cooky sheet; instead, carefully remove cornets one at a time with a broad pancake turner. Keep others warm, as they will crack if rolled when cool. Roll each gently in hands or around the handle of a wooden spoon to form cornucopias or cornets. The household departments sell cornet molds, but I find this way as convenient. Place on platter in one layer to cool. Serve plain or with Vanilla Cream.

Vanilla Cream

1 cup heavy cream, whipped
2 tablespoons confectioners' sugar

½ teaspoon vanilla
strawberry jam or 24 fresh strawberries

Combine the whipped cream with the sugar and vanilla, beating them together; spoon into cornets dotting with jam or a luscious berry. Makes 24.

The cornets may be made in advance and stored in an airtight tin. Do not fill them too early, as they may become soggy.

Mocha Cream is a delicious filling. Top with a strawberry.

Ice cream, your choice of flavor, is always good.

Note: do not bake more than 4 at one time.

HEIRLOOM COOKIES

Crust

¼ pound butter or margarine, softened	1 3-ounce package cream cheese, softened

1 cup plus 2 tablespoons flour
Walnut Filling

Combine ingredients except filling, mixing well; roll to ¼ inch thickness. Cut with 3-inch round cooky cutter. Place rounds loosely into 2½-inch muffin tins; fill with Walnut Filling.

Walnut Filling

¾ stick butter or margarine	1 cup chopped walnuts
¾ cup sugar	1 cup chopped raisins
3 egg yolks, well beaten	3 egg whites, well beaten

1 teaspoon vanilla

Melt butter and add sugar; add egg yolks, nuts and raisins. Fold mixture into egg whites; fold in vanilla. Fill pastry-lined cups and bake in 325° oven about 40 minutes. Watch carefully the last 10 minutes of baking so that cookies do not brown too much. Makes approximately 2 dozen.

'LASSES LACE

1 cup sifted cake flour	¼ teaspoon cinnamon
⅔ cup sugar	⅛ teaspoon salt
2 teaspoons instant coffee	½ cup molasses

½ cup butter or margarine

Sift flour, sugar, coffee, cinnamon and salt together. Pour

molasses into saucepan; bring to boil and add butter; stir until melted. Add flour mixture gradually, about ¼ cup at a time, blending well after each addition. Drop by level teaspoonsful, 4 inches apart, on greased cooky sheet. Place in 350° oven and bake 7 to 8 minutes, until bubbling stops and cookies are lightly browned around edges. Remove from oven and let stand 1 minute. Raise cookies from sheet with a 4-inch spatula; if they start to crinkle, delay a moment until they become firm enough to lift from pan. Remove and roll into cornucopias, placing seam side down on wire rack. While one batch is baking, start second batch on another sheet. If wafers become too firm to roll, return to hot oven for a second and they will become pliable. Timing is the secret here; after you have made the first few, the rest will proceed easily and are a distinct achievement. Makes about 4 dozen.

For a "conversation piece" dessert, make larger cookies and fill with ice cream or Coffee Cream. Use a generous rounded teaspoon of batter for each; roll the cornucopia with a wide flare. Makes about 30.

Serve in a wheel on a lace paper doily and border with green leaves. They will keep well for an indefinite time in airtight containers or plastic bags. Pack carefully in single layers.

Note: bake only 3 at one time.

PUNCH COOKIES

¾ pound butter or margarine	3 cups flour
3 egg yolks	1 teaspoon vanilla
1 cup sugar	currant jelly

Cream butter, egg yolks and sugar together. Add flour and vanilla; blend thoroughly. Refrigerate dough overnight. Pinch off pieces of dough to form round marble-sized cookies; punch a depression in the center with finger or thimble. Drop about ½ teaspoon jelly in each depression. Refrigerate again until firm, and bake on ungreased cooky sheet at 350° for 12 minutes. Makes about 4 dozen.

SOUTHERN PECAN BARS

Cooky Crust

1⅓ cups flour
½ teaspoon baking powder
⅓ cup butter
½ cup firmly packed dark brown
    sugar

¼ cup finely chopped pecans
30 pecan halves
Pecan Topping

Sift flour and baking powder together. Cream butter; add sugar gradually and cream until fluffy. Mix in dry ingredients until very fine; use a wooden spoon or electric mixer. Stir in chopped pecans and mix well. Pat firmly into bottom of well-greased 13″ x 9″ x 2″ pan. Bake in 350° oven 10 minutes. Pour Pecan Topping over, and dot evenly with pecan halves to center each bar. Bake in 350° oven 25 to 30 minutes. Let cool in pan, then cut into 30 bars. Stores well in airtight containers. Makes about 2½ dozen bars, 3 inches x 1¼ inches.

Pecan Topping

2 eggs, well beaten
¼ cup firmly packed dark brown
    sugar
¾ cup dark corn syrup

3 tablespoons flour
½ teaspoon salt
1 teaspoon vanilla
¾ cup coarsely chopped pecans

Beat eggs until foamy and cream with sugar; blend in corn syrup. Add flour, salt and vanilla; then stir in coarsely chopped pecans. Mix thoroughly.

Happy Ending

The Light Touch: Soufflés and Mousses

CHARLOTTE RUSSE

2 dozen ladyfingers   Bavarian Cream

Line Charlotte mold, or 9-inch spring form pan, with lady-fingers, fitting them into the bottom so they radiate from the center. Stand them around the sides, close together. Fill with Bavarian Cream.

Bavarian Cream

1 tablespoon unflavored gelatine	1 cup milk
2 tablespoons water	2 teaspoons vanilla
⅓ cup sugar	1 cup heavy cream, whipped
3 egg yolks	3 egg whites, stiffly beaten

Add gelatine to water and let stand 5 minutes to soften. Beat sugar and egg yolks until smooth and creamy. Scald milk; add to egg yolk mixture gradually. Return to saucepan in which milk was scalded and cook slowly, stirring constantly, until it comes to the boiling point. Do not allow to boil. Remove from heat; add vanilla and gelatine. Cool; stirring vigorously at first, while it is still hot and then occasionally to prevent a skin from forming on top. Before mixture becomes stiff, fold in whipped cream and stiffly beaten egg whites. Pour into prepared mold and refrigerate. To serve, turn out on platter; border with a row of whipped cream and stud with candied cherries. Serves 10 to 12.

CHERRY KÜMMEL SOUFFLÉ CAKE

¾ cup sugar	½ teaspoon salt
¼ cup butter	2½ teaspoons baking powder
1 egg	⅔ cup milk
1 teaspoon Kümmel (a liqueur)	1 cup pitted fresh sweet
½ teaspoon lemon extract	cherries or 1 cup canned
1¾ cups sifted flour	sweet cherries, drained

Cherry Sauce

Cream sugar and butter; add egg and beat until smooth and fluffy. Blend in Kümmel and extract; sift flour, salt and baking powder together; add to batter alternately with milk, beating each time until smooth. Fold in cherries, and pour into an 8" x 8" greased pan. Bake at 350° for 35 to 40 minutes or until middle tests done. (A knife slipped into center will be clean when withdrawn.) Cut into 9 squares and serve with Cherry Sauce.

Cherry Sauce

1 cup pitted fresh cherries, halved or 1 cup canned sweet cherries, drained	¼ cup water
	¼ cup sugar
	1 tablespoon cornstarch
	1 cup orange juice
¼ teaspoon almond extract	

Combine cherries, water and sugar; simmer for 5 minutes. Make a paste of cornstarch and ¼ cup orange juice; add to cherry mixture with remaining orange juice. Cook until clear and thickened, then add almond extract. Serve warm. Serves 6.

CHOCOLATE IGLOO

1 tablespoon unflavored gelatine	3 egg yolks, slightly
¼ cup cold water	beaten
⅓ cup sugar	1 teaspoon vanilla
¼ teaspoon salt	3 egg whites
1¾ cups milk	⅓ cup sugar
1 4-ounce package German's	1 8-inch devil's food layer
sweet chocolate	cake

Add gelatine to cold water to soften; combine ⅓ cup of sugar, salt, milk, in saucepan and add chocolate. Cook over medium heat, stirring constantly until chocolate is melted. Add a small amount of this mixture to egg yolks, stirring vigorously; then return to hot mixture. Cook over low heat until slightly thickened. Remove from heat; add softened gelatine; stir until dissolved. Pour into large bowl, cool and blend in vanilla. Chill until partially thickened. Beat egg whites until thick; add second ⅓ cup of sugar, 2 tablespoons at a time, and continue beating until stiff peaks form. Fold into chilled chocolate mixture. Spoon into well greased 6-cup mixing bowl; place in refrigerator and chill until firm. To serve, select a platter. Remove mold from refrigerator; loosen by running a sharp knife around top edge; place in warm water a few seconds, then shake gently. Place cake layer evenly over molded chocolate, then place platter over cake; invert, lowering carefully onto platter so that mold rests on top of cake. Spread generously with the following topping.

Topping

> ½ pint heavy cream, whipped   1 teaspoon vanilla
> 1 tablespoon confectioners' sugar

Combine ingredients and spread over cake. Garnish with lemon leaves or a fresh daisy or two. Sprinkle with maraschino cherries for color. Serves 10.

For the devil's food layer cake use a package mix or 1 layer of Wonderful Chocolate Cake.

CHOCOLATE SOUFFLÉ

2 tablespoons butter or margarine	1½ squares unsweetened chocolate
2 tablespoons flour	5 tablespoons sugar
½ cup milk	5 egg yolks
1-inch piece of vanilla bean	5 egg whites

Melt butter in saucepan, add flour and stir until smooth and golden. Scald milk with vanilla bean; add chocolate and stir until melted, then add to roux with 2 tablespoons sugar. Cook until thickened, stirring, about 5 minutes. Beat egg yolks with remaining sugar and stir into chocolate mixture; remove bean. Beat egg whites and fold into chocolate batter. Grease a 6-cup soufflé dish; sprinkle it with sugar. Fasten a 2-inch band of foil around rim of dish. Pour in batter and place in a 375° oven; bake about 20 minutes or until puffed and delicately browned. Dust with powdered sugar. Serve at once with Sauce Marsala. Serves 6.

One teaspoon vanilla extract may be substituted for vanilla bean. Add with the egg whites.

Chocolate plus

For mocha flavor, add 2 tablespoons instant coffee with chocolate. For rum flavor, add 2 tablespoons light rum with chocolate.

Timing is of utmost importance with soufflés, and this recipe is unusual in its short-time baking. Delicious and delicate, it must be served when puffed and browned. It will fall slightly if overbaked, but will retain delicate texture and flavor.

COFFEE SPONGE

1 tablespoon unflavored gelatine	½ teaspoon vanilla
¼ cup cold water	¼ teaspoon salt
1 teaspoon instant coffee	2 egg whites, beaten stiff
¼ cup sugar	prepared whipped topping (optional)
	1 cup skim milk, scalded

Sprinkle gelatine on water; mix and let stand 5 minutes. Add softened gelatine, coffee and sugar to milk; stir until dissolved.

Cool; add vanilla, then chill until of jellylike consistency. Add salt to egg whites; beat until stiff, then fold into gelatine mixture. Pour into 5 individual molds or a 1-quart mold; refrigerate until firm; dip quickly in hot water and invert on individual sherbets or platter. Dot with prepared whipped topping. Serves 5 to 6.

CREAM PUFFS JERMYN STREET

The setting was a fine French restaurant on quaint Jermyn Street, a favorite rendezvous of sophisticated Londoners. This dessert climaxed a superb dinner.

½ cup heavy cream, whipped
1 tablespoon sherry
1 recipe Crème Anglaise

20 Tiny Cream Puffs
2 10-ounce packages frozen
   strawberries, defrosted

Fold the cream and sherry into the Crème Anglaise. Form a pyramid of the puffs, with eight at the base, covered with Crème; a second layer with six puffs, covered with Crème; then alternate Crème with puffs — three, two and a topknot of one. Pour remaining Crème over all. Chill well and serve with border of strawberries. Use a shell-like serving dish, or one with a rim for custard overflow. Serves 6.

CRÈME RENVERSÉE

1 cup sugar
1 teaspoon vanilla
½ cup boiling water
2 tablespoons sugar

4 eggs, slightly beaten
2 cups milk, or half and half
   cream, heated
6 maraschino cherries

Pour sugar into saucepan; add vanilla and heat until it melts to a brown syrup, then add water and simmer 5 minutes. Coat bottom of a 4-cup mold, or six 4-ounce molds, with syrup, spreading so that bottom and sides are well coated; set aside to cool. Beat 2 tablespoons of sugar with eggs; pour in cream or hot milk slowly, beating continuously, then pour into prepared mold or molds. Place in a shallow pan of hot water.

Bake at 350° about 40 minutes, or until knife inserted in custard
comes out clean. Small molds bake in about 30 minutes. Place
serving dish over custard mold and invert quickly. The top will
be caramelized and syrup will drain onto custard as a sauce.
Garnish each serving with a cherry. Serves 6.

Gay Seville, home of Carmen, Don Juan and Figaro, of fiesta
and flamenco, has literally danced her way through two thou-
sand years of historical figurations. A typical Spanish dinner,
accompanied by a native punch, Sangría, ended on a French note
with Glazed Crêpes for finale.

GLAZED CRÊPES

2 eggs, well beaten	2 tablespoons melted butter
¾ cup milk	or salad oil
1 cup flour	2 tablespoons cognac or Cointreau
¼ teaspoon salt	(optional)

½ teaspoon grated orange peel

Glaze

3 tablespoons sugar   ¼ cup slivered almonds

Combine eggs and milk; blend well with flour and salt; add
melted butter, orange peel and cognac. Set in refrigerator for a
minimum of one hour to "rest" batter. Grease a 6-inch skillet
lightly; pour in 2 tablespoons of batter; tilt pan so that batter
fully covers bottom; cakes should be thin. Brown lightly on
one side, then brown reverse side. Remove from pan; roll and
arrange in a single row in an oven proof dish. Sprinkle with nuts
and sugar; place under preheated broiler about 3 inches from
heat until sugar melts and cakes are heated. Serve at once, with
Strawberry Sauce. Makes 12 pancakes.

Strawberry Sauce

1 10-ounce package frozen   1 tablespoon lemon juice
    strawberries, thawed   ¼ cup slivered almonds

Combine all ingredients in a sauce pan and bring to a boil; simmer 2 or 3 minutes. Serve hot or cold. May be prepared in advance.

For variety

Try a dash of anise extract in Strawberry Sauce for a change of flavor.

Pour 2 tablespoons brandy into small aluminum ladle; warm over stove heat and pour over crêpes. Ignite before or after pouring; just don't get your face too close.

Winged Pancakes have a different texture, but are equally delicious prepared with the glaze.

STRAWBERRY CRÊPES

8 thin 7-inch pancakes (crêpes)	1 tablespoon cognac
1 quart strawberries, sliced	1 tablespoon Cointreau
½ cup orange juice	1 tablespoon Grand Marnier

Fill crêpes with fresh strawberries and roll into packages. Heat orange juice, cognac, Cointreau and Grand Marnier in a skillet; add the filled pancakes and simmer until heated. They may be flamed with additional cognac.

If you wish, sugar the strawberries to taste before filling crêpes. Use batter recipe for Glazed Crêpes.

MARRON BAVARIAN

1 tablespoon unflavored gelatine	1 cup preserved marrons (1 11-
¼ cup water	ounce jar), drained and
4 egg yolks	coarsely chopped
⅓ cup sugar	1 cup heavy cream, whipped
½ cup hot milk	1 tablespoon sherry

Topping

½ cup heavy cream, whipped
2 tablespoons chopped candied cherries or
2 tablespoons angelica

Combine gelatine and water and let stand 5 minutes to soften.

Beat yolks and sugar in top of double boiler until very light; add milk and softened gelatine; place over hot, not boiling water. Cook while stirring until mixture thickens and coats the spoon. Cool; then fold in marrons, whipped cream and sherry. Pour into greased 5-cup mold, place in refrigerator and chill several hours or overnight until set. Turn out on platter, pipe and border with additional whipped cream, sprinkle with cherries. Serves 8 to 10.

So often one feels the need for cake or a cooky with a dessert. To complete this Bavarian, and offset the need for another service, I line a 9-inch spring form with 24 split ladyfingers, curved side out, then pour in the Marron cream. To serve, remove rim of spring form, pipe top and base with whipped cream in attractive pattern and top with cherries and/or angelica.

Bavarian Cream is a basic preparation for many variations which include Marron Bavarian.

Bavarian Cream

Substitute 2 teaspoons vanilla for the sherry, omit marrons. Pour into greased melon mold; unmold on platter, serve plain or with sauce variations. See recipe for Marron Bavarian.

Nut Bavarian

Substitute 1 cup ground hazelnuts for the marrons.

Bavaroise au Liqueur

Omit vanilla and marrons, add 2 tablespoons of any liqueur, brandy or rum. Fruit flavors are excellent.

Strawberry Bavarian

Defrost 1 10-ounce package frozen strawberries (or raspberries). Drain thoroughly and mash lightly. Add to recipe with whipped cream. Use syrup for sauce.

Coffee Bavarian

Omit marrons and vanilla, add 1½ tablespoons instant coffee to the scalded milk.

Sauces for Bavarian Cream

Fruit Sauce

Defrost 1 10-ounce package strawberries or raspberries; serve separately over Bavarian Cream.

Sauce au Marron

1 cup sour cream
⅓ cup syrup from preserved marrons (see recipe
for Marron Bavarian)

Just blend well, refrigerate and serve separately with Marron Bavarian. Both these sauces are simple and good accompaniments.

MOCHA CRÈME

When I first met the very young Freida Zylstra, she was teaching school, then in quick succession became a news photographer, and a columnist. Our paths now cross again in common interest; her newspaper column highlights the favorite recipes of movie personalities. Here is one she especially enjoys.

1 cup semi-sweet chocolate bits	⅛ teaspoon salt
¾ cup evaporated milk	2 teaspoons sugar
1 egg, well beaten	1 teaspoon vanilla

Mocha Topping

Melt chocolate bits in upper part of double boiler over very hot water. Add milk slowly, whipping quickly with a fork or wire whisk. In a bowl, combine egg with salt, sugar and vanilla; beat with rotary beater. When chocolate mixture is scalding hot, pour over egg, beating steadily. Pour into 6 dainty sherbet glasses; refrigerate. Prepare Mocha Topping.

Mocha Topping

1 teaspoon gelatine	6 teaspoons coffee liqueur
2 teaspoons cold water	⅓ cup heavy cream

2 teaspoons sugar

Add gelatine to cold water; let stand 5 minutes, then add liqueur and heat over water until gelatine is dissolved. Chill for 1 minute. Whip cream, add sugar and fold in gelatine mixture. When crème begins to set, top each glass with liqueur mixture, using a cake decorator or pastry tube for decorative designs. Finish with cherry or shaved chocolate. Refrigerate 3 to 4 hours before serving; this dessert may be made a day or two in advance. Serves 6.

MOUSSE AU CHOCOLAT

¼ pound sweetened chocolate	dash salt
⅓ cup sugar	4 egg yolks
¼ cup water	2 teaspoons light rum
4 egg whites, beaten stiff	

Melt chocolate in top of double boiler. Combine sugar, water and salt in saucepan; cook till bubbly, about 3 minutes. Pour sugar syrup slowly into chocolate while stirring. Add yolks one at a time, beating thoroughly with a rotary beater after each addition. Remove from heat, blend in rum, then fold in egg whites. Spoon into bowl or individual serving dishes. Chill a minimum of 6 hours in refrigerator. Pipe edge with whipped cream or dot with mounds, using pastry tube. Serves 6 to 8.

Pots de Crème cups are a lovely service for the Mousse.

RUM MOCHA RUSSE

1 tablespoon gelatine	1 tablespoon instant coffee
¼ cup cold water	1 cup boiling water
2 dozen ladyfingers	6 tablespoons rum
50 marshmallows	2 cups heavy cream, whipped
shaved chocolate	

Sprinkle gelatine over cold water and let stand about 5 minutes. Butter and line a 9-inch spring form pan with split ladyfingers. Cover bottom completely, using crumbled ladyfingers to fill in. Combine marshmallows, instant coffee and boiling water in top of double boiler. Cook over hot water until marshmallows are melted. Remove from heat; stir in gelatine until dissolved; add rum and continue stirring until cool. Refrigerate 15 minutes, then fold in 1 cup of whipped cream gently. Pour into pan over ladyfingers and refrigerate for several hours. Before serving, remove rim of pan; whip second cup of cream and swirl over the top; sprinkle with shaved chocolate. Serves 8 to 10.

SOUFFLÉ GRAND MARNIER

1⅔ cups sugar	¼ cup cornstarch
1 pint milk	⅓ cup Grand Marnier
½ cup butter or margarine	5 egg yolks, well beaten
8 egg whites	

Melt sugar in milk; boil slowly to obtain a light cream. Melt butter and add cornstarch. Mix well and add the milk mixture gradually; cook until evenly thickened. Remove from heat; add Grand Marnier and yolks slowly, and blend well. Beat egg whites until stiff; fold into egg yolk mixture. Pour into a 6-cup greased soufflé dish; sprinkle with sugar and bake in 350° oven 16 to 18 minutes. Serve immediately. Serves 6 to 8. It is well to sugar the greased dish before adding batter.

In Copenhagen soufflés were served individually, piping hot. The waiter pierced the center of each with a fork, opened each soufflé slightly and poured about 1 teaspoonful of Grand Marnier into the aperture. The aromatic liqueur was suavely fused into the pouf! I could sense the captain's expectant anxiety as he waited for my reaction, and I did not disappoint him. The soufflé was unexcelled.

Italian Humor

Sometimes I think I cook by name. What could be more intriguing or beguiling than "Zuppa Inglese," only to discover that it isn't a soup at all, but the Italian version of the English Trifle. And it is good!

An Italian cook attempted to follow a recipe for Trifle to
please English guests, with the following results. Being a
rather moist version, it was hilariously named "Zuppa."

ZUPPA INGLESE

4 egg yolks	¼ cup light rum
½ cup sugar	4 egg whites
⅓ cup flour	⅛ teaspoon salt
¼ teaspoon salt	¼ cup sugar plus
2 cups milk, scalded	1 teaspoon sugar
1 teaspoon vanilla	candied ginger or orange peel

2 cake layers, sponge or sunshine

Break yolks into top of double boiler; beat slightly and set aside.
Combine ½ cup sugar, flour, and ¼ teaspoon salt, then add milk
gradually, beating until smooth. Pour slowly into yolks, beating with a whisk to prevent curdling. Cook over hot water,
stirring constantly until smooth and thickened, about 10
minutes. Cool and add vanilla; set aside. Place 1 cake layer in
shallow ovenware dish and sprinkle with 2 tablespoons rum;
spread with half of custard mixture; repeat with second cake
layer. Beat egg whites until frothy, add teaspoon salt and beat
until stiff but not dry. Add ¼ cup sugar very gradually, beating
until stiff and glossy. Cover the "zuppa" carefully, sealing top
with the meringue. Sprinkle with 1 teaspoon sugar and place in
325° oven until lightly browned. Border top with candied fruit
and chill. Serves 8.

The English Trifle has an extra layer of tart jelly over the cake
below the custard; and is topped with whipped cream instead
of meringue.

Substitute 2 dozen almond macaroons for the sponge cake, if
desired.

Frozen Desserts

ICE CREAM AD INFINITUM

Ice cream is the cook's "manna from heaven." Practically a commodity, it ranges from simple goodness to lavish lusciousness in endless variety. Let's start with a dish of ice cream and go on from there.

For the youngsters

Crown a ball of vanilla with a cone, give it spice drop features — you have a clown.

Long spice drops for ears — you have a bunny.

And for all

Soften ice cream and pour it into 4-ounce molds of various forms; refreeze.

Add to the softened ice cream any of the following; nuts, grapenuts, marrons, puréed or sliced fruits, then freeze.

Ice cream may be tinted to match decor. Soften it and add vegetable coloring, darker than desired. It becomes lighter as it freezes.

Use cookies or cake to line or border small or large molds.

Enhance a serving with sauces and toppings

shredded coconut	fresh fruit
chopped nuts	canned fruit
shaved chocolate	various sauces
candy decorettes	stud with slivered almonds, porcupine-like

Serve sherbets as first course, as dessert or as meat accompaniments.

Freeze fruit soup on a stick like a sherbet.

Have a do-it-yourself ice cream bar — don't forget the cones.

Forerunner to the ice cream cone was a paper cone filled with ice and flavored with syrup.

BLUEBERRY CANTALOUPE À LA MODE

2 cantaloupes   1½ quarts vanilla ice cream

Slice the cantaloupe in ½-inch rings; there should be 8. Peel and set each on dessert plate. Center with a scoop of ice cream and cover with Wine-Blueberry Sauce. Serves 8.

A simple and satisfying summer dessert. Black Walnut Fluff Cake would add good flavor.

Wine-Blueberry Sauce

2 cups blueberries	1½ teaspoons arrowroot or
1 tablespoon lemon juice	1 tablespoon cornstarch
½ teaspoon grated lemon or	½ teaspoon cinnamon
orange peel	⅓ cup water or port wine

dash salt

Wash and pick over the berries. Mash 1 cup, then place both mashed and whole berries in saucepan. Combine remaining ingredients, blending arrowroot smoothly. Add to berries; bring to boil; reduce heat and simmer for 5 minutes, or until clear.

I like to keep prepared grated orange and lemon peel on hand as a convenient time-saver. This, too, is true of the lemon juice, and I always have it on the shelf.

As always with creatively busy people, Ruth Lee found time to send me this "freezer ready" delectable.

CAREER GAL'S FROZEN PIE

1 pint chocolate ice cream	1 pint coffee ice cream
1 pint orange or raspberry	¼ cup crushed pecans or
sherbet	cashew nuts

Graham Cracker Pie Shell

Have ice cream slightly softened. Spread layer of chocolate ice cream over graham cracker crust with back of wooden spoon; add layer of sherbet; top with a third layer of coffee ice cream.

Sprinkle crushed pecans or cashew nuts over the top; freeze solid, then wrap and replace in freezer overnight. Serve with a fruit sauce if desired. Serves 12.

This dessert will keep well in freezer for a week or more.

Graham Cracker Pie Shell

> 1 cup crushed graham cracker crumbs
> 4 tablespoons melted butter or margarine

Combine ingredients and press firmly and evenly into bottom and against sides of a 9-inch buttered pie plate. Chill in refrigerator about one hour until firm.

CHERRIES JUBILEE

1 1-pound can bing cherries, drained	2 jiggers Kirsch (¼ cup)
	2 jiggers Cointreau (¼ cup)
½ cup juice from cherries	1 teaspoon grated orange peel
2 jiggers cognac (¼ cup)	1 quart vanilla ice cream
2 ounces brandy	

Place cherries in bowl with ½ cup juice; add cognac, Kirsch, Cointreau and orange peel; marinate a minimum of 2 hours. Pour into chafing dish and heat. Place a scoop of ice cream on each of 6 individual dishes. Pour brandy in ladle; warm it, set it alight and pour over cherries. While blazing, pour cherries and liqueured liquid over ice cream. Serves 6.

CHOCOLATE COCONUT NESTS

½ cup sweetened condensed milk	½ teaspoon vanilla
1 ounce unsweetened chocolate	2 cups shredded moist coconut
⅛ teaspoon salt	1 quart pistachio ice cream

Pour sweetened condensed milk, chocolate, and salt in top of double boiler. Cook over rapidly boiling water, stirring frequently until thick, about 10 minutes. Turn mixture into large mixing bowl. Stir in vanilla and blend in coconut. Grease 8 muffin pans thoroughly. Place about ¼ cup of mixture in each cup. Form into nests by pressing with back of spoon firmly around bottom and sides, allowing mixture to extend ½ inch above rim. This mixture is firm enough to hold shape until it is baked. Bake in a 350° oven until top edges are browned and firm, about 20 minutes. Let stand in pans 10 minutes. Loosen edges and lift gently to remove. Cool. To serve, fill each nest with ball of pistachio ice cream. Serve with Chocolate Sauce. Serves 8.

Line a pie shell with Coconut mixture and use this recipe for Coconut Chocolate Ice Cream Pie.

FLOWERPOT PARFAIT

6 flowerpots, 2 inches in diameter	1 pint chocolate ice cream
aluminum foil	1 pint pistachio ice cream
soda straws	1 cup Chocolate Sauce
	6 bright, stemmed flowers

3 tablespoons chopped pistachio nuts

Line flowerpots with foil. Holding straw upright in center, layer alternate chocolate ice cream, sauce and pistachio ice cream, topping with pistachio. Freeze until serving time, then slip the flower into the straw; sprinkle ice cream with nuts. Serve on doilies. An extra posy on the plate is charming. Serves 6.

The hostess can look as cool as the dessert, for the preparation may be made days in advance.

For simpler arrangement, fill pots with either flavor and top with nuts and/or Chocolate Sauce.

FROZEN ANGEL TOFFEE

1 7″ x 4″ angel food loaf cake (11 ounces)	1 quart coffee ice cream
	½ pound English toffee, crushed

Caramel Sauce

Slice cake in 3 layers lengthwise. Spread half of ice cream on bottom layer and sprinkle with ⅓ of the toffee. Repeat with

next layer, reserving sufficient ice cream for frosting, and cover
with third layer of cake. Frost with remaining ice cream (plus
that which will ooze from the layers). Place in freezer until
firm. Approximately 15 minutes in advance of the serving,
remove from the freezer. Sprinkle remaining toffee over the top;
pass with the Caramel Sauce, hot or cold. Serves 6 to 8.

May be prepared two weeks in advance. Store in freezer.

To serve 12, double the quantity of ice cream and candy, and
use a 9-inch round angel food or 6-egg chiffon cake. Double the
Caramel Sauce recipe, too.

Peanut brittle and butter pecan ice cream is also a good
combination. This is a wonderful dessert to have on hand for
last-minute planning, and is deliciously complete even without
the added glamour of Caramel Sauce. Whipped cream piped over
the top is always an attractive touch.

Most home freezers do not provide the same intensity of cold
as the commercial, which freeze more solidly. You must judge
your own timing for removal.

An electric beater, a freezer, and this pie is a matter of sleight of
hand. "Lovely to look at" and delightfully refreshing. In
addition, one to have on hand in the freezer for that last-minute
need.

ICY LIME PIE

1 quart lime sherbet, softened
1 9-inch Graham Cracker Crust
1 pint strawberries, sliced thick

Pour sherbet into bowl of mixer and beat until fluffy and aerated.
It should stand in peaks. Turn into prepared crust and place in
freezer several hours to refreeze. To serve, border with overlapping sliced berries. The cool combination of colors is garnish
enough. Serves 6 to 8.

The berries may be sprinkled with sugar before placing on
sherbet, but I have omitted it as sweetening is a matter of taste.

ORANGE TORTE

1 8-ounce angel food cake	1 quart vanilla ice cream
½ cup orange juice	1 large banana, diced (optional)
concentrate, defrosted	½ cup Toasted Coconut

Garnish: whipped cream, galax leaves, orange segments

Line a 6-cup bowl or mold with plastic wrap. Break cake into chunks about the size of a walnut, and layer in bottom of mold. Cover thickly with tablespoons of ice cream; moisten with undiluted orange juice concentrate; distribute banana. Repeat layers of cake, ice cream, banana and juice until all are used, ending with cake. Place in freezer until firm, then cover mold tightly with foil. To serve, remove from freezer, turn over onto serving platter, peeling off plastic wrap. Cover with mounds of whipped cream; sprinkle with Toasted Coconut. Decorate with border of galax leaves and orange segments. Serves 6 to 8.

Toasted Coconut

Place in shallow pan in 350° oven; stir gently or shake pan frequently until coconut is delicately browned. Watch closely that it does not burn.

RAINBOW ICE CREAM

1 pint strawberry ice cream	1 pint lime sherbet
1 pint orange sherbet	1 quart vanilla ice cream
whipped cream (optional)	

Chill a 6-cup ring mold or melon mold. Line smoothly with aluminum foil; allow ends to extend. Using a small ice cream scoop, form balls of strawberry ice cream, orange, and lime sherbets. Place the balls on a cooky sheet; chill in freezer until firm. Soften vanilla ice cream; whip until fluffy. Place a layer of colored balls in bottom of mold; fill in spaces with vanilla ice cream. Repeat until mold is filled. Freeze overnight. At serving time; turn out onto a chilled plate and peel off foil. Frost with ribbons of whipped cream if you like. Fill center of ring mold with a variety of cut fresh fruit; cherries, peaches, pears, berries.

Select the most attractive berries and arrange as border. Serves 12 to 16.

A bit of glamour presentation for prosaic ice cream.

SUNDAE RING

½ cup molasses   2 teaspoons butter or margarine
¼ cup sugar   6 cups cornflakes
¼ teaspoon salt   1 quart vanilla ice cream

Mix molasses, sugar, and salt. Cook slowly, stirring occasionally, to 250° (when a small amount dropped into cold water forms a firm ball). Remove from heat and add butter. Pour over cornflakes and toss gently with a fork. Press mixture lightly into a buttered 8-inch ring mold. Cool, unmold, and fill center with scoops of ice cream. Serve with Chocolate Sauce. Serves 6.

Try it with frozen strawberries or raspberries, defrosted, or with butter pecan ice cream and Caramel Sauce.

TORTONI GLACÉS

1 quart vanilla ice cream,   ¼ cup chopped maraschino
    softened   cherries, drained
½ teaspoon anise flavoring   ¼ teaspoon each: grated
½ cup slivered pistachio nuts   orange and lemon rind
           2 7-ounce milk chocolate bars
               candy finely shaved

Combine all ingredients and mix well; turn into individual paper cupcake holders. Place in muffin tins until frozen to retain shape, or use freezer containers. Freeze until firm. Top with a rosebud of whipped cream and a sliver of maraschino cherry. Serves 6 to 8.

This is a good dessert to make in larger quantity. It freezes well and may be stored in plastic bags when it becomes solid.

Fruit Desserts

BLUEBERRIES IN CHEESE RING

1 envelope unflavored gelatine
¼ cup cold water
1 8-ounce package cream cheese
½ cup sugar

½ teaspoon almond extract
dash salt
1¼ cups milk
1 cup heavy cream, whipped

1 quart fresh blueberries

Soften gelatine in cold water. Dissolve over hot water. Combine softened cream cheese, sugar, extract, and salt, blending until smooth. Gradually add milk and gelatine. Chill mixture until partly set. Fold in cream; pour into greased 1-quart ring mold; chill until firm. Unmold and fill center of ring with fresh blueberries, slightly sweetened if you wish. Serves 6.

Fresh or frozen strawberries or raspberries are good flavor contrasts.

From Brazil comes this mousse!

CREMA DE RÍO

4 ripe avocados
1 teaspoon lemon juice
1 6-ounce can evaporated milk

⅓ cup sugar
¼ cup Crème de Cacao or
¼ cup Curaçao

Peel avocados, remove pits and place in blender with lemon juice, milk, and sugar. Give it a whirl for a few seconds or until thoroughly blended. Place in bowl in refrigerator to chill. Serve this cool green mousse in frosted sherbet glasses; pour the liqueur over each after it is served. Serves 6.

Variegated Strawberries

The wild strawberries in France are a seasonal delight and are often served with Crème Fraiche. Neither the berries nor the sauce are obtainable here. A young friend, Susan, who lives in Paris, gave me this version of Crème Fraiche. We served it with our own cultivated berries and found it as delicious.

CRÈME FRAICHE AMÉRICAINE

1 cup heavy cream   ½ cup sour cream

Whip cream to a velvety softness, not too stiff. Combine with sour cream, blend well. Serve with Strawberries au Kirsch.

STRAWBERRIES AU KIRSCH

1 quart strawberries   2 tablespoons Kirsch
⅓ cup confectioners' sugar,   ½ cup slivered almonds
   or to taste   (optional)

Wash and hull strawberries; place in bowl; sprinkle with sugar and Kirsch. Chill in refrigerator a maximum of 2 hours, no longer, as they become too soft. Serve from large glass bowl or in individual sherbet cups. Pass Crème Fraiche Américaine and nuts separately.

STRAWBERRIES CHANTILLY

2 pints whole strawberries   ⅔ cup Marsala or white wine
2 tablespoons sugar   1 cup heavy cream, whipped
         2 teaspoons confectioners' sugar

Wash and hull berries, saving 6 or 8 with stems for garnish. Drain hulled berries; place in bowl; sprinkle with sugar and toss lightly. Pour wine over berries and refrigerate one hour. Blend with whipped cream and confectioners' sugar. To serve, fill sherbet cups with berries, adding wine-berry liquid; garnish with a dollop of whipped cream topped with a reserved whole berry. Serves 6 to 8.

HONEYED STRAWBERRIES

1 pint strawberries, washed and hulled
1 cup Honey Cream

Place in bowl and top with Honey Cream.

Honey Cream

Combine 2 tablespoons honey with 1 cup sour cream and blend well. Serves 4.

STRAWBERRIES GLACÉES

1 pint vanilla ice cream, slightly softened
1 pint strawberries, hulled

Combine lightly. Serve topped with whole berries. Serves 6.

STRAWBERRIES IN WINE

Port and Sherry are happy berry affinities.

STRAWBERRIES ANISETTE

One day I added a teaspoon of anisette to the Chantilly recipe and found it an intriguing flavor.

BUBBLY STRAWBERRIES

An elegant touch; chilled sugared berries, in tall footed glasses; drenched with iced champagne, poured as each guest is served.

Refreshingly simple!

MANDARIN CHANTILLY

2 16-ounce cans Mandarin oranges   ¼ cup Cointreau
½ pint heavy cream, whipped   ½ cup coconut flakes, toasted

Drain oranges thoroughly; blend carefully with cream; stir in
Cointreau lightly. Refrigerate ½ hour. Stir again before serving. Sprinkle with coconut and serve in your prettiest sherbet
dishes. Serves 6.

To toast coconut

Line a cooky sheet with foil and spread coconut in thin layer.
Place in 350° oven for about 5 minutes or until browned. Watch
closely as coconut browns more quickly around the edges. Move
outer edges toward center when sufficiently brown.

A wonderful light dessert to follow a substantial entrée.

PEACHES MARIANNE

8 large freestone peaches   1 pint fresh raspberries
2 10-ounce packages frozen   (optional)
raspberries, defrosted   ⅓ cup slivered almonds
Mocha Crème Custard or Coffee Cream

Spear each peach on a 2-pronged fork and dip (blanch) in boiling
water for a minute. Peel off skins and place in a bowl. Press
defrosted raspberries through a food mill or coarse sieve, then
strain a second time through a fine sieve to remove all seeds.
Pour over peaches and place in refrigerator a minimum of 12
hours turning frequently to marinate evenly. Peaches become a
lovely bright red. To serve, place each in a low glass bowl or
sherbet glass, spoon raspberry juice over and arrange fresh berries
around in the liquid; sprinkle with almonds and serve Mocha
Crème Custard separately. Serves 8.
      The peaches should be firm but ripe and are sometimes a bit

slippery as a result. Serve them with a fork and spoon for helpful manipulation. If the peach seems too large for 1 portion, cut in half and remove the stone before covering with sauce. Serve cut side down, to show a similar rounded effect.

PEARS MOCHA

1 1-pound can pear halves	1 cup whipping cream
1 12-ounce package semi-sweet chocolate pieces	1 teaspoon vanilla
⅓ cup pear syrup	¼ cup pistachio nuts, coarsely chopped
1 tablespoon instant coffee	

Drain pear halves. Melt chocolate over hot water. Heat pear syrup, dissolve coffee in it and add to chocolate. Beat until smooth and cool, but not firm. Whip cream; fold gently into chocolate mixture; add vanilla and pour half of mixture into serving bowl. Slice half of pear halves and place in circular arrangement on sauce; pour on remaining sauce; slice and swirl remaining pear halves. Chill thoroughly and sprinkle with pistachio nuts just before serving. Serves 8.

This simple recipe has the "gourmet" look.

TOP BANANA

1 recipe Marvelous Pie Crust	6 teaspoons dark brown sugar
6 small ripe bananas	½ teaspoon powdered ginger

Prepare crust; divide in half and roll each half into a rectangle 6" x 8", then cut into 3 6-inch squares. Place a banana diagonally on each; press a teaspoon brown sugar in a line the length of banana and dust with ginger. Bring corners of dough over banana and seal ends. Place seam side down. Make 3 diagonal slashes across top; repeat with remaining dough and bananas. Place on buttered cooky sheet and bake in 450° oven 15 minutes or until lightly and evenly browned. Serve plain, with Mandarin Sauce, or with vanilla ice cream. Serves 6.

Top Bananas may be served warm or cooled. I like them warm and with ice cream they are superb.

Wrap the bananas in the crust 1 or 2 hours in advance and refrigerate before baking. If baked one hour before serving they will cool to the right temperature.

Dessert Sauces

BLUEBERRY SAUCE

2 cups blueberries	1 teaspoon arrowroot
2 tablespoons sugar	1 teaspoon lemon juice
⅛ teaspoon cinnamon	

Mash 1 cup berries; combine with sugar; mix arrowroot with lemon juice and add with cinnamon. Bring to boil; cook until clear, about 5 minutes; add remaining whole berries; boil 1 minute. Makes about 1 cup.

BUTTERSCOTCH SAUCE

⅔ cup light or dark corn syrup	⅛ teaspoon salt
1¼ cups brown sugar	⅔ cup evaporated milk, or
4 tablespoons butter or margarine	cream

Combine syrup, sugar, butter, salt, and boil slowly until a small amount forms a soft ball when dropped into cold water. Cool and add milk or cream. Serve hot or cold. May be stored in refrigerator. To heat, place in top of double boiler. Makes about 1½ cups.

CARAMEL SAUCE

25 candy caramel squares	2 egg yolks, slightly beaten
⅓ cup cream	1 teaspoon vanilla
4 teaspoons lemon juice	

Melt caramels in cream over low heat, stirring until blended.

Mix in egg yolks very gradually and boil 1 minute or until thick, stirring constantly. Blend in vanilla and lemon juice. Refrigerate.

One hour before serving, remove from refrigerator. Heat just before serving.

This sauce keeps well for several days under refrigeration.

COFFEE CREAM

1 cup heavy cream	2 tablespoons confectioners'
1 tablespoon instant coffee	sugar
½ teaspoon vanilla	

Combine all ingredients in bowl and chill several hours. Whip with rotary or electric beater until stiff. Use for cake roll, cream puffs, frostings, fillings or topping. Makes about 2 cups.

CRÈME ANGLAISE
(Soft Custard)

1½ cups scalded milk	pinch of salt
⅓ cup sugar	1 teaspoon cornstarch
3 egg yolks, well beaten	2 teaspoons vanilla extract

Scald milk in top of double boiler. Add sugar gradually to yolks, beating until mixture is creamy. Beat in salt and cornstarch. Pour milk gradually into egg mixture, then return to double boiler. Cook over simmering water, stirring constantly until mixture is thickened. Do not let it boil. It should coat a silver spoon when removed from custard. Add vanilla. Strain into a cold bowl; cool and chill. Cover surface with a piece of wax paper to prevent skin from forming. It is also well to stir occasionally. Makes about 2 cups.

Crème Anglaise has many adaptations, and is typically French. It is served warm or cold, on puddings, cakes, fruit, or ice cream; in fact, as an alternate sauce wherever whipped cream is indicated.

The flavoring may be varied by adding a tablespoon of brandy, Kirsch, or rum.

Mocha Crème Custard

For nonalcoholic flavor, add 2 teaspoons instant coffee to the scalded milk or 2 1-ounce squares of German's sweet chocolate, melted.

DUTCH CHOCOLATE CREAM

1 cup heavy cream	½ teaspoon instant coffee
2 tablespoons Dutch style cocoa	¼ cup confectioners' sugar

Combine cream, cocoa and coffee; sift in sugar. Place in refrigerator a minimum of 2 hours or as long as overnight. Whip until stiff and fluffy, then chill until ready to use. Holds consistency well. Makes about 2 cups.

1 cup heavy cream equals 2 cups whipped.

Though I originally used this recipe for cake filling and frosting, I find it a delicious Crème Chantilly as a sauce. It has many versions:

Omit the coffee and use ½ teaspoon vanilla.

Use 1 teaspoon rum or ½ teaspoon rum flavoring.

Use almond, lemon or any other flavoring which will combine with your accompanying recipe.

GOLDEN SAUCE

2 tablespoons flour	3 egg yolks, beaten
1 cup sugar	¼ cup orange juice
1 cup milk	⅓ cup lemon juice
¼ cup butter or margarine	1 tablespoon sherry

Mix flour, sugar, and milk; cook over low heat until slightly thickened. Add butter and egg yolks. Cook 5 minutes, then add juices and sherry.

A good sauce for gingerbread and steamed puddings.

HOT CHOCOLATE SAUCE

1 6-ounce package chocolate   ½ pound marshmallows, cut in
   bits   4ths, or ½ pound small
1 cup milk   marshmallows
     1 square unsweetened chocolate

Place bits and square of chocolate in top of double boiler with milk. Cook over hot water until melted. To serve, add marshmallows to hot chocolate mixture and stir until partially melted. Serve hot or cold. Makes about 2 cups.

RASPBERRY SAUCE

Our frozen fruits offer simple and piquant variety with a minimum of effort.

     1 10-ounce package frozen raspberries,
     strawberries or blueberries

Defrost and serve au naturel.

Combine with 1 tablespoon lemon juice and sugar to taste; whirl it in the blender or use a rotary beater.

For a thicker sauce, make a paste of 1 tablespoon cornstarch and ¼ cup of defrosted fruit juice. Place defrosted berries in saucepan; add cornstarch mixture and 1 tablespoon lemon juice; bring to boil and then simmer until clear and thickened. Add sugar if you wish, then refrigerate.

May be served hot or cold. Makes 1¼ cups.

SABAYON

6 egg yolks   ½ cup sherry or Marsala
½ cup sugar   angel food cake or 12 ladyfingers
4 tablespoons Cointreau   (approximately)

Pour yolks into top of double boiler; add sugar and beat with wire whisk until smooth and lemony. Add Cointreau and sherry, then place over hot water; cook, stirring until thickened. Pour

into cake-lined sherbet dishes and serve warm. May be used as
a sauce for other desserts, omitting cake. Serves 4 to 6.

Use the egg whites for a white cake or toward an Angel Food.

SAUCE MARSALA

2 eggs	4 tablespoons Marsala or dry
2 egg yolks	white wine
4 tablespoons sugar	1 tablespoon Kirsch (optional)

Combine eggs and yolks with sugar and Marsala in top of double
boiler, beating with rotary beater, over hot, not boiling water,
until thick. Add Kirsch. Use at once, if served hot, or cool and
chill thoroughly.

TOPPING HARD SAUCE

1 2-ounce package dessert topping mix
1 teaspoon vanilla, coffee, rum, brandy

Prepare dessert topping mix according to package directions.
Add flavoring and chill in refrigerator overnight. The whipped
mix becomes thickened to the consistency of hard sauce, and is
delicious and convenient. Makes 2 cups.

If you wish, flavor half the amount for the Hard Sauce,
reserving the balance for another use, such as whipped cream
topping, or for Vanilla Cream Pudding.

It may be softened with a small amount of milk.

TRADITIONAL HARD SAUCE

⅓ cup butter or margarine	⅛ teaspoon salt
1 cup confectioners' sugar,	1 teaspoon flavoring of your
sifted	choice, vanilla, rum, lemon

Cream butter and sugar together with spoon or in electric mixer
until smooth and fluffy, then beat in flavoring. Pile into your
prettiest serving bowl and refrigerate until thoroughly chilled.
Makes about 1 cup.

Figuring 2 tablespoons per serving, this makes 8 portions.

The sauce may be rolled into balls after chilling, and rolled in grated orange peel; chill again to serve.

Serve the sauce on mince pie, cobblers, or steamed puddings and vary the flavors to match the recipe.

Dine with Wine

Our burgeoning appreciation of fine dining keeps pace with other aspects of a broadening culture. Wine has been endorsed as a delightful adjunct, though ofttimes considered an extravagance. The fine quality of our American wines, however, refutes this misconception, since our vintages successfully vie with the more expensive imported product.

Proper selection need not present a problem. The study of wines is unending, but these simple suggestions are offered as a basic beginning.

Dry wines accompany entrées.

Serve sweet wines with dessert.

As a general rule, serve dry white wine with poultry, fish, or veal.

For beef, game, and cheese, the heavier red wines are preferred.

Do not allow yourself to be intimidated by what others say is correct! Enjoy the convivial cup; let your taste be your guide.

A bit of assurance — Champagne and rosé wines may be used with almost everything, from appetizers to dessert. When in doubt, use either for a one-wine dinner.

CAFÉ BRÛLOT

2 lumps sugar	1-inch stick cinnamon
2 pieces lemon peel	2 tablespoons brandy
2 cloves	⅔ cup strong hot coffee

Warm a heat-resistant bowl; add sugar, lemon peel, cloves and cinnamon. Pour brandy into ladle and warm it over a glamorous candle — or prosaically, over stove heat. Ignite and when flame dies, pour over spices and sugar. Add very hot coffee gradually and ladle into demitasse cups. Serves 2.

A small chafing dish or fondue dish would serve charmingly for the bowl.

It is essential to warm brandy in order to ignite it.

CAFÉ DIABLO

6 whole allspice	peel of 1 lemon
4 cloves	6 tablespoons cognac
1 bay leaf	4 cups hot coffee
6 juniper berries	2 tablespoons Cointreau
20 coffee beans	4 cinnamon sticks
peel of 1 orange	granulated sugar

Heat allspice, cloves, bayleaf, juniper berries, and coffee beans in chafing dish, over high flame. Add peelings. Press peelings against bottom of pan to extract oil. Keep stirring to prevent burning of spices until berries are hot. Add cognac to heated spices; it will flame instantly. Let it burn a few minutes, then add coffee. Simmer until very hot. Remove peelings and spices.

Heat Cointreau in ladle over flame, ignite and add to coffee. Serve immediately in Café Diablo or demitasse cups. Place cinnamon stick and a teaspoon of sugar on each saucer. Dip cinnamon stick first into coffee, then into sugar and then back into coffee. Sweeten coffee as desired in this fashion. Stir, using cinnamon stick for muddler. Serves 4.

CAFÉ ROYALE

Fill demitasse cups with piping hot black coffee; have each guest heat a teaspoon by dipping it into coffee; place a small cube of sugar in bowl of spoon; add cognac to fill, and ignite. When flame dies, stir contents of spoon into coffee and drink at once.

MULLED FRUIT PUNCH

1 quart pineapple juice	1 46-ounce can grapefruit-orange juice
1 2-inch stick cinnamon	1 orange
1 teaspoon nutmeg	1 lemon
1 quart cranberry juice	12 whole cloves
	½ cup honey

Mix pineapple juice, cinnamon and nutmeg in saucepan and simmer 20 minutes. Add cranberry juice and grapefruit-orange juice. Stick orange and lemon with cloves and add to liquid. Heat to boiling, stir in honey and remove from heat. Pour into warmed bowl. Makes about 3 quarts.

MULLED WINE

1 gallon apple cider	1 lemon, sliced
2 quarts domestic sweet grape	1 orange, sliced
wine	1 apple, peeled, quartered, and
2 3- to 4-inch cinnamon sticks	sliced
	12 whole cloves

Combine all ingredients in large kettle; bring to a boil then reduce heat and simmer 5 minutes. Remove all fruit and spices except apple slices. Serve very hot or very cold. Makes 6 quarts.

Spanish Punch

At Las Barracas, a fine old restaurant in Madrid, we first saw icy pitchers of this ruby-red beverage served at a family dinner party. At a sophisticated restaurant in Sevilla a bodega (cellar) rendezvous for flamenco devotees, the wine punch literally flowed. We reached Torremolinas on the Mediterranean, sauntered through the quaint streets and into a charming boutique. There we were lulled with glasses of Sangría into complete approval of the lovely merchandise, and presented with this recipe.

SANGRÍA
A traditional Spanish drink

1 quart red wine
juice of 1 lemon
¼ cup sugar, or to taste

2 tablespoons Cointreau or rum
(optional)

Sliced fresh fruit: 2 oranges, 2 peaches, 8 slices pineapple,
or others of your choice
ice to fill pitcher

There was no particular selection of red wine, and we were informed it need not be of the best vintage. Pour it into a 2-quart pitcher; stir in lemon juice, sugar, and Cointreau until well blended. Add fruit and sufficient ice to fill pitcher. Serve icy cold with luncheon or dinner. Serves 8.

Versatile Is
the Name for Cheese

•♡•♡•♡•♡•♡•

"Food fit for the gods" apparently referred to cheese as it was offered to the Greek Gods on Mount Olympus. A godsend, indeed, to the hostess — versatile is the name for cheese.

To cook, or eat "as is," grate or slice; it forms a delicious partnership with fruit, greens, casseroles of vegetables, and pastas, meats, and poultry, running the gamut from appetizer to dessert.

An early American cheese factory started in Oneida, New York, in 1851; today Wisconsin leads with unparalleled quality and variety. Numberless recipes include cheese; its adaptations are limitless.

A cheese platter induces conversation with cocktails. Center with red-wrapped Gouda or Edam, surrounded with smaller wrappings of Camembert and Blue or Roquefort. Cubes of Cheddar may be scattered between; crackers of varied shapes, with and without spread, make an interesting border. For additional color, intersperse slices of apple and small bunches of grapes.

A similar arrangement may be the perfect dessert to follow a substantial dinner. Serve it on cart or tray in the living room with coffee, for a relaxing finale. A wheel of Brie is a fine accompaniment to the salad course. England's Golden Cheshire and the purple-veined Stilton are gourmet delights to any cheese devotee.

A simple tray with a limited variety is always in order. Gorgonzola, Liederkranz, and wedges of Gruyère combine with a tasteful flare. A knowing touch, recommended by the French, is to combine wine and cheese from the same province.

Don't overlook the wonderful small packages of cheese and crackers so welcome when touring, or the cheese combinations with other fillings, for interesting sandwiches.

Ever a favorite is Cream Cheese with Bar-le-Duc, and many other Cream Cheese assortments (see section on Hors d'Oeuvres).

CHEESE SOUFFLÉ

For

1½-quart or 2-quart			1½-quart or 2 quart	
3	4 tablespoons butter		1	1½ cup grated Cheddar cheese
3	4 tablespoons flour			
1	1 teaspoon salt		3	5 egg yolks, well beaten
½	½ teaspoon dry mustard		1	2 tablespoons cognac
	dash cayenne pepper		3	5 egg whites, stiffly
1	1½ cups milk			beaten

Melt butter in saucepan; blend in flour, salt, mustard and cayenne pepper. Gradually add milk and heat to boiling, stirring constantly. Simmer 5 minutes; stir in cheese and continue stirring until cheese is melted. Add this mixture to egg yolks, stirring steadily to prevent curdling. Mix in cognac, then cool 10 minutes. Fold in egg whites carefully, but thoroughly. Pour into buttered 1½-quart or 2-quart soufflé dish or casserole. Bake in 375° oven 40 minutes or until browned and set. Serves 4 or 6.

To form crown, make a shallow indentation with a knife in complete circle about 1 inch from rim of dish.

A well-recommended luncheon dish, served with green salad and a fruited dessert.

COTTAGE CHEESE QUICHE

9-inch pie shell	1½ teaspoons salt
½ cup grated Swiss cheese	⅛ teaspoon white pepper
1½ cups chive cottage cheese	¾ cup canned French
4 eggs	fried onion
⅓ cup half and half cream	rings

Bake pie shell 10 minutes in 450° oven to set; cool. Sprinkle with Swiss cheese. Beat together cottage cheese, eggs, cream, salt and pepper. Pour into shell and bake 40 to 45 minutes at 350°. About 10 minutes before done, sprinkle top with onion rings and return to oven to complete baking. Cool slightly before serving. Serves 6.

CREAM CHEESE AND BAGEL

1 8-ounce package cream
   cheese, softened
3 tablespoons sour cream
⅛ teaspoon freshly
   ground pepper

3 tablespoons drained capers
   (optional)
¼ pound smoked salmon (lox)
12 miniature bagels

Mix cheese, sour cream, pepper, and capers together; blend very well. Cut salmon in small pieces and stir in cheese mixture. Slice bagels in half and toast cut side; spread toasted surface with cheese mixture and broil 3 inches from heat for 1 to 2 minutes. Serves 6.

PETIT SUISSE TRIANON

1 8-ounce package cream
   cheese, softened
2 tablespoons confectioners'
   sugar

¼ teaspoon salt
⅛ teaspoon onion juice
2 tablespoons half and half cream
1 cup heavy cream, whipped

Bar-le-Duc

Combine the cream cheese with sugar, salt, onion juice, cream, and blend well; then fold in whipped cream. Turn into a 4-cup mold and chill. When firm, unmold on platter. Serve with a border of Bar-le-Duc (red currant jam), or chill the cheese in a ring mold; unmold and serve with Bar-le-Duc in the center. Border with salted crackers and Melba toast. Serves 6 to 8.
   Any tart jellies may be substituted for the Bar-le-Duc.

The Swiss are past masters at the art of conviviality, and more often than not, it is over the Traditional Cheese Fondue. The bubbling hot fondue is placed in the center of the table in a chafing dish or comparable container; long fondue forks are convenient, but please don't allow the lack of them to deter you. Have on hand two loaves of French bread, cut in cubes. Each person spears a cube of bread, then twists it in the fondue so that it is well covered. Do not lose your bread, for the fondue sticklers demand a forfeit: the presentation of the next bottle of wine.

TRADITIONAL SWISS FONDUE

1 clove fresh garlic, halved	3 tablespoons cornstarch
2 cups dry white wine	⅛ teaspoon paprika
1 pound Swiss cheese, cubed	3 tablespoons kirsch or brandy
⅛ teaspoon nutmeg	1 tablespoon lemon juice
½ teaspoon salt	(optional)

2 loaves French bread, cubed

Rub the top of a double boiler with garlic; add wine and heat just until bubbles rise to the surface; do not boil. Combine cheese, nutmeg, salt, cornstarch, paprika, and add by handfuls to the wine, stirring constantly until cheese is melted. This takes about 20 minutes. Add kirsch, lemon juice, and blend. Transfer it to a table container and keep fondue at a simmer over a candle or sterno heater. However, the most desirable container is a chafing dish. Serves 4.

It would be remiss not to give the traditional form of the Fondue, but our favorite recipe is our own interpretation and I can't resist its inclusion.

We use ½ pound Herkimer cheese and ½ pound Swiss cheese, reduce the wine to 1½ cups and the Kirsch to 1 tablespoon. The choice is yours. Take your fork in hand, stab a chunk of bread, and dip, very carefully.

Unexpected guests are a culinary challenge. One morning I learned our California relatives would be able to drop in for cocktails between planes. I left the telephone for a dash to the convenience cupboard. Invariably cheeses are at hand, and the conviviality of the Fondue seemed right. The limited supply of Swiss or a comparable cheese did not deter me as I venturesomely added a yellow type. The flavor had more the tang of Welsh Rabbit, but it adhered smoothly to the speared bread cubes, and disappeared with dispatch.

YELLOW FONDUE

1 8-ounce jar Cheddar cheese spread	1 tablespoon cornstarch
	1 tablespoon kirsch
4 ounces Swiss cheese	dash paprika
1½ cups dry white wine	¼ teaspoon garlic powder or
1 tablespoon kirsch	cut garlic clove

Combine cheese spread, Swiss cheese, wine, and 1 tablespoon kirsch in a saucepan. Stir over low heat until melted and bubbly. Blend cornstarch and 1 tablespoon kirsch together and add to melted cheese; stir in paprika. Cook, stirring, just until thickened. Rinse fondue or chafing dish pan, and shake out excess moisture. Sprinkle garlic powder over bottom or rub with cut clove; pour in Fondue and keep hot over flame. Serves 4 to 6.

The seasoning in the spread is sufficient and additional is unnecessary. True Fondue is made practically the same, using all Swiss or half Emmenthaler; add a pinch of nutmeg and freshly ground pepper.

In lieu of a garlic clove, I found sprinkling the garlic powder another good emergency measure and now use it frequently in other recipes.

In France even sandwiches are male and female.

CROQUE-MONSIEUR

1 slice boiled ham	2 slices Swiss cheese
2 slices Fried Bread	1 slice tomato
1 teaspoon chopped parsley	

Place ham on Fried Bread; cover ham with 1 slice of cheese and second slice of bread. Top with last cheese slice and bake in 350°

oven until cheese melts. Top with tomato slice and parsley. Makes 1 sandwich.

CROQUE-MADAME

This sandwich becomes feminine by substituting the lighter chicken for the more hearty ham. Try them both.

Freezing sandwiches

Sandwiches are a convenient addition to the freezer.

Wrap each one individually.

Both Monsieur and Madame may be frozen; remove from freezer and bake as directed.

Those fillings which freeze well, among others, are cooked meats, chopped or sliced; cooked poultry, baked ham, cheeses and canned tuna or salmon. See Frozen Assets.

Complements
and Accents

•♡•♡•♡•♡•♡•

BREAD CANAPÉS
(Fried Bread)

6 slices white bread   1½ tablespoons butter

Remove crusts from bread; cut each slice into triangles or into a round, using a cooky cutter. Heat butter in skillet, add bread and fry until golden brown on both sides. Remove and use the rounds for tournedos of beef; for chicken breasts use the triangle toast points. This "Fried Bread" is typically French and does add flavor to the usual toast points.

FRIED PARSLEY

Wash and dry a large bunch of parsley; divide into 6 little bouquets and drop them into hot fat. Fry for about 2 minutes or until crisp. A "must" with smelts and good garnish for other fish, or meat.

The Desert Blooms

Out of its dessert obscurity, the prickly alligator pear has evolved into a shiny green avocado, autocrat of the vegetable counter. It is a lovely addition to a fruit bowl, before it is fully ripened; to be eaten later when time has mellowed it. It must be thoroughly ripened to attain its subtlest flavor, and the pulp should be soft but not mushy. To hasten ripening, wrap in brown paper or foil and let stand in a warm, not hot, place for a day or two. Versatile and equally good served hot or cold.

As a garnish

Peel avocado; cut in half lengthwise; remove pit; sprinkle with lemon juice. Warm it in the sauce of prepared chicken or meat with which it will be served. Remove to serving plate; cut in ½-inch slices, crosswise, allowing ¼ avocado for each serving.

SAUCED AVOCADO

3 avocados	2 tablespoons butter
2 tablespoons catsup	1 tablespoon soy sauce
1 tablespoon Worcestershire	2 tablespoons sugar
2 tablespoons wine vinegar	

Peel avocados; remove pits; cut in half lengthwise and place in shallow pan. Combine remaining ingredients in saucepan; heat and pour over avocados. Place in 350° oven and bake about 15 minutes until quite warm. Remove from oven; cut each half in 3 strips, retaining original pear shape; pour sauce over each. Use as a garnish around a platter. Serves 6 or more.

APRICOT JAM

1 pound dried apricots	3 pounds (6 cups) sugar
6 cups water	grated rind and juice of 1 lemon

Cut apricots in small pieces and soak overnight in water; do not drain. Add sugar, juice and grated rind of lemon. Bring to boil, reduce heat and simmer gently ½ hour or until thickened. Pour into jars; cool, then cover and refrigerate. Stores well.

BRANDY PEARS

26 Seckel pears	½ cup brown sugar
1½ tablespoons liquid sweet- ener	¼ teaspoon salt 3 cups water
15 cloves	2 teaspoons lemon juice
1 3-inch stick cinnamon	¾ cup brandy

Peel the pears whole, without removing stems; add all ingredients except brandy and simmer 40 minutes or until fork tender.
Add brandy; cool and chill well. Because fruits vary, test each
pear and remove when it is done. For dessert, serve with Crème
Anglaise or Sabayon; good served hot or cold as a meat accompaniment. They store well when refrigerated. To preserve for
out of season use, pour into hot sterilized jars. The proportion
of brandy for syrup is ¼ cup brandy to ¾ cup water.

CRANBERRY CHUTNEY

1 pound fresh cranberries	½ cup seedless raisins
1 cup white vinegar	1½ cups firmly packed brown
½ teaspoon garlic powder	sugar
½ teaspoon garlic salt	2 tablespoons granulated
1 teaspoon grated fresh ginger or powdered ginger	sugar dash cayenne
¼ cup slivered almonds	

Pick over cranberries, carefully removing softened berries. Place
in saucepan with all ingredients except almonds. Simmer, stirring frequently, for 20 minutes. Add almonds and cook another
10 minutes or until thick. Pour into 3 sterile 8-ounce glasses and
seal. Chutney may be cooled and refrigerated. It will keep 4
weeks if it is still on hand. Makes 3 cups.

CRANBERRIES FROM THE OVEN

2 cups cranberries   1½ cups sugar
½ orange, thinly sliced, then quartered

Pick the cranberries over carefully; wash and turn into a
6″ x 10″ ovenproof cake pan. There should be at least an inch

rim so that the cranberries will not boil over. Sprinkle with the sugar and toss the berries to coat them. Place in 325° oven; bake until syrup comes to a boil, about 20 minutes, then add orange slices, distributing them underneath the berries while tossing lightly with a spatula. Bake a total of one hour. Remove from oven, toss again to separate berries; cool and refrigerate. They will keep well for a week or two.

FRUIT COMPOTE MAYFAIR

1 pound dried apricots
1 1-pound can pitted black cherries, drained, juice reserved

1 1-pound can sliced peaches, drained
juice and grated rind of 1 orange
juice and grated rind of 1 lemon

½ cup brown sugar

Wash apricots and combine with drained cherries and peaches. In a large bowl, mix cherry juice, orange juice and rind, lemon juice and rind and brown sugar. Add fruits. Pour into a greased 6-cup casserole and bake in 350° oven one hour, or until apricots are soft. Serve hot as accompaniment to meat course. Serve cold as a sauce or dessert. Serves 8 to 10.

Prepare early in the day for baking; chill. Remove from refrigerator and let stand at room temperature ½ hour before placing in the oven.

FRUIT PYRAMIDS

6 slices canned pineapple (1 1-pound can)
½ pound jar cinnamon apple slices or whole spiced apples
1 14-ounce jar preserved kumquats

Place the pineapple slices in a flat baking dish with a slice of apple or whole apple over each, then top with kumquat. Secure with toothpicks. Place remaining kumquats in bottom of dish. Pour Golden Sauce over all. Place in 350° oven and bake 15 to 20 minutes, or until heated. Border meat or poultry platter. Serves 6.

These may be served as a course, or as accompaniment to hot entrées with plate service.

FROSTED GRAPES

1 pound seedless grapes   1 egg white, slightly beaten
1 package lemon-flavored gelatin

Break grapes into small clusters, dip into beaten egg white and drain on paper toweling. Sprinkle evenly and well with gelatin. Chill until dry, about 3 hours. Use as garnish. Grapes may be stored overnight in refrigerator.

Grapes may be frosted by being dipped into slightly beaten egg whites, drained and dredged in granulated sugar, then chilled.

GREEN TOMATO RELISH

6 medium green tomatoes   15 whole cloves
1 cup thinly sliced onion rings   1 teaspoon mixed pickle spice
1 green pepper, thinly sliced   ½ teaspoon turmeric
   in rings   ⅔ cup cider vinegar
2 tablespoons salt   ⅓ cup water
1-inch stick cinnamon   2 tablespoons granulated sugar
⅓ cup brown sugar

Slice off both ends of tomatoes, then cut in ¼-inch slices. Place in bowl in alternate layers with onion and green pepper rings, sprinkling each with salt. Cover and let stand overnight. In the morning, drain; rinse with cold water; drain well again. Combine cinnamon, cloves and pickle spice in a bag and tie to close well (if you have no bag, use a small piece of fresh cotton or linen and tie into a bag). Place in saucepan with drained vegetables and remaining ingredients. Bring to a boil, reduce heat and simmer 20 minutes; remove spices. Cool, pour into covered container and store in refrigerator. Makes about 3 cups. Keeps 2 weeks.

PEACH CHUTNEY

1 cup water
¼ cup sugar
3 tablespoons wine or white vinegar
½ teaspoon ground allspice
2 teaspoons soy sauce
3 or 4 dashes Tabasco

¼ teaspoon salt
1 teaspoon dry mustard
1 teaspoon dry ginger
2 tablespoons orange juice
1 teaspoon grated orange rind
6 peaches, peeled and coarsely chopped

Combine all ingredients in saucepan; bring to boil; cover and reduce heat. Simmer slowly, 30 minutes. If a thinner condiment is desired, add orange juice or peach nectar. Makes about 1½ cups.

Delicious with curries, seafood, barbecued ribs, etcetera.

PEARS AND SPICE

1 16-ounce can pears, drained
¼ teaspoon cinnamon
⅛ teaspoon garlic salt
¼ cup currant or grape jelly

¼ teaspoon seasoned salt
¼ cup raisins
¼ teaspoon ginger

Place pears, rounded side up, in saucepan. Combine remaining ingredients, blend well and pour on pears. Heat slowly for 2 minutes; turn pears, hollow side up and fill with raisins. Simmer just until thoroughly heated. Serve as border or accompaniment for meat or poultry.

PICKLED ONIONS

3 pounds onions, sliced
½ cup salt
1 quart white vinegar
2 cups sugar
2 tablespoons mustard seed
1 teaspoon powdered alum

2 tablespoons pickling spice
2 tablespoons celery seed
1 tablespoon ground ginger
½ teaspoon dry mustard
1½ teaspoons turmeric

Toss onions with salt; let stand 1 hour, then drain. Combine vinegar, sugar, and mustard seed in saucepan. Place pickling spice, celery seed, ginger, dry mustard, and turmeric in cheesecloth bag; tie securely. Bring vinegar mixture to rolling boil; add bag of spices and cook 10 minutes. Add drained onions and cook until slightly yellow but not soft; add alum. Pour into sterilized jars while hot, and seal.

PRECIOUS ORANGE

3 whole oranges	1 cup water
water to cover	1 cup sugar
3 tablespoons finely sliced crystallized ginger	6 drops red food coloring

Topping

6 maraschino cherries   9 large grapes, halved and seeded

Place oranges in water and boil about 20 to 30 minutes or until tender. Cool; cut in halves, remove center core and seeds, if any. Drop ½ teaspoon ginger in center of each and place on baking sheet. (Cover sheet with foil to protect it from sticky syrup.) Combine 1 cup water, sugar, and food coloring in saucepan, simmer 10 minutes; pour over orange halves and place in 400° oven to glaze. Baste frequently until shiny. Remove, center with cherry cut in 6 petals, and 3 halved grapes tucked under for leaves. Serve warm or cold. Serves 6.

A scoop of orange ice to top the glazed fruit is refreshing. These are a beautiful garnish for meats as well as a dessert.

Orange slices make a colorful border. Slice ½-inch thick, place in skillet, cover with the syrup and simmer until glazed and tender.

SPICED PECANS

1 egg white	½ cup sugar
1 teaspoon cold water	¼ teaspoon salt
1 pound pecan halves	½ teaspoon cinnamon

Beat egg white and water until frothy, but not stiff; add pecans and mix lightly until each one is coated evenly. Combine sugar, salt, and cinnamon in a quart-sized bowl; mix together and add pecans. Toss pecans lightly until covered with the sugar mixture. Butter a 10″ x 15″ jelly roll pan and spread nuts evenly over buttered surface. Bake in 225° oven 1 hour, stirring every 15 minutes. Remove and cool.

These are delicious, and elegant.

STRAWBERRY PRESERVES

1 tablespoon cider vinegar	4 cups hulled, washed straw-
3 cups sugar	berries

Add vinegar to strawberries in large pot. Bring to a boil slowly; cover and boil 1 minute. Add sugar; boil uncovered, gently, for 20 minutes. Stir occasionally and carefully so as to not break berries. Pour hot berries into deep platters and let stand overnight. Next day, ladle cold fruit into sterilized jars. Cover immediately with melted paraffin. Makes 5 or 6 small glasses.

TOASTED ALMONDS

1 tablespoon butter   ¼ cup slivered almonds

Heat butter, add almonds. Sauté slowly, stirring until almonds are brown (about 5 minutes). Watch closely that they do not burn.

Prepare 2 cups whole almonds and store in airtight container; have on hand to serve with cocktails or after dinner.

Art in the Kitchen

• ♡ • ♡ • ♡ • ♡ • ♡ •

Flowers

Just as a woman's grace is accented by tasteful adornment, so a recipe's appeal is increased by appropriate trimmings. In arranging foods, the use of color and composition is irresistible. Nature endows us with an abundance of beauty in many media. Masterpieces of art portraying food are among our treasured inheritance.

The housewife, like other artists, enjoys her creative materials. The dish she develops can have tasteful appeal for eye and tongue. The "props" are unending; here are a few suggestions proffered to stimulate your own ingenious touch.

TOMATO ROSES

Blanch 2 or 3 small tomatoes in boiling water for a minute. Peel in circular fashion so that peel is removed in one spiral. Rewind it around your finger, spreading top edges for petal effect. Secure the ends with a toothpick.

TOMATO BUDS

Remove stem of cherry tomato; make 8 cuts from stem end almost to base and gently spread the sections to open flowerlike.

RADISH ACCORDIONS

Cut off both ends of long radishes. Cut crosswise into very thin slices, to, but not through the opposite side. Refrigerate in ice water a minimum of one hour. Drain. The slices will open attractively.

GRAPEFRUIT ROSES

Whenever we have grapefruit, I am impelled to make a rose. The decoration makes every meal a party.

The method involves two peelings; first, peel off the outer skin, "zest," thinly, leaving the white membrane exposed. Next peel off this membrane, ¾ inch in width, in a single spiral, if possible. Sometimes it will tear, but that only alters the size of the "posy." (As you peel, leave the pulp exposed to enable you to remove segments more easily.) The roses may be made in any size, the complete rind making a large flower. Roll the membrane back on its natural spiral so that any exposed fruit left on the membrane will be at the bottom. Fasten securely with toothpicks at the base and if edges seem too ragged, trim them with scissors. Place in a bowl of water and add sufficient fruit coloring to tint to your desired intensity and color. Smaller flowers may be made for an old-fashioned bouquet with a fresh crisp parsley border.

The petal edges of the "flower" may be tinted, using a cotton swab; oftimes the natural color of the membrane is good contrast.

The fragility of flowers restricts their adornment of heartier foods and to this cause, we can add the simulated vegetable posies which are such fun to make.

CUCUMBER LILIES

The end of cucumbers are a waste as a rule and so they become a lily. Cut off the end about 1 inch in length. Make diagonal cuts along the edge to make a sawtooth-edged rim. Hollow it slightly and then stick a sliver of carrot into the center as a "stamen." Nest it in a bunch of watercress with 2 or 3 carrot daisies.

CARROT DAISIES

Flower cutters are available in the specialty shops, or a truffle cutter does very well. Cut carrot or turnip in ⅛-inch slices. Press out flower with cutter. I remove the eraser from a pencil and use the hollow as a cutter for the center. On the carrot daisy center a turnip disk and reverse the procedure for the turnip daisy. Spear with a toothpick and group the daisies in a bouquet with bright parsley or watercress. For height, spear them into an orange for a base, and twine the toothpicks with parsley.

RADISH TULIPS

Have radishes with bright leaves if possible. Outline petals from the top to the leaves and release them with a sharp knife, ¾ of the way. Let them soak in ice water and the blossoms will open.

ONION CHRYSANTHEMUMS

Start with a nicely rounded onion; peel it smoothly. Cut down through center, quartering onion, cutting to but not through bottom; then cut each quarter in half, dividing into 8ths, and again cut the 8ths in half, making 16ths. Place in bowl of red-tinted water to cover, and refrigerate a minimum of 2 hours. The larger the onion, the larger the flower and they do spread as they open. Consider the platter you use. One Chrysanthemum with 2 smaller flowers on a bed of greens is most attractive.

TANGERINE CHRYSANTHEMUMS

Remove peel from 3 tangerines by cutting each into four sections from stem end just to the bottom. Do not cut fruit; remove the sections for other use. With scissors cut peel in ¼-inch strips, completely shredding it into petals. Place the stripped peelings, one inside the other, to form chrysanthemum. Center with 3 or

4 tangerine sections speared to bottom with toothpicks.

They make delightful receptacles for tiny containers of relishes and jellies, omitting tangerine sections.

APPLE EGGS

6 eggs	6 sprigs crisp watercress
6 cloves	red food coloring

Place eggs in water to cover; bring to a boil. Cover, remove from heat and let stand 15 minutes. Drain; cover with ice water and drain again. Peel, and while still warm, press ends between palms, rolling to form a ball. Paint egg with red coloring and chill 2 to 3 hours. To complete apple concept, inset a clove for base, and use the sprigs appropriately for stem end. A tasteful garnish for most cold platters.

CUCUMBER CUPS

2 firm cucumbers about 7 inches long

Peel cucumbers; slice off ends, then cut each remaining cucumber into 3 pieces, 1½ to 2 inches long. Scoop out center of each piece to form cup. Use a French cutter for slicing or notch top side of cup for an attractive edge. Makes 6 cups.

The scooped out pieces and ends may be added to other vegetables and used as a filling for Cucumber Salad Cups.

Use unpeeled ends of cucumbers to make Cucumber Lilies for garnish.

Eye Appeal for Appetites

Add interest to a simple chowder, cream soup, or bisque with

frankfurter slices	dollop of sour cream
croutons	grated hard-cooked egg yolk or
dollop of whipped cream	white
	paprika

For clear soups, consommés, or broths, add

avocado cubes
sliced zucchini
julienne-sliced pancake strips
beaten egg dropped from a spoon
   to make a fluff
croutons
fine noodles
lemon slice

snipped parsley
snipped shallots
sliced mushrooms
rice
toasted almonds
toasted bread and grated
   cheese
tiny dumplings

For cold platters

a splash of pomegranate seeds
   on crisp greens
Apple Eggs
olives
fresh or vegetable flowers

carrot strips slipped through
   pitted olives
asparagus spears
chopped aspic
pears, tinted a blushing pink

For poultry or meats

peach halves, hollow-side up,
   filled with chutney, hot or
   cold
oranges, slices or wedges
spiced fruit
clusters of kumquats, some
   peeled in petals

sliced avocado, cold or warmed
persimmons in wedges
a variety of canned fruits, tinted
   with vegetable coloring
lemon wedges and slices, paprika
   dipped
parsley and watercress bouquets

beet cups filled with horseradish cream

Spices

The spices of the Old World led Columbus to the unchartered waters which dashed him against our shores. Spices today take us on flavorful tours transported by exotic recipes of other lands. Cinnamon was so revered as a love potion by the ancient Greeks that offerings to its honor were made on Mount Olympus. The Persians inherited the predilection for this spice, and cinnamon-spiced meats are a modern means of travel fantasy, and away we go!

Most spices are familiar to cooks, and are used unquestion-ingly, a few just occasional participants in the saucepan. This is a brief review of limited uses.

PEPPER — an indispensible item for eggs, meats, and vegetables

CLOVES — use in beef, ham, dried fruits, puddings, spice cakes, marinades

CINNAMON — similar in use to cloves

NUTMEG — another ally of cinnamon

MACE — for cooked fruits, stuffings, chowders; related to nutmeg

ALLSPICE — a requirement in pickle relish, tongue, pork, shrimp

GINGER — good in fruit and fruit dressings, candy, fish sauces, and puddings

CARDAMOM — for cakes, drinks, sauces

VANILLA — reliable standby in ice cream, cakes, puddings, drinks

CURRY — for poultry, meats and seafood

SAFFRON — in curries, rice, cakes

CAPERS — good in chicken and seafood salads, dressings

PAPRIKA — a must for meats, fish, poultry, sauces for these three

Herbs

The use of herbs in an encompassing manner is still experimental with most housewives; testing has proven them a delicious accent and their inclusion is gaining in popular favor.

The following is a list of those most frequently used:

ANISE — for salads, baking, cooked fruits, and candy

BASIL — in soups and sauces

BAY LEAVES — for bouquet garni

CELERY SEED — soups, stews, salads

CARDAMOM — in baking
CHERVIL — in fine herbes — to replace parsley
CHIVES — for a delicate onion flavor
CORIANDER — in cookies and candies
CARAWAY — in baking; with few vegetables, such as cabbage and beets.
CRESS — salads
CUMIN — cookies, sauces and gravies
DILL — in pickles, in salads and vegetables
FENNEL — in sauces and soups
GARLIC — in poultry, meats, dressings, salads, sauces. A pungent herb, truly a personal choice
HORSERADISH — an accompaniment to beef, seafood, an inclusion in sauces
MARJORAM — use with meat and in salads
MINT — to flavor sauces, vegetables, beverages
MUSTARD — cooking and preserving
ROSEMARY — for lamb or veal
SAFFRON — flavor and color for rice and fish
SAGE — best known as a stuffing ingredient
SAVORY — meats, poultry and sauces
SESAME — used in baking
TARRAGON — sauces, poultry, meats and salads
THYME — in herb bouquets, sauces, and soups

FINES HERBES

A mixture of herbs used for seasoning sauces, omelets, eggs. One good combination is

parsley   tarragon
chervil   chives

You may substitute herbs of your choice in many combinations.

BOUQUET GARNI

A faggot of herbs and plants tied together and used as seasoning in sauces, stews, soups, and gravies. They can be large, small, or medium and the combination depends upon the seasoning needed in the preparation. They are assembled in bouquets so that they may be easily removed at the end of cooking time. Parsley, thyme, celery, and bay leaf are the popular plants and other plants and herbs, such as basil, tarragon, chervil and rosemary, are choices.

The Marrying Kind

There is true affinity between specific foods, and this awareness becomes a challenge, especially when one is confronted with a leftover ingredient. So it was after preparing Crabmeat Mushrooms; with a wealth of the mushroom stems left over, a compatible mate was needed. A glance through the files and a bit of cogitation provided a Mushroom Barley Casserole for dinner the following night as an accompaniment to the Sauerbraten entrée.

CELERY LEAVES

A very commonly rejected item is the delectable celery leaf. There are innumerable uses for this fragrant foliage, and disposing of it is wasteful and a real loss of flavor. Don't toss celery leaves out, toss them in, fresh or dried.

Use them in sauces.

Cut the more tender leaves into tossed salads.

Shred and cook with potatoes or carrots.

Use as a base for cream of celery soup.

Sauté them with the onions and vegetables in stews and pot roasts.

They have an exceptional flavor for dressings.

Indispensable for soup stock.

BEET GREENS

Beet greens are a premium often discarded. Remove from the beets and cut into strips with the tenderest of the stems. The kitchen scissors are a handy implement for this procedure. Cook in ½-inch of boiling salted water, using ½ teaspoon salt for each cup; boil 20 minutes or until tender. If amount is sufficient, drain and serve with butter, a sprinkling of lemon juice, and freshly ground pepper. If meager, prepare in like fashion, and serve with whole or sliced hot beets.

CABBAGE

The core of a cabbage adds fine flavor to soup; cooked until tender, it may be diced and added to a vegetable potage, hot or cold. Or cook, cube, and toss over slices of hot corned beef served traditionally with fresh cabbage wedges. My Dutch friends add it, well cooked, to a few cooked carrots, and mix it with fluffy mashed potatoes.

STALE BREAD

Dried bread, unused crusts, or ends of a loaf should be utilized for crumbs. Leave them uncovered to dry thoroughly, then place in paper bag and roll until smooth, or crush in a blender.

COURT BOUILLON
(Poaching stock for meat or fish)

1 quart water	6 peppercorns
Bouquet Garni	½ teaspoon salt
1 small onion	¼ cup white vinegar or
1 clove garlic (optional)	½ cup white wine

Combine all ingredients in saucepan and bring to boil. Reduce heat and simmer 20 minutes. Excellent with meat or fish; for fish, use the bones and head of fish for marked flavor. Makes approximately 1 quart.

For large quantities, recipe may be increased as needed.

SEASONED FLOUR

½ cup flour　　　　1 tablespoon salt
½ teaspoon pepper　　1 teaspoon paprika

Mix and blend well. Celery salt, garlic salt, herbs or other seasonings of your choice may be added.

Kitchen Schoolroom

Simple Equations

A GREAT PART of enjoying "housewifery" to the fullest is good organization.

A kitchen list, religiously kept, from cleansers to capers, can offset many frustrating situations. With a one-item shelf of standard stock, each item immediately goes on the shopping list as it is used. Like the Lord High Chancellor, have it on your list!

Things Equal to the Same Thing
Are Equal to Each Other

A few simple equations

3 medium cooked poatoes	equal 1 cup mashed (approx.)
1½ pounds apples	equals 1 quart, pared, sliced
1 cup heavy cream	equals 2 cups whipped
3 medium bananas	equal 2 cups, mashed
1 medium grapefruit	makes ¾ cup juice
1 medium orange	makes ½ cup juice

1 medium lemon	makes 3 tablespoons juice
1 medium onion	makes ½ cup, chopped
3 medium raw potatoes (1 pound)	makes 2½ cups, diced
1¼ pounds raw carrots	serves 4
1 cup grated raw carrot	use 1 large
12 square graham crackers	make 1 cup fine crumbs
1 envelope unflavored gelatine	equals 1 tablespoon; use for 2 cups liquid
1 pound brown sugar	makes 2¼ cups, packed
1 pound granulated sugar	makes 2¼ cups
1 pound confectioners' sugar	makes 3½ cups
1 pound all-purpose flour	makes 4 cups, sifted
1 pound cake flour	makes 4¾ cups, sifted

Figure ½ pound dressing for each pound of turkey

3 cups diced cooked meat	1 pound, cooked
2 cups ground cooked meat	1 pound, cooked
2 cups diced chicken	1 pound, boned and cooked
4 cups diced cooked chicken	1 5-pound chicken, cooked
1 8-ounce package spaghetti	makes 4 cups, cooked
1 cup raw rice	makes 3 to 4 cups, cooked
2 slices bread	make 1 cup soft crumbs
2 slices bread	make 1 cup small cubes

Weights and Measures

Dry Measure

3 teaspoons = 1 tablespoon
4 tablespoons = ¼ cup
8 tablespoons = ½ cup
16 tablespoons = 1 cup
a dash = less than ⅛ teaspoon

Fluid Weight

2 tablespoons = 1 fluid ounce
4 ounces = ½ cup
8 ounces = 1 cup
2 cups = 1 pint
4 cups = 1 quart
4 quarts = 1 gallon

For liquid measure, the cup with a lip is an aid; also a convenience is the 2 cup measure.

The glass variety enables one to see the amount needed.

For dry measure, use a one cup lined rimless type and a set of of the nested smaller measures.

For accuracy, use the leveled measuring spoons which come in
  sets of sizes.
Use a spatula for leveling measurements.

Butter

  2 cups = 1 pound   ½ cup = ¼ pound
    1 cup = ½ pound   ¼ cup or 4 tablespoons = ⅛ pound

Approximate Measurement of Cans in Terms of Cups

#1 can — 10½ ounces, or 1¼ cups (approximately)
#2 can — 16 ounces, or 2 cups
#2½ can — 1 pound, 13 ounces, or 3½ cups
#300 can — 15 ounces, or 2 cups
#303 can — 1 pound, or 2 cups

Soups

10½ ounces, or approximately 1¼ cups

Evaporated milk

small can — 6 ounces, or ¾ cup
tall can — 14½ ounces, or 1¾ cups

Sweetened condensed milk

15 ounces, or 2 cups

Gadgets and Semantics

GADGETS are for the convenience of all, including our new cooks, the brides, but sometimes they prove a boomerang for the manufacturers.

Take the case of the pressure cooker. One was sold to a bride in Leeds, England. She used it, and returned it to the manufacturer complaining that it did not cook her potatoes. A new pot was sent her and returned with the same complaint. The public relations office was perturbed, and sent their most charming representative to adjust the matter. Upon inquiry, the customer proceeded to demonstrate her problem. She peeled the potatoes; placed them in the cooker; pushed them to one side, then placed a glass of water in the pan, next to the potatoes. In dismay, the investigator exclaimed, "My dear, there is your trouble. The potatoes should be *in* the water." "Well," said the bride, "the directions say 'put a glass of water in the cooker with the potatoes' and that is just what I did."

Needless to say, the printing was immediately changed to read "*Pour* a glass of water into the cooker with the potatoes."

Then there was the note I received from a bride-to-be, in which she said:

Dear Mrs. Hirschfeld:
I was in desperate need of a cookbook that would be a kind of a guiding light. Just between us, I am the kind of cook who, if instructed to separate six eggs, will put three over here and three over there.

Pretty and practical appliances and work-savers contributed mightily to the renaissance of the kitchen.

So much of kitchen simplification is taken for granted. My recent assessment credits many helpers for which I usually reach with unconscious habit; I list a few.

apple corer and sectioner
ball cutter — to pretty a platter of vegetables or fruits
baster, with a bulb
candy thermometer — no wondering about "spinning a thread"
decorating cutters
deep-frying thermometer — again, no "proper heat" worry
flour sifter (2-cup)
French fluted cutter — lovely for slicing
kitchen mitts — wonderful protection from steam when un-
    covering a Dutch oven
kitchen scale — a joy
kitchen shears — try the kind that come apart for easy cleaning
long-handled brushes — good to the hands
measuring cups — all sizes and some with spouts
meat grinder — speaks for itself
meat thermometer — relief from roasting worry
metal spatula (4″) — to lift cookies, patties, etcetera.
pastry brush
pastry tube
rubber spatulas — to clean a bowl of batter with neatness and
    dispatch — other preparations, too
slotted spoon — drain before dripping
spiral whisk — for an egg or two or other small amounts
tongs — to lift potatoes, eggs, and "too hot to handle" things
toy ladle — for reaching obscure recesses of a roasting pan
toy pancake turner — for dollar-size pancakes
vegetable peeler
wire whisk
wooden spoons — irreplaceable old-timers

These are my special addictions; I did not mention all the es-
    sentials and many other gadgets which may be your favorites.

Frozen Assets

FROZEN SANDWICHES

Have a do-it-yourself family sandwich party and stock up the freezer. Ingredients and combinations which do *not* freeze well are:

cooked eggs   mayonnaise
gelatine molds   fresh tomatoes
crisp vegetables with high water content, to be eaten raw
smoked meats, ham, etcetera
highly seasoned preparations (they lose flavor)

Wrap sandwiches separately and do not keep longer than 2 weeks.
Seal well and label each with name and date.
Thaw before unwrapping.

Pack the lunchbox with frozen sandwiches in the morning and they will be thawed by lunchtime.

Ingredients and combinations which *do* freeze well are

cooked chicken	turkey	fish
meat	egg yolk	sandwich meats
butter	apple sauce	sour cream

Do not refreeze sandwiches.

FROZEN MEATS

Wrap air-tight; label carefully with date and type of cut. Thaw in refrigerator in wrapping and cook as soon as possible. For quicker thawing allow meat to stand under cool running water, then cook at once.

Most frozen meats may be cooked before thawing. Allow 1½ times as long as for fresh or thawed meats, especially with large cuts.

Time Chart For Frozen Meats

The following is the recommended maximum time for storing frozen meats.

Beef, veal and lamb, roasts or chops	12 months
Ground beef, lamb or veal	8 months
Pork roasts and chops	8 months
Pork frankfurters and sausage	4 months
Liver, tongue and kidneys	3 months
Poultry, raw	8 months
Poultry, cooked	3 months
Poultry giblets	3 months
Fish, lean	10 months
Fish, fat	8 months
Seafoods	8 months

To freeze soups

Pour soup into bowl and freeze quickly. When solid, dip bowl for a moment into hot water and turn frozen soup into plastic bag. Saves room and possible breakage.

Appetizers

A true bonus item. Many can be popped in the oven for re-heating, others partially cooked. Freeze and store in bags or on trays ready for the oven. Pastry wrapped hors d'oeuvres may be partially baked and then frozen.

Casseroles

Many combinations may be frozen and on hand for an emergency. Some may go from freezer to oven. Check first, as it may be that your oven ware should stand at room temperature before baking.

Cakes and Ice Creams

Freeze first then remove and wrap; return to freezer as quickly as possible.

Remember that if foods are well wrapped and air tight, they will not dry out. Keep wrapped while defrosting.

Do not re-freeze raw meats, or cooked foods which have been defrosted and heated.

Use plastic wrap or bags, wax-coated paper cartons, or heavy duty aluminum foil.

Expel all air from package before sealing.

Do not reuse wrappings.

Containers may be washed and reused if in good condition.

Reviewing Stand

To PREVENT unflavored gelatine from lumping and to dissolve evenly, always sprinkle it on the water or other dissolving liquid. 1 tablespoon equals 1 envelope.

Spices lose strength after a time and should be replaced. This can be observed by the diminishing taste and darkening color. Refrigerate in summer as they deteriorate more quickly in heat.

Do not butter pans when baking angel food, chiffon, sponge or sunshine cakes. Almost all other cakes are turned into buttered pans; when batter contains solids such as nuts or candies, flour the pans as well to prevent bits from sticking.

If uncooked confectioners' sugar frosting is too thick, add a small amount of heated water, cream or coffee until of spreading consistency. If too thin, add more sugar. Do not despair.

To decorate a cake simply without frosting, place paper doily on top; sift powdered sugar thickly over and remove doily carefully, leaving its design clearly marked.

To rehabilitate a cracked aspic mold, nonchalantly cover the damage with a bit of garnish.

To prevent crust from forming on a custard, lay a piece of wax paper directly on partially cooled surface and allow it to remain until served.

Save the ends of ribs of beef for braising. The bone of a leg of lamb may be used for delicious broth.

When buying boned chicken breasts, take home the bones to use as a base for stock; likewise head and bones of fileted fish for stock or court bouillon.

When butter is the sautéeing agent, you may substitute ½ vegetable shortening for extra browning. Butter burns very easily and the shortening acts as a stabilizer.

Caution: To avoid weeping when peeling onions blanch them in boiling water, or peel under cold running water.

Butter: The regulation pound package to which we have been accustomed contains either a full uncut pound, or 4 quarters, individually wrapped. Each stick or quarter pound equals ½ cup. Please note, however, that the one-pound package of *whipped butter* is divided into 6 separately wrapped pieces or sticks.

A *dash* or a *pinch* of an ingredient is less than ⅛ teaspoon.

Try adding ¼ teaspoon garlic salt to water when boiling vegetables such as spinach, broccoli or others of your choice.

When boiling dumplings or matzo balls, add bouillon cubes to water for extra flavor.

To clear beaters of an electric mixer, remove them from mixture slowly while gradually reducing speed.

Add 4 or 5 marshmallows to the syrup of stewed fruits. They act as a self-baster. Especially helpful when coloring with cinnamon drops or vegetable coloring.

Cream

Heavy sweet cream and sour cream may often be used interchangeably. Both may be whipped, though the sour cream will not become as stiff, but rather fluffy. Be certain that both bowls and beaters are icy cold.

Sweet cream triples in volume; sour cream doubles.

Use either one as dessert dressing with a suggestion of flavoring, orange, lemon, vanilla or almond.

Do-it-yourself-Hibachi may be improvised with medium-sized flowerpots filled with glowing charcoal. Use new flowerpots or wash thoroughly and line generously with heavy metal foil. Placed on their matching clay saucers they will not burn table or floor. They will amuse guests aromatically while the hostess is bringing in cocktail franks, squares of beef and other tidbits to be charbroiled. A smart curtain-raiser to the anticipated entrée.

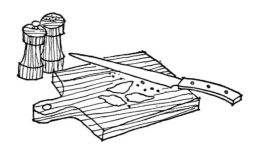

Truth and Consequences

Today the U.N. works around the world to correct nutritional fallacies and wipe out taboos which prevent the hungry or underdeveloped countries from making use of valuable indigenous foodstuffs. Yet here in our own highly sophisticated area many baseless superstitions persist.

To lift the veil of ignorance covering the foods we eat, let's take a look at some of the more popular food fallacies, and at factual answers founded on scientific evidence. By following truth, not fancies, you may consequently enjoy better nutrition in more appetizing meals.

Aside from color, the only difference between a white and a brown *egg* is the breed of hen that laid it. There is no difference in nutritive value.

The nutritive values of *vegetable juices* and *vegetables* are approximately the same. Whole vegetables are an important source of bulk in the diet.

No experimental or clinical evidence indicates that the combination of *milk* and *fish* is poisonous, or even harmful. The idea doubtless originated before the era of good refrigeration, when people eating spoiled fish happened to be drinking milk at the same time.

No single food is responsible for making blood. Some wines contain a small amount of metallic iron, essential to the manufacture of hemoglobin.

Oysters, raw eggs, lean meat, and *olives* contribute to general health and well-being, but none has any special quality which increases sexual potency.

It is the nutrients in food, hot or cold, not the *temperature* at which they are served, that determine how nourishing they are. A popular misconception is that a good hot meal is more nutritious than a cold one.

The old wives' tale that *hot biscuits* and *bread* aren't good for you until they've cooled is completely false. Hot bread, fresh from the oven, is just as nutritious and digestible as cold bread — and to many people, more delicious.

Although a few food acids may dissolve a little of the iron, it is perfectly safe to leave food in an *open can*, if refrigerated and covered.

Fresh foods are seldom perfectly "fresh" these days, and are usually over a week old by the time they reach the consumer market. Frozen foods, on the other hand, are fresher because they are prepared shortly after picking. Both have approximately the same nutritional value.

Another Day
A Different Way

T<small>HE FOLLOWING</small> are recipes which can be prepared with left-overs:

Index

❤ ❤ ❤ ❤ ❤